Please renew or return items by the date
shown on your receipt

www.hertsdirect.org/libraries

Renewals and enquiries: 0300 123 4049

Textphone for hearing or 0300 123 4041
speech impaired users:

L32

Hertfordshire

THE NEW GROVE
TWENTIETH-CENTURY
ENGLISH MASTERS

THE NEW GROVE
DICTIONARY OF MUSIC AND MUSICIANS

Editor: Stanley Sadie

The Composer Biography Series

BACH FAMILY
BEETHOVEN
EARLY ROMANTIC MASTERS 1
EARLY ROMANTIC MASTERS 2
FRENCH BAROQUE MASTERS
HANDEL
HAYDN
HIGH RENAISSANCE MASTERS
ITALIAN BAROQUE MASTERS
LATE ROMANTIC MASTERS
MASTERS OF ITALIAN OPERA
MODERN MASTERS
MOZART
NORTH EUROPEAN BAROQUE MASTERS
RUSSIAN MASTERS 1
RUSSIAN MASTERS 2
SCHUBERT
SECOND VIENNESE SCHOOL
TURN OF THE CENTURY MASTERS
TWENTIETH-CENTURY ENGLISH MASTERS
TWENTIETH-CENTURY FRENCH MASTERS
WAGNER

THE NEW GROVE®

Twentieth-century
English Masters

**ELGAR   DELIUS
VAUGHAN WILLIAMS   HOLST
WALTON TIPPETT BRITTEN**

Diana McVeagh

Anthony Payne

Hugh Ottaway

Imogen Holst

Ian Kemp

Peter Evans

MACMILLAN

First published in
The New Grove Dictionary of Music and Musicians®,
edited by Stanley Sadie, 1980

The New Grove and *The New Grove Dictionary of Music and Musicians*
are registered trademarks of Macmillan Publishers Limited, London

First published in UK in paperback with additions 1986 by
PAPERMAC
a division of Macmillan Publishers Limited
London and Basingstoke

First published in UK in hardback with additions 1986 by
MACMILLAN LONDON LIMITED
4 Little Essex Street London WC2R 3LF
and Basingstoke

British Library Cataloguing in Publication Data

English 20th-century Masters: Elgar, Delius,
    Vaughan Williams, Holst, Walton, Tippett, Britten.
    —(The Composer biography series)
    1. Composers—England   2. Music—England—
    20th century—History and criticism
    I. McVeagh, Diana   II. The new Grove dictionary
    of music and musicians   III. Series
    780'.92'2   ML286.4

ISBN 0-333-40241-3 (hardback)
ISBN 0-333-40242-1 (paperback)

First American edition in book form with additions 1986 by
W. W. NORTON & COMPANY
500 Fifth Avenue, New York NY 10110

ISBN 0-393-02285-4 (hardback)
ISBN 0-393-30351-9 (paperback)

Printed in Great Britain

Contents

List of illustrations

Abbreviations

Preface

Edward Elgar   *Diana McVeagh*
I	Life	1
II	Works	24
	Work-list	51
	Bibliography	59

Frederick Delius   *Anthony Payne*
I	Life	69
II	Works	74
	Work-list	88
	Bibliography	92

Ralph Vaughan Williams   *Hugh Ottaway*
I	Life	97
II	Works	108
	Work-list	132
	Bibliography	139

Gustav Holst   *Imogen Holst*
I	Life	145
II	Works	155
	Work-list	166
	Bibliography	170

William Walton   *Hugh Ottaway*
I	Life	175
II	Works	178
	Work-list	193
	Bibliography	196

Michael Tippett	*Ian Kemp*	
I	Life	201
II	Works	206
	Work-list	231
	Bibliography	234
Benjamin Britten	*Peter Evans*	
I	Life	239
II	Instrumental music	247
III	Solo vocal music	253
IV	Choral works	264
V	Music for children and amateurs	269
VI	Dramatic works	273
	Work-list	289
	Bibliography	294
Index		297

List of illustrations

1. Edward Elgar and his wife, Alice, *c*1891 — 4

2. Edward Elgar wearing the insignia of the Order of Merit — 16

3. Autograph MS from an intermediate stage in Elgar's composition of 'The Dream of Gerontius' (British Library, London, Add.47902, f.255*r*) — 31

4. Part of an autograph letter from Elgar to Jaeger (Elgar Birthplace, Lower Broadheath) — 34

5. A performance of Elgar's 'The Kingdom' in Gloucester Cathedral, 6 September 1922 — 38

6. Edward Elgar and George Bernard Shaw, 1929 — 46

7. Nina and Edvard Grieg, Johan Halvorsen, Frederick Delius and Christian Sinding at a card party — 70

8. Title-page of the first edition of the vocal score of Delius's 'Fennimore and Gerda' — 79

9. Frederick Delius: portrait by Jelka Delius (Grainger Museum, Melbourne) — 85

10. Ralph Vaughan Williams and Gustav Holst — 103

11. Scene from the first production of Vaughan Williams's 'Job' — 120

12. Autograph MS from the first movement of Vaughan Williams's Symphony no. 5 (British Library, London, Add.50372, ff.2*v*, 3, 4) — 125

13. Ralph Vaughan Williams — 129

14. Gustav Holst: portrait by Millicent Woodforde (National Portrait Gallery, London) — 152

15. Sketch for the opening bars of Holst's 'The Hymn of Jesus' (Edwin Evans Collection, Central Music Library, Westminster, London)   158

16. Gustav Holst, aged 59   163

17. Screen for the 1923 performance of Walton's 'Façade'   180

18. William Walton   189

19. Michael Tippett   204

20. Scene from Act 3 of Tippett's 'The Knot Garden'   214

21. Autograph MS from Tippett's 'The Vision of St Augustine'   218

22. Benjamin Britten and Eric Crozier, 1949   242

23. Benjamin Britten and Peter Pears, 1967   258

24. Benjamin Britten in conversation with a Squirrel during a rehearsal of 'Noye's Fludde'   271

25. Scene from the first production of Britten's 'Peter Grimes'   274

26. Autograph sketch from Britten's 'Curlew River'   284

27. Benjamin Britten, 1976   287

Cover: 'Landscape of the Malvern Distance': painting (1943) by Paul Nash (Southampton Art Gallery)

Illustration acknowledgments

We are grateful to the following for permission to reproduce illustrative material: Elgar Birthplace Trust, Lower Broadheath, Worcester (figs.1, 2, 4); Elgar Will Trust, Williams and Glynn's Trust Co. Ltd, London/photo British Library, London (fig.3); Times Newspapers Ltd, London (fig.5); Trustees of the Sir Barry Jackson Trust, Birmingham (fig.6); Delius Trust Archive, London (fig.7)/ photo Grainger Museum, University of Melbourne (fig.9); Holst Birthplace Museum, Cheltenham/photo W. G. Whittaker (fig.10); Theatre Museum, Victoria and Albert Museum, London (fig.11); Mrs R. Vaughan Williams, British Library, London, and Oxford University Press (fig.12); photo Allan Chappelow, London (fig.13); National Portrait Gallery, London (fig.14); Central Music Library, Westminster City Libraries, London, and Stainer & Bell Ltd, London (fig.15); John Gay, London/photo Martha Stern (fig.16); photo Christina Burton, London (fig.18); Sunday Times, London/photo Michael Ward (fig.19); photo Stuart Robinson, Redruth (fig.20); Sir Michael Tippett and Schott & Co. Ltd, London (fig.21); BBC Hulton Picture Library, London (fig.22); Executors of the Britten Estate, Aldeburgh/photo Clive Strutt, Leiston (fig.23); Peter Hutten, Wollongong/photo Kurt Hutton (fig.24); Harvard Theatre Collection, Cambridge, Massachusetts/photo Angus McBean (fig.25); Executors of the Britten Estate, Aldeburgh, and Faber Music Ltd, London (fig.26); photo Clive Barda, London (fig.27); Southampton Art Gallery (cover).

Music example acknowledgment

We are grateful to the music publishers Schott and Co. Ltd, London, for permission to reproduce copyright material in the essay on Sir Michael Tippett.

General abbreviations

A	alto, contralto [voice]	inc.	incomplete
ABC	American Broadcasting Company	inst	instrument, instrumental
		ISCM	International Society for Contemporary Music
acc.	accompaniment, accompanied by		
appx	appendix	K	Köchel cataogue [Mozart]
aut.	autumn		
		LPO	London Philharmonic Orchestra
B	bass [voice]		
b	bass [instrument]	LSO	London Symphony Orchestra
Bar	baritone [voice]		
BBC	British Broadcasting Corporation		
		mand	mandolin
bn	bassoon	Mez	mezzo-soprano
BWV	Bach-Werke-Verzeichnis [Schmieder, catalogue of J. S. Bach's works]	movt	movement
		n.d.	no date of publication
c	circa [about]		
CBSO	City of Birmingham Symphony Orchestra	ob	oboe
		obbl	obbligato
cl	clarinet	off	offertory
collab.	in collaboration with	orch	orchestra, orchestral
conc.	concerto	orchd	orchestrated (by)
cond.	conductor, conducted by	org	organ
Ct	countertenor	ov.	overture
db	double bass	perc	percussion
		perf.	performance, performed (by)
edn.	edition		
EMI	Electrical and Musical Industries	pf	piano
		pic	piccolo
		PO	Philharmonic Orchestra
fl	flute	prol	prologue
facs.	facsimile	pubd	published
frag.	fragment		
FRCO	Fellow of the Royal College of Organists	qnt	quintet
		qt	quartet
gui	guitar		
		R	photographic reprint
hn	horn	r	recto
hpd	harpsichord	RAF	Royal Air Force

RAM	Royal Academy of Music, London	transcr.	transcription, transcribed by/for
RCM	Royal College of Music, London	trbn	trombone
rec	recorder	U.	University
repr.	reprinted		
rev.	revision, revised (by/for)	v, vv	voice, voices
RPO	Royal Philharmonic Orchestra	*v*	verso
		va	viola
		vc	cello
S	soprano [voice]	vn	violin
sax	saxophone		
SO	Symphony Orchestra	WoO	Werke ohne Opuszahl [works without opus number]
str	string(s)		
sym.	symphony, symphonic		
		ww	woodwind
T	tenor [voice]		
timp	timpani		
tpt	trumpet	YMCA	Young Men's Christian Association
Tr	treble [voice]		

Symbols for the library sources of works, printed in *italic*, correspond to those used in *Répertoire International des Sources Musicales*, Ser. A.

Bibliographical abbreviations

DNB	*Dictionary of National Biography* (London, 1885–1901, suppls.)
Grove 2	*Grove's Dictionary of Music and Musicians*, 2nd edn.
JEFDSS	*The Journal of the English Folk Dance and Song Society*
ML	*Music and Letters*
MMR	*The Monthly Musical Record*
MO	*Musical Opinion*
MQ	*The Musical Quarterly*
MR	*The Music Review*
MT	*The Musical Times*
NOHM	*The New Oxford History of Music*, ed. E. Wellesz, J. A. Westrup and G. Abraham (London, 1954)
PRMA	*Proceedings of the Royal Musical Association*
SMA	*Studies in Music* (Australia)
SovM	*Sovetskaya muzïka*

Preface

This volume is one of a series of short biographies derived from *The New Grove Dictionary of Music and Musicians* (London, 1980). In their original form, the texts were written in the mid-1970s, and finalized at the end of that decade. For this reprint, they have been brought up to date, some small corrections have been made, and the information in the work-lists has (in most cases) been substantially expanded. This emendation has been undertaken by the original authors for the essays on Elgar, Tippett and Britten. The essay on Delius has been prepared by Lionel Carley, that on Holst by Colin Matthews (assisted by Lowinger Maddison), and those on Vaughan Williams and Walton by Stewart Craggs.

The fact that the texts of the books in the series originated as dictionary articles inevitably gives them a character somewhat different from that of books conceived as such. They are designed, first of all, to accommodate a very great deal of information in a manner that makes reference quick and easy. Their first concern is with fact rather than opinion, and this leads to a larger than usual proportion of the texts being devoted to biography than to critical discussion. The nature of a reference work gives it a particular obligation to convey received knowledge and to treat of composers' lives and works in an encyclopedic fashion, with proper acknowledgment of sources and due care to reflect different standpoints, rather than to embody imaginative or speculative writing about a composer's character or his music. It is hoped that the comprehensive work-lists and extended bibliographies, indicative of the origins of the books in a reference work, will be valuable to the reader who is eager for full and accurate reference information and who may not have ready access to *The New Grove Dictionary* or who may prefer to have it in this more compact form.

S.S.

EDWARD ELGAR

Diana McVeagh

CHAPTER ONE

Life

Elgar's abundant invention, largeness of vision, and strength and singularity of musical character place him high among European Romantic artists and at the peak of British music of his time. He drew inspiration from the culture and landscape of his own country, resourcefulness from the study of his continental colleagues; and he worked in all the major forms except opera, creating a significant body of symphonic literature, the finest oratorio by an Englishman, and in his popular music a style of direct national appeal.

I Early years

Edward William Elgar was born in Lower Broadheath, near Worcester on 2 June 1857. His father, William Henry Elgar (1821–1906), a Dover man, was apprenticed to a London music firm, then in 1841 settled in Worcester, establishing a piano-tuning round and in 1863 opening a music shop. Among his early clients was the dowager queen Adelaide, and through this appointment W. H. Elgar came to tune the instruments of the local county families. Though a Protestant until later in life, he was engaged in 1846 as organist of St George's Roman Catholic Church, Worcester, and, a handy violinist and pianist as well, quickly became an influence in the city's musical life. In 1848 he married Ann Greening (1822–1902), a country woman from the nearby village of Claines, with taste and inclination for the arts.

Edward, the fourth of their seven children, was born in the country cottage where the Elgars briefly lived (1856–9), and his formative years were spent in Worcester, from 1863 over the shop, Elgar Bros., at 10 High Street. He can have composed no music at the cottage of his birth. But he was sent back to Broadheath for holidays at a farm, and the hamlet – its beauty, isolation, and view of the Malvern Hills – took hold of his imagination. That he alone of his brothers and sisters was born there must early have set him apart. About the age of ten he composed music for a family play on which he later drew for the *Wand of Youth* suites (1907, 1908) and *The Starlight Express* (1915).

His schooling was local and Catholic, first at a dame school, then just outside Worcester at Spetchley Park and (1868) at Littleton House. At 15 he had to earn his living, and briefly worked in a solicitor's office (1872–3). He won praise as a child for his piano improvisations, but he had no formal training in music beyond violin lessons from a Worcester teacher and, in 1877 and 1878, from Adolf Pollitzer in London. He absorbed what he could, in his father's shop and organ loft, in the cathedral services and in the city's music societies. Plans for studying at the Leipzig Conservatory foundered for lack of means. At 16 he left business and became, for the rest of his life, a freelance musician, never again holding a regular secure post.

There was plenty of local work. He became assistant, then successor (1885), to his father as organist at St George's. As a violinist his name appeared regularly from 1873. He led the Worcester Amateur Instrumental

Society (1877) and the Worcester Philharmonic (1879), accompanied then conducted (1879) the Glee Club, played the bassoon in a wind quintet (with two flutes and no horn), coached and conducted (1879–84) the staff of the County Lunatic Asylum at Powick, and established a violin teaching practice. There was more music-making in Worcester than in many a comparable English city for, with Hereford and Gloucester, it was host once in three years to the Three Choirs Festival, which involved the townspeople as well as the Anglican cathedral choirs. Elgar played in the violins for the Worcester festivals of 1878 (in the seconds), 1881 (in the firsts) and 1884 (under Dvořák), and indeed in many subsequent festivals. He became conductor of the Worcester Amateur Instrumental Society (1882–9) and in 1882 took his first regular job outside his city as a first violin in W. C. Stockley's orchestra at Birmingham. There, on 13 December 1883, Stockley performed Elgar's *Intermezzo: Sérénade mauresque* (Suite in D). On 1 May 1884 the Worcester Philharmonic Society under the cathedral organist gave his *Sevillana*; Elgar had shown the score to Pollitzer, who brought about a London performance under August Manns at the Crystal Palace on 12 May 1884.

Such all-round activity would have satisfied and supported many a young musician. But Elgar, who had relinquished the idea of becoming a concert violinist, had been composing all the time, in moments snatched between travelling, or at the end of a day's teaching – and he was not robust. Original music exists for choir, orchestra, wind quintet and string ensembles as well as arrangements and exercises. His school was the sharp one of performance; if he lacked guidance, he suffered

3

1. *Elgar and his wife, Alice, c1891*

no false influence; and he acquired craft and speed. Though some of the early music is personal, none is exceptional, and Elgar must have been sustained at this time by an inward sense of power. In his private life he had suffered a rebuff. Helen Weaver, daughter of a tradesman in his own street, was studying music in Leipzig, and Elgar had joined her and her friend for a brief holiday, packed with concert-going, early in 1883. That summer they became engaged; but the Weavers were chapel-goers, and it came to nothing – unless Elgar's later music enshrined his love. But in 1889 he found a partner to share his belief in himself. He had extended his teaching to Malvern, and there in 1886 Caroline Alice Roberts came to him as a piano pupil. She was a person of some consequence, the daughter of Major-General Sir Henry Gee Roberts, KCB. She had been born in India (on 9 October 1848) and, when she met Elgar, was living with her widowed mother at Redmarley d'Abitot. She had accomplishments a little beyond those of the traditional daughter-at-home: she had published a novel, had a facility for verse, knew German, and sang in a choir. In Elgar she saw a slight, dark, youngish man, whose aloof manner could not hide his nervous sensibility and his dissatisfaction with his manner of life. She was prepared to take instruction in the Catholic faith – Elgar was born a Catholic, his mother having in 1852 entered the Church her husband served as organist. They were married quietly, with little family support, in a side-chapel at Brompton Oratory, London, on 8 May 1889.

II The 1890s
Resigning most of his Midlands appointments, Elgar moved to London, first to a rented house, then to a

borrowed house in Norwood, close by the Crystal Palace, where he was able to hear the enterprising programmes Manns was conducting there. Elgar is reckoned of provincial origin, but Alice gave him the independence to absorb the most recent music the capital could offer. In March 1890 they moved to 51 Avonmore Road, West Kensington, and in August their only child, Carice, was born. Elgar tried to establish himself. Some small violin pieces were in print, and he sold some more, including *Salut d'amour* – for years his most frequently played piece – for only a few guineas. Manns conducted the orchestral version on 11 November 1889, and the Suite in D the following February. Elgar did not secure other London performances and no pupils came. His disappointment was acute. But he composed there his first major work, the assured and uninhibited *Froissart*, in response to an invitation from the Three Choirs Festival, and conducted it in the Worcester Public Hall on 10 September 1890. London did not take it up, and after a cold, hard winter the Elgars retreated; in June 1891 they took a house, Forli, in Malvern, and Elgar resumed his old activities.

It was, to his mind, defeat; and some humiliation was bound to be felt by a composer who had made a bid for London and had to fall back on Kapellmeister-ish jobs in the provinces. But Elgar had other reasons to feel an outsider. He was a Catholic in a staunchly Protestant community. Though from early days he had cherished the Romantic belief that the artist was a visionary and a man apart, his neighbours knew him as a shopkeeper's son; and to be in trade, according to the rigid class structure of small English towns of the time, was to be unacceptable. He had made his position the more equivocal by marrying above him, taking a wife conscious of niceties of convention which meant little to him. He disliked any work other than composing (teaching, he once said, was in general like turning a grindstone with a dislocated shoulder); but few composers have been able to live without supplementary uncongenial work. Elgar felt his divided position keenly. By temperament volatile, proud and shy, he developed during these years a tendency to violent and severe depressions, masked by a manner sometimes jocular, sometimes touchy. At the time of Queen Victoria's Diamond Jubilee in 1897, when he was a national figure, he sent a card on the morning of a formal luncheon party which he had previously accepted: 'You would not wish your board to be disgraced by the presence of a piano-tuner's son and his wife'.

That was an extreme moment. His happier nature, and the trust and tenderness between him and his wife, are revealed at the central point of his existence, his autograph scores and sketches. There is a skeleton draft of *The Black Knight* signed 'C. Alice and E. Elgar, Aug: 29, 1889', three months after their marriage; and 'Braut' (as he had called Helen, and now called Alice), occurs in many such jottings as 'Braut helped a great deal to make these little tunes' or 'Mrs Edward Elgar begs to say that these pens are infinitely too good for a wicked Braut'.

During the 1890s his achievement and reputation in the provinces grew steadily. *Froissart* had been accepted by the London publishers Novello, who specialized in the cantatas then popular at provincial festivals. Elgar turned his attention to that market. *The Black Knight* was completed, and produced on 18 April 1893 by the Worcester Festival Choral Society. 1896 saw the first performances of his oratorio *The Light of Life* (*Lux Christi*) at the Worcester Three Choirs Festival on 10 September and of *Scenes from the Saga of King Olaf* during the North Staffordshire Festival at Hanley on 30 October. His first real London success came on 19 April 1897 with the *Imperial March* composed for the Jubilee; and Queen Victoria accepted the dedication of a commission for the Leeds Festival, the large-scale cantata *Caractacus*, which Elgar conducted on 5 October 1898. From the start he was involved in the production of his music, and performances increasingly took him to London and the regional centres. In 1898 the Worcestershire Philharmonic Society was formed, as recognition of his growing status (though he was still teaching), and this he conducted until 1904, introducing works by men he was now meeting professionally, such as Bantock, Cowen, Walford Davies, Mackenzie, Parry, Stanford and Sullivan, and also playing the classics and much French music.

The plots of the cantatas are historical romances, at several removes from Elgar's life (though in each is a point of self-identification). But they show clearly that, if he was looking to the British festival for their promotion, he was also looking across the channel for matters of style and vocabulary. Friends had taken the Elgars holidaying to Germany in the 1890s and he had heard much Wagner, and at home he had studied and performed other men's scores, from Weber to Gounod. The avoidance of a national boundary in the cantatas is inspiriting. When after Elgar's death they went unheard, there was speculation about how he had developed so suddenly as to produce *Enigma* and *Gerontius*. It was not sudden at all. Some of his music of the 1890s is trite or overblown, a good deal is no more than picturesque, but the proximity of the masterpieces is to be heard at every other turn. Released from words altogether into an orchestral variation set, or disciplined by fine words on a subject both personal and universal, he found the freedom and the pressure he needed.

III Fame

The Variations on an Original Theme ('Enigma') op.36 were begun 'in a spirit of humour and continued in deep seriousness', Elgar recalled in 1911. They acquired a threefold interest. Quite simply, the music is the most distinguished British orchestral work to that date. Then there was the entertainment of identifying the friend 'pictured within' each variation: the genesis of the work had been Elgar's improvising at the piano from one theme in the manner of a dozen friends, all met during the previous weeks. These quickly became known and were found to include G. R. Sinclair (the organist of Hereford Cathedral); 'Nimrod' (A. J. Jaeger, publishing office manager at Novello); Worcestershire friends, some of them amateur musicians, some not (an author, a country squire, an architect); Alice Elgar (the first variation) and Elgar himself (the last). But this was still not the solution of the 'enigma' which has teased musicians ever since. Elgar wrote: 'the Enigma I will not explain – its "dark saying" must be left unguessed ... further, through and over the whole set another and larger theme "goes", but is not played'. (The second tune, if it exists, has often been sought.) His wife and Jaeger are thought to be the only people who knew the answer. In the early years Elgar seemed to want the secret guessed, but later he avoided the subject. In letters of the time he spoke always of 'my Variations', and, though the work is now known as the 'Enigma Variations', 'enigma' applies to the theme only, and was added in pencil to the autograph. At the end of the score Elgar quoted from Tasso: 'Bramo assai, poco spero, nulla chieggio' ('I long for much, I hope for little, I ask for nothing'), and in *The Music Makers* (1912) he quoted the music of the theme to symbolize the loneliness of the creative artist.

The Variations brought him to national prominence on their production by Hans Richter at St James's Hall, London, on 19 June 1899. That autumn Clara Butt introduced his orchestral song cycle *Sea Pictures* at the Norwich Festival. By then he was considering a commission, offered on the strength of *Caractacus,* for the major choral work for the Birmingham Triennial Festival of 1900. As if to emphasize and fully to face one element in his isolation, he chose as his text the greater part of the outstanding English Catholic poem of the day, John Henry Newman's *The Dream of Gerontius* (1866). It had meant so much to him that, even before their engagement, he and Alice had indicated in their copies those passages that had sustained General Gordon during the Khartoum siege. Elgar began work early in 1900. His progress is vividly, searingly told in the letters exchanged between him and Jaeger (1860–1909), who since 1897 had become his champion, close confidant and, on occasion, critic (it was he who persuaded Elgar to lengthen the finale of the Variations, and to face a supreme moment in *Gerontius*). Elgar poured out in an unselfconscious torrent his joy in creation, in his own powers, in matching himself to his great subject; and his humility to his God, his teasing warmth to his friend, his practical sense over the printing of his music: all in letters full of the hilarious 'enharmonic' puns and phonetic 'mis'spellings he loved, decorated with lively pen-and-ink drawings.

But the performance of *Gerontius* fell short of the work. By the day, 3 October 1900, it was obvious that several factors had contributed. The chorus master had died during the preparation. The complexity and strangeness of the idiom had been underestimated. There was only one full score, the autograph, which Hans Richter had only ten days before the performance. Elgar's overwrought tactlessness at rehearsal caused some resentment. Richter was unable to prevent the chorus from sounding apprehensive and losing pitch, and Edward Lloyd, Plunket Greene and Marie Brema were not ideally cast. Though many musicians grasped the work's stature, to most of the audience it was a comparative failure. Elgar's bitter disappointment burst out: 'I always said God was against art . . . I have allowed my heart to open once – it is now shut against every religious feeling and every soft, gentle impulse *for ever*'. But quickly he was disclaiming the depths of his feeling, attributing his depression to other causes, protesting his interest in golf: trying on a defensive mask.

Cockaigne (*In London Town*), the 'healthy, humorous' overture first performed under him on 20 June 1901 in London, and dedicated to 'my friends the members of British orchestras', showed every sign of cheerfulness. But Elgar's autographs often reveal more than his printed scores, and that of *Cockaigne* bears a quotation from *Piers Plowman*: 'Metelees & monelees on Malverne hulles'. Elgar confided to Jaeger in

11

December 1898 that he needed £300 a year, and that year had earned only £200. As a reward for *Gerontius* the Elgars had to go without fires. Novello were not markedly generous, and Elgar held it against them that in the 1890s they printed only vocal, not full scores, which did not encourage performances: orchestral scores of *King Olaf* and *Caractacus* were not published until 1905. For a short time in 1899 he changed to Boosey & Hawkes. That year the Elgars had moved to a slightly larger house, Craeg Lea, at Malvern Wells, and between 1898 and 1904 they rented a summer cottage, Birchwood Lodge, in thick woods on the north slopes of the Malvern Hills, which gave Elgar the informal life he so needed (his knowledge of the country was down-to-earth and loving). But in autumn 1900 he was talking, with perhaps not much exaggeration, of having to take up a trade, and in 1904 even of teaching the violin again. He had since 1898 been wanting to compose a symphony inspired by Gordon's heroism and religious zeal, and had even offered it for the 1899 Three Choirs Festival and then withdrawn it. By 1904, asking where the money would come from while he composed such symphonies and chamber music, he was showing some cynicism – unless, once again, he was masking a deeper unease.

Yet by now he was famous. In recognition of the Variations the University of Cambridge conferred an honorary doctorate on him in November 1900, the first of many such British and foreign honours. At Jaeger's persuasion prominent German musicians had attended the production of *Gerontius* and had been so impressed that performances followed under Julius Buths at Düsseldorf in December 1901 and again at the Lower Rhine

Festival, held there in May 1902 (when Muriel Foster first sang the Angel's role complete). Elgar, present and much lauded, was hailed by Richard Strauss as the 'first English progressivist'. On the continent Weingartner, Steinbach, Busoni and Colonne, among others, began to show interest. But the second English performance (with some cuts) was by Elgar's own Worcestershire Philharmonic Society on 9 May 1901. After it, Elgar particularly asked that the *Musical Times* report should record favourably the first performance in the same concert of a piece by the orchestra's leader; if he was touchy about his own feelings, he was also alive to those of others. Performances of *Gerontius* at the 1902 Worcester Three Choirs Festival, and in Sheffield, Manchester, Hanley, Chicago and New York, came before the first in London, in the as yet unconsecrated (Catholic) Westminster Cathedral on 6 June 1903. The first two *Pomp and Circumstance* marches carried a broader appeal, and the trio melody from no.1, re-used in the *Coronation Ode* of 1902 for Edward VII, began to gain worldwide celebrity to A. C. Benson's words as 'Land of Hope and Glory'. Elgar had inquired the previous year about setting Kipling's *Recessional*, but took it no further. Could it have been as popular?

IV Hereford and London

As a boy Elgar had been struck by his schoolmaster's comment that Christ's apostles, before their calling, had been unremarkable men, and he planned a sequence of three oratorios illustrating their training and the work of the young Church. Sustained effort on the first, *The Apostles*, which he conducted at Birmingham on 14 October 1903, exhausted him, and, though this time the

13

performance was a complete success, the minor ailments of stress that plagued him most of his life – eye weakness, indigestion, throat trouble – became overwhelming. The Elgars wintered in 1903–4 in Italy, which then became, as Bavaria had in the 1890s, their favoured holiday place (with further visits in early 1907, 1907–8, 1909 and 1913). It seems that this most English of composers was at his most relaxed abroad. The hoped-for symphony, however, did not come, and it was his third concert overture, *In the South* (*Alassio*), that became the new work at the three-day Elgar Festival, devoted entirely to his music, held at the Royal Opera House, Covent Garden, 14–16 March 1904. Such an honour had never been accorded a living English composer.

After his wife's death in 1920 Elgar must have read through the diaries she meticulously kept through all their marriage, for he began a précis of the most significant dates. Her first lesson with him, 6 October 1886, is there. And there are two pages of jottings for 1904: the command to dine with the king, the levée, the Festival, Elgar's election to the Athenaeum club, his knighthood, the invitation to become Peyton Professor at Birmingham, the move to a substantial house, Plâs Gwyn at Hereford, even the installation of a telephone. It was his year.

Richard Peyton, a business man, endowed a chair of music at Birmingham University on the condition that Elgar became the first professor. Reluctant in some respects, Elgar was in others gratified, for in this way he joined the academic men from outside their ranks. He delivered eight lectures between March 1905 and November 1906, largely on the state of British music at the time (they were published in 1968). All his life he detested the world of musical commerce and held a low opinion of the taste of the British public. He allowed these feelings to show in his lectures, and he commented on the general want of fire in compositions and performances of the time. He called for better training, subsidized music and a national opera, but spoke with more common sense and courage than tact, and his remarks were given wide and controversial publicity. When, talking of Brahms's Third Symphony, he championed absolute music, Ernest Newman demanded to know why Elgar had composed so much descriptive music. He did good work in establishing a library, but was thankful merely to arrange the next series of lectures and in 1908 to relinquish the post to Granville Bantock. The Introduction and Allegro (London, 8 March 1905), the sequel to *The Apostles* called *The Kingdom* (Birmingham, 3 October 1906) and the First Symphony (conducted by Richter, Manchester, 3 December 1908) constituted his real work in the first years at Plâs Gwyn. The symphony in particular was acclaimed; there were nearly 100 performances in its first year, in cities as far apart as Vienna, St Petersburg, Leipzig and New York.

The Introduction and Allegro was dedicated to S. S. Sanford, professor at Yale University, an indication of Elgar's forthcoming American visits, to accept a Yale doctorate in 1905 and to conduct his music in 1906, 1907 and 1911. Elgar's dedications merit attention: they include 'the greater glory of God' (the prime religious works), Hans Richter (First Symphony), the memory of Edward VII (Second Symphony), the music critic Ernest Newman (the Piano Quintet); colleagues; cultivated men of substance who delighted in furthering his career, such as Rodewald in Liverpool, Kilburn in

2. Elgar wearing the insignia of the Order of Merit, 1911

Bishop Auckland, Speyer and Schuster near London; and later in life men of letters, Sir Sidney Colvin (Cello Concerto) and Bernard Shaw (*Severn Suite*). The Violin Concerto is dedicated to Kreisler, who gave its first performance in London, 10 November 1910. The man closely involved in the violin technicalities of its composition, however, was W. H. Reed, a member of the LSO and its leader from 1912, whose kindly, admiring memoir of Elgar is a source of first-hand memories, joining those which cover the earlier Malvern days by 'Dorabella', the tenth Enigma Variation, and Rosa Burley, headmistress of a school where Elgar taught. Each book tells much about its author as well as its subject who, as he passed through his 50s, presented an increasingly complex face. To an insecure man, nothing is harder to bear than success. Honestly rejoicing in the Order of Merit bestowed on him in 1911, he was to the public gaze a figure of military bearing with something of the bluff country squire. Yet in his creative self-examination he needed to re-enter his childhood (the *Wand of Youth* suites), in his letters he could one day exult in the 'emotionalism' of his music and another curse the providence that gave him gifts, and, while defending his right to privacy, invite speculation by publishing 'enigmas'.

The Violin Concerto bears the incomplete quotation 'Aquí está encerrada el alma de . . . . .' from the preface of Le Sage's novel *Gil Blas*. The 'soul enshrined' in this intimate, regretful music could be that of an American friend, Julia Worthington; of an English friend, Alice Stuart-Wortley; of the violin; or of Elgar himself. As to all Elgar's riddles, the answer may be allegorical, and yield most when it is pressed least. His music draws deeply on private sources and allusions, and in that sense, as in others, is as romantic as any composed. 'Music is in the air', he said in the 1890s, 'you simply take as much as you require!'; and, of his own music: 'It's a man's attitude to life'. In retirement he refused to write his autobiography; in effect, he had already written it.

Around the time of the Violin Concerto it seems probable that he experienced some personal crisis and that his attachment to Alice Stuart-Wortley deepened into romance. Tender themes in the concerto were known by his name for her, 'Windflower', and for some years she was his musical confidante, receiving sketches as they were composed. Five years younger than him, she was a woman of grace and sensibility, daughter of the painter Millais, and a talented amateur pianist. Her husband was Conservative MP for a Sheffield division and was made a peer in 1916. All four people concerned were loyal and circumspect, and if indeed there was a flame between the composer and his 'other' Alice, its fire was surely creative. After the deaths of her husband and his wife, there remained between them a warm bond of affection.

The last major work composed in Hereford was the Second Symphony, produced under Elgar in London on 24 May 1911. By 1912 the Elgars were living in London; the move could be seen as a vindication of their retreat from the capital at the start of their marriage, and Severn House, in Hampstead, built by Norman Shaw, was an appropriate setting for a great man. There they entertained, and could indulge their delight in theatre-going. There were composed *The Music Makers* (Birmingham, 1 October 1912) and *Falstaff* (Leeds,

2 October 1913), both conducted by Elgar, both strangely autobiographical, the ode with self-quotations from earlier works, the symphonic study, for all Elgar's learned literary essay printed at the time, less Shakespearean than Elgarian. Only two London years passed before war came. 'Land of Hope and Glory' swept through the nation, and Elgar, who had reacted to the outbreak of war with a near-hysterical cry of fear for what might happen in battle to horses, never mind the men, begged for new, less swaggering words to his tune; but quickly realized that the public was in no mood to want them. Musically, the war took Elgar further (after *The Crown of India* of 1912) into theatrical ground with *Carillon* and other dramatic recitations, incidental music (*The Starlight Express*) and ballet (*The Sanguine Fan*). Elgar loved the theatre, plays and opera, and was a frequent visitor to Covent Garden. In 1903 he went some way towards composing a ballet on a Rabelais subject, which was enthusiastically accepted by the Grand Opera Syndicate as a project, but he dropped the idea. Had he wanted above all to compose an opera, it would surely have been welcomed after his 1904 Covent Garden Festival. His continuing search, even during the war years, for a libretto, and his complaint that he was offered nothing but 'blood and lust', suggest that the writing of opera was more of a diversion than a compulsion. The symphonies are his dramas.

His most enduring war music is *The Spirit of England*, three choral settings in temper far removed from his romantic patriotism of earlier years. It has come to seem as though his 'war requiem' is the Cello Concerto, composed, with the chamber music, under the stimulus of Brinkwells, an isolated Sussex cottage in the woods, the Birchwood of his later composing days. The quartet and quintet had their first public performance at the Wigmore Hall, London, on 21 May 1919, and Felix Salmond introduced the Cello Concerto (though Beatrice Harrison soon became more associated with it) at the Queen's Hall on 27 October 1919. It was the last first performance Lady Elgar attended.

It was in fact the last first performance of a major Elgar work. Alice Elgar, who had been failing for some months, died on 7 April 1920, and with her died a part of Elgar's creativity. To attempt to understand this it might be well to consider what had first drawn the young struggling music teacher, of high aspiration, to propose to a tiny lady of gentle manners, strong in will and spirit: his pupil in music, his teacher in ways of the world, and some eight years older than him. The piety and idealism of Elgar's mother had bred in him a distrust of 'modern young women' (his phrase to Jaeger in 1898) and in Alice he found someone to cherish and revere. As the years passed and his stature grew, the nature of their bond might have changed, and it is hard to know with quite what feelings of grief, abandonment, guilt and defensiveness he may have reacted to her death. So he went out into the world alone once more – 'only I am disillusioned and old'.

V Last years

With the help of his daughter Carice, Elgar set about selling Severn House and in 1921 moved into a London flat. But in 1923 he went back to his roots, taking houses near Worcester and in Stratford until in 1929 he moved into his final home, Marl Bank, in Worcester City. His interest in horse-racing, in his dogs, in the good life, had now taken the place of such pastimes as golf, kite-flying, chemistry and heraldry, in which he had before found recreation and which may have been useful for staving off untimely inquiries. Some could discern neither the poet nor the dreamer in this courtly man of presence, hair and moustache now white and high nose more pronounced, a Master of the King's Music (1924) who brushed aside talk of music, affecting ignorance of it. Others, recognizing that the musical and moral values of his world had given way to newer, sharper attitudes, understood his reluctance to commit himself to composition, and his haunting fear that the day of his music was done.

He found companionship and comfort with his Worcester relations, and with such lifelong colleagues as the cathedral organist Ivor Atkins, whose son's account of that friendship is a most valuable supplement to the earlier first-hand memoirs. And as late as 1931 Elgar formed a most touching attachment with a young woman violinist, Vera Hockman, who found in him 'such a gorgeous medley of Michelangelesque grand faults and virtues' and became for the aging man, so briefly, 'my mother, my child, my lover and my friend'.

Some theatre music, suites and arrangements date from his retirement, but possibly his most valuable work lay in the recording studio. Fred Gaisberg of the Gramophone Company had the foresight to engage Elgar in conducting the bulk of his instrumental repertory. From the acoustics of 1914 to the last electrics of 1933, Elgar wholeheartedly cooperated, and the result is a superb series, unrivalled in documentary significance, of early composer–conductor recordings. After the Worcestershire Philharmonic days and an

LSO engagement for the 1911–12 season, Elgar only occasionally conducted other men's music, but in his own he was unmatched for elegance, vitality and justness of proportion. With the 16-year-old Menuhin he recorded the Violin Concerto in 1932, and the following year they performed it together in Paris; Elgar visited Delius at Grez-sur-Loing, and the two elderly men talked of music, books and gardens. In 1931 Elgar was created 1st Baronet of Broadheath. A brief film was made that year of him conducting (see the vivid series of stills, Moore, 1974; and the television documentary, *Hope and Glory*, 1984), and this includes his speaking a few sentences; his voice was also recorded during a rehearsal, and he can be heard playing the piano in five 'improvisations' (1929). Neither the bust by P. Hedley in the National Portrait Gallery nor the portrait by Philip Burne-Jones in Worcester Guildhall is thought to do him justice, but, as well as very many occasional snapshots, there exist fine studio photographs (see Moore, 1972).

Elgar was still under persuasion to complete the oratorio trilogy, but whether because of his deflection after 1906 to symphonic literature or whether because of growing spiritual disillusion, *The Last Judgment* was not to be. Bernard Shaw had a part in what appeared at last to be a resurgence of power. Sparkling friendship with Shaw revived Elgar's old interest in opera, and Sir Barry Jackson, director of the Malvern Festival, was drawn into helping him extract a libretto for *The Spanish Lady* from Ben Jonson's *The Devil is an Ass*. Then in 1932 the BBC, prompted by Shaw and others, commissioned a Third Symphony, which Elgar's frequent grumbles that his music was unwanted had led

people to suppose was part written. Work on both pro-
gressed fast and sketches accumulated, but in autumn
1933 a sciatic pain was found to be caused by a malig-
nant tumour. There was an operation but in November
Elgar appeared to be sinking. Carice sent for Reed, who
gave Elgar the assurance he pleaded for that no-one
should 'tinker' with the incomplete symphony. He
rallied enough to return home, to listen in his last weeks
to his own records, even to supervise by post office
circuit a final recording session in London. After dwell-
ing on his boyhood days beside his beloved river Teme,
where at one point he had wished to be buried, he died,
after being given the last rites, on 23 February 1934.

He was laid beside his wife in the place she had
chosen, St Wulstan's Church, Little Malvern, and is
commemorated by a window based on *The Dream of
Gerontius* in Worcester Cathedral (1935) and a tablet in
Westminster Abbey (1972). In 1938 the cottage at
Broadheath where he was born was opened as a museum
to illustrate his home, his fame and his work.

CHAPTER TWO

Works

I Up to 1899

Elgar began composing before he understood notation, and his phrase 'music is in the air' takes literal and imaginative force with his attempt to write down the singing of the reeds by the river. As a youth he invented copiously; much of his later music existed in some form long before publication, and he returned all his life for themes and inspiration to his early sketchbooks. They hold, for an untrained boy of his period, some adventurous fragments. The warmly romantic style of his early church pieces – suave and devotional – may be partly derived from the music of the Catholic Emancipation movement familiar to him in his own church. In *Ecce sacerdos magnus* (1888) the processional note first sounds. Violin and piano romances, written for the composer–performer, have grace and fluency and a nice balance of sentiment and display – one reason for the popularity of *Salut d'amour* may be that it is easier than most of his pieces to play. Some of the wind quintet music (1878–81) is remarkable for his thorough and stylish investigation of classical sonata forms along the lines of Haydn, Schubert and Mendelssohn, and for the young man's relish for his craft; other wind and Powick orchestra music shows the swing of Elgarian melody.

In *Sevillana* and the Three Characteristic Pieces Elgar's personal sonority can at moments be heard, and his love of sliding in a new counter-melody at a repeat, among much that is brilliant and brash; his Spanish vein, which he often mined, was purely literary – he never visited the country. In the third Characteristic Piece he contrasted the same gavotte in styles of 1700 and 1900, a curious preview, in treatment of time, of his treatment of character in *Enigma*. Up to this point Elgar, at the age of 32, had composed nothing of sustained originality, and his self-trust in removing to London is the more astonishing.

If Elgar had little to offer London, he had much to gather. In July 1889 he went three times to hear *Die Meistersinger* at Covent Garden. From October 1889 to March 1890 he attended the Crystal Palace concerts, day after day, hearing Weber overtures, Meyerbeer selections, Gounod and Massenet, Mendelssohn, Schumann and Brahms, Liszt (*Les préludes*), Berlioz (*Benvenuto Cellini* overture) and Wagner (excerpts, from *Rienzi* to *Die Walküre*). At St James's Hall he heard Hans Richter conduct Brahms's Third Symphony and Parry's Fourth. He knew by this time exactly what he needed. On 6 April 1890 he began composing his concert overture *Froissart*, and though there are plainly responses to what he had heard, his intensive course of education marvellously released his own personality. 'When Chivalry lifted up her lance on high' is quoted on the score from Keats, but it was Elgar's lance that was lifted too. The brilliant opening gesture, the generous cut of the melodies, the long, dying string cadence before the tender clarinet tune, the romantic-bravura atmosphere, are as much of Elgar as moments in the development are of *Hebrides* and *Der fliegende Holländer*.

The String Serenade, composed in 1892 but almost

certainly worked from the lost 1888 pieces, is formally slighter, but its slow movement is the first of Elgar's many with a commandingly sculptured melody held in a diatonic but tense harmonic relationship. A rather similar tune forms *Sursum corda*, though this relies more weakly on rhythmic sequences, more strongly on the aural imagination of timpani rolls and brass calling through a rich texture; and there is too at the climax a more feverish, *Gerontius*-like quality. In happy contrast are the *Spanish Serenade* and other early partsongs, and the six choral songs *Scenes from the Bavarian Highlands*. It may have been an advantage of Elgar's sometimes deplored provincial surroundings that he could write music as simple, pretty and melodious as this. It was a gift he kept all his life.

The main works of the 1890s are the substantial choral and orchestral *The Black Knight*, *The Light of Life*, *King Olaf* and *Caractacus*. All suffer from poor librettos, and the three cantatas from their hybrid form. Elgar's reading was wide and deep, as well as quirky, but here he chose texts which are sometimes muddled dramatically and often commonplace, or worse, in style. It seems that he could ignore these liabilities if he found the particular challenge he needed. He certainly found strong, picturesque situations, and while *The Black Knight* and *King Olaf* are mainly by Longfellow, a poet he was brought up on as a child, *Caractacus* is set on his own Malvern Hills. There is a further personal element that may have significance: in each story there is a character who is an outsider. The Black Knight attacks the established court and castle, King Olaf takes Christianity by force to a heathen land, and the Blind Man and the Bard are cast out by their companions when they gain vision. Possibly without realizing it, Elgar, rejected by the metropolis, identified with these situations. That may not make the cantatas better or worse, but it makes their strengths and weaknesses more easily understood.

In performance the want of niceties in the words is only just noticeable, for on the whole the pace is strong and swift. More damaging is the curious form of the dramatic cantata, which half cries out for staging, but in which 'onstage' murders, for example, have to be narrated. Elgar's talent does at points seem operatic; there is a love duet and a lover's curse in *Olaf*, a 'resolution' trio and a thanksgiving quartet in *Caractacus*, where in particular the voices expand and bloom; had he been born in a continental town with an opera house, he might have developed that way. But he wanted to describe *The Black Knight*, which has no soloists, as a symphony founded on the poem, and there is little doubt that his heart all this time was with the orchestra. No wonder he grudged Novello's not printing full scores: the vocal scores give scant account not only of their colour but of their complexity. Apart from the lavishness of the orchestral writing, there is a most skilful use of solo strings, of registers, of tremolo and other effects, and of expressive percussion (as in the awe-inspiring rolled cymbal in *Caractacus*).

In all four works Elgar used leitmotifs, most freely and imaginatively in *King Olaf* (1896), most intricately in *Caractacus* (1898). He claimed to have learnt the technique as a youth from Mendelssohn's *Elijah*, but in 1892 he had heard *Parsifal*, *Tristan* and *Die Meistersinger* at Bayreuth, and in 1893 the complete *Ring* in Munich. If his leitmotif system did not derive

27

from Wagner, other things did, for he was consistently expanding his harmonic resources by chromatic and augmented progressions, and there are passages in all these works of real 'Wagner sound'. There are other influences, as wide apart as Gounod and Schumann, and though Elgar's personality is strong enough not to be subdued, in sum the works are uneven. At times the mood turns mawkish or aggressive, and then the inter-action of melody, harmony and rhythm seems too easily come by. There is some dull invention (mostly in *The Light of Life*), and some trivial (for example, the choric measure in *Caractacus*). But in the best of *The Light of Life* there is intensity, and of *The Black Knight*, direct-ness. The whole of the first five scenes of *King Olaf* is memorable, with a young man's athletic vigour, almost Verdian, and wide-ranging in mood with grand, rolling passages anticipating the symphonies; both choral bal-lads go with a swing. *Caractacus*, though larger and grander, is stiffer, but the control of pace over certain spans – the long diminuendo of hope dying into the Lament, for instance – is characteristic of Elgar at his best. All the four big choral works of the 1890s can still be heard with genuine enjoyment, not simply as a fore-taste of things to come.

II 1899–1907

Whatever the 'enigma' of the Variations on an Original Theme (1899), one puzzle is how Elgar should in the year 1898–9 have so shrewdly diagnosed his need, after the loosely narrative choral works, for the discipline of variations (the work was not commissioned, and does not seem to have been prompted by Parry's Symphonic Variations of 1897). Concentration on short, separate pieces, on drawing the utmost variety from a restricted source, defined his style and enlarged his capacity. The work was his self-discovery: after trying on 13 personalities over his theme, in the 14th variation he 'came to himself'. Understandably, this final variation is the only one with a trace of assertiveness; otherwise, the sureness of voice matches the technical skill and, for all that they are delicious character-pieces, the variations are impressive as an absolute structure. The G minor–major–minor theme's ending on a major chord implies more contrast of tonality than in fact there is, though variations 5–7 move to C major–minor, and 'Nimrod', the Adagio core of the work, drops with serious, intimate effect from a single sustained G to the key of E♭. 'Nimrod' is among Elgar's most impassioned utterances, a great-hearted melody, the 7ths built by characteristic sequences into a magnificent long crescendo, the climax diffusing gently to end in humility. There are 'dark sayings' in the Variations, but in sum it is the lightly-worn skill, the spontaneity of the theme transformations, and the natural thinking in orchestral terms that give the work its lustre.

Elgar's scoring is so much part of his composition that invention and colour are indivisible. The brilliance of his flamboyant moods has been found almost suspect. But as essential are his melancholy chording for clarinets, bassoons and horns; his string textures which sometimes give a tune wings, sometimes hold it in tranced stillness; and his sombre brass calls. His repeats are particularly intensified, with a new thread of melody (Larghetto, Symphony no.2), or a sense of fresh illumination ('C.A.E.', *Enigma*) or withdrawal ('R.P.A.', *Enigma*), that checks the heart. His pages look fuller than they sound, for, although his orchestra is generally large, his doubling is selective; he gives the doubling instruments only an odd note or two, not the complete melody. It has the curious, wholly personal effect of making even his most assured tunes not wholly self-confident, given as they are through shifting sonorities. Sometimes he reinforces the rhythm (opening of *In the South*), sometimes he adds delicate points of colour (Symphony no.1, cue 66). Elgar in fact phrased with his whole orchestra. He probably learnt this colouring and clarifying technique from late 19th-century composers, Chabrier, Saint-Säens, and particularly Delibes, whose music he chose to conduct at Worcester. The blend of German warmth and French sparkle in the English *Enigma* is irresistible.

Sea Pictures (1899) can most sympathetically be listened to as the composer's reaction to the success of *Enigma* and his intention to strive in the future. The two ambitious songs have a sense of commitment and expanding horizons. 'Sabbath Morning at Sea' is very nearly a great song – it approaches the solemnity of Mahler's then unwritten 'Um Mitternacht', and the contralto tone foreshadows the *Gerontius* Angel. 'The Swimmer', though awkwardly strenuous, carries great excitement. 'Sea Slumber Song' shares with the opening of *King Olaf* and the Enigma 'Romanza' an atmosphere of distance and wonder.

In *The Dream of Gerontius* (1900), widely considered as among his three or four finest works, Elgar found a subject of private but universal significance: an ordinary man on the point of death – dramatic, mysterious and inescapable – and facing his judgment. Gerontius's predicament touched Elgar's own anxieties. His need of faith was the more urgent because of his

3. An intermediate stage in Elgar's composition of 'The Dream of Gerontius', composed 1899–1900; this page was copied in pencil and ink from an earlier sketch, with the change of octave in bars 8–10 written in red ink; the deleted passage in bars 5–7 is the 'Novissima hora est' motif, and the placing of the Soul's entry over the 'Proficiscere' chords was later modified; the large K (in red crayon) stands for 'Koppied'

outwardly exuberant temperament, his late self-discovery, and his near-acceptance of the materially prosperous world around him. *Gerontius* is an affirmation, yet the note of doubt and despair in Part 1 rings as true as the vision of eternity in Part 2. The words of Newman's poem are of higher quality than those Elgar usually set, and give unity to the music which is shaped in wide strong arches for all its close derivation from representative motifs. Some of these motifs modulate inside their own length (partly because they are sequential) and so offer great harmonic mobility. For the role of Gerontius Elgar developed the fluent vocal line of Olaf's Return, which moves easily between speech-rhythms and lyrical expansion (his sketches show how assiduously he worked at this). Though *Gerontius* is the first major English work in which the orchestra is as expressive as the voices, the choral writing is almost as much of an advance; and the integration of chorus and orchestra is complicated and subtle. Yet the weaker moments of invention are in 'Praise to the Holiest' and the Demons' Chorus.

Elgar was more artist than theologian and a few early reactions against the Catholicism of *Gerontius* were largely against the words. But the stress on human sin, shame and guilt, and the idea of Purgatory, where the soul 'lies motionless and happy in my pain', are bound to be alien to some people, who may also find the music so intense as to be oppressive. Not only in *Gerontius* but in many of Elgar's major works there are passages so exposed and vulnerable that most find them a welcome education in sensibility while a few flinch, as they might from elements in Franck, Liszt, Tchaikovsky and Messiaen, or from *Parsifal*.

Elgar could not fail to be influenced by the dedicated seriousness of *Parsifal*, which he saw twice at Bayreuth in 1892. *Parsifal* Act 1 and *Gerontius* Part 1 have strikingly in common their anguished chromatics, for Amfortas and Gerontius (though one is a baritone, the other a tenor), the distant unaccompanied semichoruses, the evocation of the liturgy in the Dresden Amen and the 'Noe' litany, and the closing ritual marches, with ostinatos in *Parsifal*, pedal points in *Gerontius*. The 'Grail' motif (Dresden Amen) and the 'Spirit of the Lord' motif in *The Apostles*, both diatonic, are later transformed by similar harmonic dislocations. The Lord's Supper in *The Kingdom* may owe its place to the Communion in *Parsifal*. A memory of the opening theme of *Parsifal* lies behind the motto theme of Elgar's First Symphony (both are in A♭) and a memory of the Herzeleide motif behind the Cello Concerto. Wagner's writing of his own librettos surely encouraged Elgar to compile his for *The Apostles* and *The Kingdom*; the trilogy was to be his *Ring*, 'oratorio reviewed in the light of Wagnerian music-drama'.

However, *Gerontius* moves much more swiftly than *Parsifal*: the words are uttered faster (English being the lighter language) and Elgar's rate of harmonic change, compared with Wagner's, is lively, even restless. Many of Elgar's motifs are longer, more lyrical and self-sufficient than Wagner's (particularly in Elgar's two later oratorios, with the drawback that they are less malleable). One reason for their length may be the greater part the chorus has in the concert work. At 'Praise to the Holiest' Bayreuth gives way to the needs of Birmingham. But 'Firmly I believe' and 'Softly and gently' are nearer in style to *Lohengrin* or *Meistersinger*, to

4. Part of an autograph letter (dated 7 July 1906) from Elgar to Jaeger referring to the reduction to vocal score of a passage ('The Sign of Healing') from 'The Kingdom'

Verdi or Dvořák, than to anything in *Parsifal*. The triumph of *Gerontius* lies in how surely Elgar took what he wanted from his own past and from his predecessors to form a work conditioned by his country's festival demands at that moment when his religious and romantic fervour were perfectly matched, thereby creating music of such vigour, generosity and startling candour.

The two linked oratorios, *The Apostles* (1903) and *The Kingdom* (1906), were begun as a single work, then planned as the first two in a trilogy (Elgar's earliest scheme), which was to expound the schooling of the young Church, the result on earth, then the result in the next world. Elgar designed them with some didactic thought, choosing Mary Magdalene as a sinner who repents, Judas as one who despairs, and selecting the words from throughout the Scriptures (Powell, 1948) to amplify and make his own comments on the New Testament story. The oratorios share many motifs and gain greatly by being performed in sequence, as Elgar intended. They are charged with being episodic, and defended by reason of this being Elgar's purpose, that he wanted to create a series of frescoes. The finest pages are ardent and mystical, ecstatic contemplations. The most interesting character is Judas, seen as a misguided zealot who attempts to force Christ into a display of supernatural power; Judas dominates Part 2 of *The Apostles* and has a gripping monologue on the transience and hopelessness of life, set against an ironic psalm in the background. *The Apostles* is a curious, individual work. It touches extremes of self-abasement in Mary Magdalene's music and of glory at the end, when the 'Ascended Lord is received by the hierarchy of

Heaven'. It is as progressive as anything he composed: the parallel triads, whole-tone progressions and false relations, and the exoticism of the Morning Psalm, are unmatched elsewhere. But there are also in both works conservative elements: the two Marys sing sensuous lines that recall Massenet, and it is easy to visualize them as pre-Raphaelite figures. Though the trilogy was unfinished, the oratorios revitalized the tradition to some extent; their real successors may be Walton's *Belshazzar's Feast* and, by reaction, Britten's church parables.

The splendid concert overtures *Cockaigne* (1901) and *In the South* (1904), with their physical delight in energy and their frank tunefulness, follow another line. Both are to some extent programmatic – the brass bands in the earlier work, the pugnacious Roman passage in the later – and easily bear comparison with Richard Strauss. *In the South*, lasting some 18 minutes, is really a tone poem (the opening theme is one of several composed earlier as a 'mood' of Dan, G. R. Sinclair's famous bulldog; they are listed in Young, 1955). These overtures' advance over *Froissart* lies largely in Elgar's more refined handling of sonata structure, and his growing ability to bring into relationship images which start as opposites. That principle underlies the Introduction and Allegro for strings, quartet and orchestra (1905), in which the concerto grosso is realized in Romantic terms and finally resolved in song. This intricate piece, rich and free in invention, grand and haunting in resonance, might by analogy pose the question 'where does certainty end and speculation begin?', so poignantly do bold formal statements yield to more tentative impulses. The fugue, which seems to be quite new material, is shown to be connected with the Introduction when a phrase from the bass in bars 7–8 sings out over it. Such a method of development is fundamental in Elgar. His contrapuntal thinking is seldom disciplined for its own sake, and it is not a consequence of harmonic emancipation as it was in late Mahler or early Schoenberg; in this he was not adventurous. But by his free Romantic polyphony he linked apparently unrelated themes in a poetic and individual manner.

Of the five military marches for symphony orchestra called *Pomp and Circumstance* (what an ear for a quotation Elgar had!), no.1, with the popularity of its big tune, has outshone the others. All are stirring, but nos.2 and 3 are in minor keys: the opening of no.2 is tonally ambiguous, of no.3 oddly suppressed, and in each horn calls rip through the Allegro. These are not unthinking celebrations of military might, but the grim tread that stalked Elgar's deeper reflections. However, his unaffected love of English ceremonial, and of the grand moments in Meyerbeer and Verdi, prompted him to compose marches all his life: independent pieces like these, or for particular occasions (*Imperial March*, 1897; *Coronation March*, 1911; *Empire March*, 1924), or as parts of larger works (*Caractacus*, *The Crown of India*). Mostly they are magnificent display pieces, apt for their time, and still of worth, if they can be listened to without nostalgia or guilt for an imperial past. The 'heroic melancholy' that Yeats found in the funeral march from *Grania and Diarmid* is that of the symphonic slow movements. Elgar's march style causes embarrassment only where it sits uneasily, as in the finales of some early choral works, or as an occasional bluster in symphonic contexts. Part of his strength, his appeal to a wide public, lies in that simplicity which enabled him to

37

5. The performance of Elgar's 'The Kingdom' in Gloucester Cathedral (6 September) during the Three Choirs Festival of 1922 in which 'The Apostles' and 'The Kingdom' were performed on successive days; the composer stands to the left of the rostrum

gather an open, honest emotion and cast it into a tune which has entered the national consciousness.

As he approached 50, and the challenge of a symphony could no longer be evaded, Elgar returned to his childhood sketchbooks. The two *Wand of Youth* suites (1907 and 1908), like *Enigma*, concentrated his instrumental thinking. In any medium his style is so assured that a couple of bars are recognizably his, and most numbers in the suites, though brief, are significant. They helped him redefine and single out some of the emotions shortly to be mixed in his symphonic works, and to reach deep into the earliest stirrings of his imagination. It is this that touches off such profound tenderness in, say, 'Slumber Scene', such fun and brightness in the scherzandos – their deft execution is a match for Bizet or Tchaikovsky. Elgar's comment in 1921 that 'as a child . . . no single person was ever kind to me' is an appalling example of how he could colour one experience with the resentment of another. In this music he knew better. He wrote very little for children to perform, but his withdrawals into the adult's world of childhood (*Dream Children*, 1902; *The Starlight Express*, 1915; the *Nursery Suite*, 1931; also often in larger works) are ravishingly beautiful, the music of a loving nature.

III   After 1907

The two symphonies, in A♭ (1908) and E♭ (1911), rank high not only in Elgar's output but in English musical history. Both are long and powerful, without published programmes, only hints and quotations to indicate some inward drama from which they derive their vitality and eloquence. Both are based on classical form but differ from it to the extent that, compared with Brahms (then an accepted model in England), they were considered prolix and slackly constructed by their critics. Certainly the invention in them is copious and their developments are not strictly motivic or fundamentally to do with key contrast. In Elgar the contrasts are between states of mind. Themes act out their dramatic potentials. For instance, the calm processional melody which opens the First Symphony, the 'motto theme' of the whole work, is scarcely drawn on thematically; it returns like a presence or a vision, and changes the course of what it touches.

In all Elgar's larger works, as in the Introduction and Allegro, unexpected likenesses between themes are often disclosed, sometimes as late as the restatement. This kind of allusiveness, by glancing cross-references, even by a texture or a colour, is more poetic than classically symphonic. A rare example of Elgar's showing an allusion as it comes about is the metamorphosis of the theme common to the two middle movements of the First Symphony; here the likeness is candid, the transition itself magical. The symphonic works literally need the passage of musical time, for some themes are recalled in later movements as if a remembered emotion is relived. Elgar needed length, as a novelist sometimes does, to uncover the significance of the past by looking back through more recent experience. His nervous instability of harmony, his sequential writing, avoidance of root positions and fluctuations from active to withdrawn tonal planes all propose key relationships that need time and space for their resolution.

Though Elgar has none of Bruckner's monumental patience and little of Mahler's self-parody, familiarity with their lengthy symphonies has helped to raise critical opinion – which had begun to drop in the 1920s – of Elgar's. Both in Mahler and in Elgar an emotional narrative is held together by the force and sensibility of the composer's musicianship. Elgar's Second, which he called 'the passionate pilgrimage of a soul' as well as heading it with the Shelley quotation 'Rarely, rarely comest thou, Spirit of Delight', contains a transformation of a weird theme in the first movement into a horrifying nightmare in the third; the seeds of that horror are found in a passing progression in the symphony's first full bar. Occasionally a refined idea is provoked to a reaction violent enough to seem raw. Such inflation is common to many Romantic composers; in Elgar, a latecomer, it was intensified by a sophisticated technique being at the service of a complex but unsophisticated man. If the symphonies are to some extent autobiographical, admitting frailties and doubts as well as strengths and visions, then their occasional overworkings, rhythmic monotony and inferior ideas can be accepted as part of a comprehensive and adult perception of his world.

The Violin Concerto (1910), expertly composed for Elgar's own instrument, is rare in combining bravura with such a confidential manner (Berg's concerto comes near it). The solo personality is ardent and sweet, made the more affecting by the rubato common to all Elgar's music, but most persuasive in this context, where a single figure sways a crowd. This rubato, partly deduced from his liberal expression marks, is held to be a secret of Elgar's performing style; played without it, or with too much, his music lacks flow. His own recorded performances are never indulgent; he pounces on to the crux of a phrase and draws a keen, supple line. The opening of the Violin Concerto is a group subject of four shortish phrases, an example of his composing method sometimes criticized as short-winded; but Elgar's own performance (or indeed a fine one by any conductor and soloist) sweeps them into a single paragraph.

Falstaff, Elgar's most explicit programme music, is a ripe and genial portrait of a big-spirited man. It is his largest instrumental movement, masterly in having so many strong themes which can be treated in witty fugal devices or run together as counter-melodies to illustrate the action. Elgar's attitude to Falstaff was protective, his view partial, drawn only from Shakespeare's *Henry IV* and *Henry V* and realized through his own tempera-ment. Flatterer, braggart, charmer and law-breaker, this Falstaff is above all a gentleman. The tavern scene is mild, neither bawdy nor erotic. Though Elgar is a Romantic, and could compose a passionate apotheosis, there is scarcely a trace of eroticism in his music. Bearing in mind the voluptuous sounds of such contemporaries as Rakhmaninov, Strauss or Puccini, it would seem that his chaste instincts were fostered by the Victorian world in which he grew up. Chaste is a word few would use about Falstaff, yet it describes the interludes, both of innocence regained, first in a dream of youth, then in a country orchard. Falstaff's final rejection by the new king and his death are so heart-rending that one sees in them Elgar's own fears – he was not deaf to the changes of taste in 1913 – that he too might be rejected by the new musical regime.

Elgar's solo songs range from conventional drawing-room ballads to intimate utterances of great charm. More important as a body, however, are his choral songs. Prompted by interest in the competitive festivals, he composed a skilful set from the *Greek Anthology* for unaccompanied male voices, and for mixed voices elaborate pieces such as *Go, song of mine, There is sweet music* and *Love's Tempest* which, while very singable, are scored almost instrumentally. Elgar believed with O'Shaughnessy in *The Music Makers* (1912) that the artist, set apart though he is, shapes the world's destiny; and, in his wish to identify with that sentiment, he used apt quotations from his earlier works (listed in Kennedy, 1968). This use has been questioned, but the quotations fall movingly into place. It is some of the new invention that, curiously, seems less strongly motivated, apart from the promising opening and the soloist's profoundly disturbing 'Great hail! we cry to the comers from the dazzling unknown shore'.

Elgar's anthems for the Anglican rite are not greatly distinguished; the most personal is *O Hearken Thou*, for the 1911 coronation. His last choral work, *The Spirit of England* (1915–17), the finest of his patriotic and war-time music, is grand and melancholy. 'The Fourth of August' (in which the demons from *Gerontius* represent the enemy) has something of Parry in it – Elgar probably learnt about broad choral writing from the older man. The opening of 'For the Fallen' is a dead march; later, at 'They went with songs to the battle', comes a quick march tune, rangy and awkward as the scarecrow army in *Falstaff*, a direct and bitter Mahlerian irony rare in Elgar.

Some works from the London years are tantalizing because they contain worthwhile music but are dependent on their original circumstances. Elgar himself approved suites drawn from *The Crown of India* (1912) and *The Starlight Express* (1915). Both were theatrical, the former a spectacular masque to celebrate the Delhi Durbar, the latter a play for 'children of all ages'. Reaction in taste in the 1940s and 1950s against sentiments thought to be imperialist or whimsical kept the music unknown. Some of *The Crown of India*, hastily put together from sketches, is trumpery in a colourful and dashing manner; but some equals *The Wand of Youth*; and the Interlude is as rapt a self-communion as 'The Sun goeth down' in *The Kingdom. The Starlight Express* is a different case. Blackwood's novel *A Prisoner in Fairyland*, though long and rambling, is a sensitive allegory on the clearsighted sympathy shared by children and artists. Elgar's music put back the poetry partly lost in the stage version, but because much of it was to be played behind speech it is not wholly independent. The songs are only part of a long score which is a captivating blend of Edwardian light music and Elgar's more thoughtful tones. What might be called the 'creative fire music' is as stirring as any he imagined. He drew on *The Wand of Youth*, not only quoting but developing the themes, and the complete music is more fluent than might be expected; a radio broadcast (as in 1965) provides an ideal medium for play and music. Had Elgar lived at another time or place the work might have taken the form of a *Hänsel und Gretel* or *Little Sweep*.

For *The Sanguine Fan* (1917) Elgar composed his only ballet score, some 20 minutes of floating, continuous music, reminiscent of sweet, lyrical moments in his symphonic as well as his light style. The scenario was 18th-century pastoral, based on a fan design drawn in sanguine by Conder. *The Fringes of the Fleet, Carillon* and two other recitations with music, and *Polonia* depended more for their success on the mood of wartime audiences, and so have other problems than the theatre music in revival. Attractive in its various ways as all this music is, it does suggest that Elgar's ideas were less significant than those that concerned him during the first decade of the century. Over-simplifying, it could be said that he turned either towards propaganda or fantasy, and, viewing his career at 1917, it is not his virtual stop to composing after 1920 that is unexpected, but the sudden pressure of his being engaged on four abstract instrumental works in 1917–19.

As a group, the three chamber works are conservative, both for their own date, and if compared with Elgar's earlier big works. Possibly, recognizing in himself no wish to absorb recent idioms, he went his own way easily; and his affections turned to the music he had played as a violinist during his youth. The noble Adagio of the Piano Quintet and the first movement of the Violin Sonata are markedly Brahmsian. Both outer movements of the sonata are unusual for Elgar in how exactly they fulfil the promise of their opening bars – no less, but no more. In the central Romance he returned to clichés of his early salon and Spanish styles, but now they are 'used' – if not quite stylized, then compressed elliptically into fantasy. The String Quartet has most of the old nervous energy, but with some difference. The first movement shares with the Introduction and Allegro and the Cello Concerto a questioning, speculative mood, but without the zest of the earlier work or the open heartache of the later. The mood is wry, the rhythmic gestures at odds with the hollow, irresolute harmonies: a possible third-period style may be discerned, an

6. Elgar and
George Bernard
Shaw, 1929

experienced but undogmatic voice. The Piano Quintet is larger, and the implications of conflict in the opening (which caused Shaw to declare it the 'finest thing of its kind' since *Coriolan*) lie behind it all and come up to trouble the surface in the last movement; but, grand though it is, it has occasionally an improvisatory air.

It was into a virtuoso form that he confided his most private thoughts. So much is made of the poignancy of the Cello Concerto that its daring can be overlooked. But there is consummate technical confidence in opening a concerto with a solo recitative of such panache, allowing it to die to nothing, and then presenting so gentle and unobtrusive a main theme for violas alone. In the tension between the risks taken by the craftsman and the shyness of the aging man, Elgar turned his disillusion to positive account. The concerto is in simple lyrical and rondo forms. The scherzo is a shadowy, fantastic *moto perpetuo*, the Adagio a passionate lament. The Falstaffian last movement runs a humorous course before the stricken cadenza, in which soloist and orchestra sing the pain and poetry of Elgar's most searching visions, reaching stillness in a phrase from the Adagio. Elgar cut resolutely into this with the formal recitative of the opening; and the end is abrupt.

After that, Elgar published nothing of real consequence. He took refuge behind other music, in the vigorous, unselfconscious transcriptions for full orchestra of Bach (1921–2), Handel (1923) and (less interestingly) of Chopin (1933), and in motets for specific Three Choirs Festival programmes. He could easily produce a piece for a carillon (1923), a civic fanfare (1927), and music for the Wembley British Empire Exhibition (1924). The theatre still attracted him, and his music for *Arthur* (1923) contains passages he was preparing to re-use in the Third Symphony. The *Severn Suite* (1932), commissioned for the National Brass Band Contest, is of slight distinction, though the similarity between two fugatos for two great riverside cathedrals is a pleasant reminder that Elgar admired Schumann's symphonies. The *Nursery Suite* (1931) has the charm of the earlier children's music and of the Serenade, and in two pieces rather more: under its pictorialism 'The Wagon passes' offers the fears and apprehensions, and 'Dreaming' the sweetness, of Elgar's truest nature.

The works he left unfinished, in particular the opera and the Third Symphony, cannot be completed from the remaining sketches. His method of composing has been described in detail by Reed (1936) and Maine (1945) who observed it, and by Kent (1978, 1982) and Moore (1984) who have studied it. Elgar would amass cogent material, some old, some new; some mere pencil scraps, some fully scored. Then he worked at the piano until, he told Sanford Terry in 1911, 'in every movement its form and above all its climax were very clearly in his mind ... But withal there was a great mass of fluctuating material which *might* fit into the work as it developed in his mind to finality'. 'In his mind' is the crux: Elgar did not lay out a continuous short score on paper: his sketches were on loose sheets, to be arranged and rearranged. Any comparison with Mahler's Tenth is inappropriate, for that gave a continuing thread which allowed a reconstruction for a performing edition. Though brief passages from Elgar's Third could be performed orchestrally, much was still uncomposed, and he had not ordered even the extant sketches in their final relationship. He habitually preserved sketches from completed works, affording exceptional insight into his mind, which the Elgar Complete Edition is gradually revealing.

Elgar's voice is individual enough to be instantly recognizable. Melody, harmony and sonority are equally striking and combine into a personality which provokes strong reactions. Not all such reactions have been purely musical. The first years of this century, the decade of his highest achievement, have acquired some dubious shadows as they recede, but it would be as limiting to deny the element of celebration in Elgar's music as to overrate that of nostalgia. To a large extent he worked in traditional forms, but inside the boundaries of development and recapitulation he allowed himself poetic and allusive discursiveness. Though some of his most moving passages are diatonic, he stretched chromatic implications to their limits without departing from fundamental tonality.

Unlike Vaughan Williams, he was not interested in the revivals of Tudor music or folksong, and his Englishness can be felt more easily than defined. For a time his countrymen adopted a proprietorial air towards him which began to disperse in the 1960s when he came to be more widely performed by international interpreters. Less radical than Holst, less hermetic than Delius, he was more complex than either, and the inner conflicts of his personality, when they are not resolved, are held in a creative tension which give his music its depth. It took a man of high courage and receptivity to embrace all that he did.

WORKS

Edition: *The Elgar Complete Edition*, 43 vols., ed. R. Anderson (London, 1981–) [E; vols. in square brackets are in preparation]

Numbers in right-hand margins denote references in the text.

STAGE

op.

— Humoreske Broadheath, 1867, and Music for the Elgar children's play, 1869 or 1871, unpubd; used in orch suites The Wand of Youth   21

42 Grania and Diarmid (G. Moore, W. B. Yeats), 1901: Incidental Music, Funeral March, There are seven that pull the thread [song]; Dublin, Gaiety, 21 Oct 1901   2

— ballet (after Rabelais), 1902–3, inc.   37

66 The Crown of India (imperial masque, H. Hamilton), A, B, chorus, orch, 1911–12, sketches from 1902 onwards: 1a Introduction, 1b Sacred Measure, 2 Dance of Nautch Girls, 2a India greets her Cities, 3 Song: Hail, Immemorial Ind'l, 3a Entrance of Calcutta, 3b Entrance of Delhi, 4a Introduction, 4b March of the Mogul Emperors, 5 Entrance of John Company, 5a Entrance of St George, 6 Song: The Rule of England, 7 Interlude, 8a Introduction, 8b Warriors' Dance, 9 The Cities of Ind, 10 March: The Crown of India, 10a The Homage of Ind, 11 The Crowning of Delhi, 12 Ave Imperator; M. Beeley, H. Dearth, cond. Elgar, London, Coliseum, 11 March 1912; see also orch suite   19, 37, 43, 44

78 The Starlight Express (V. Pearn, after A. Blackwood: A Prisoner in Fairyland), incidental music, melodrama and songs, S, Bar, orch [incl. music from The Wand of Youth, 1915, unpubd]: 1 To the Children, 2 The Blue-eyes Fairy, 3 Curfew Song (Orion), 4 Laugh a little ev'ry day, 5 I'm everywhere, 6 Night Winds, 7 Oh stars shine brightly, 8 We shall meet the morning spiders, 9 My Old Tunes, 10 Dandelions, Daffodils, 11 They're all soft-shiny now, 12 Oh, think beauty, 13 Hearts must be soft-shiny dressed, duet; C. Hine, C. Mott, cond. J. Harrison, London, Kingsway Theatre, 29 Dec 1915 [nos.1, 2 and 9, pubd 1916]   2, 19, 39, 44

81 The Sanguine Fan (ballet), 1917, unpubd; cond. Elgar, London, Chelsea Palace, 20 March 1917   19, 44

— The Fringes of the Fleet (R. Kipling), 4 Bar, orch, 1917: The Lowestoft Boat, Fate's Discourtesy, Submarines, The Sweepers; C. Mott, H. Barratt, F. Henry, F. Stewart, cond. Elgar, London, Coliseum, 11 June 1917; Inside the Bar (G. Parker), 4 Bar unacc., added 25 June 1917   44

— Arthur (incidental music, L. Binyon), unpubd; cond. Elgar, London, Old Vic, 12 March 1923; suite ed. A. Barlow   49

— The Pageant of Empire (A. Noyes), 1v/SATB: 1 Shakespeare's Kingdom, 2 The Islands, 3 The Blue Mountains, 4 The Heart of Canada, 5 Sailing Westward, 6 Merchant Adventurers, 7 The Immortal Legions, 8 A Song of Union; Empire March; cond. H. Jaxon, Wembley, 21 July 1924   48

— Beau Brummel (incidental music, B. Matthews), unpubd; cond. Elgar, Birmingham, Royal, 5 Nov 1928

89 The Spanish Lady (opera, 2, Elgar, B. Jackson after Jonson: The Devil is an Ass), inc. [sketches use material from 1878 onwards]; 2 songs ed. P. M. Young (1955); suite for str orch ed. P. M. Young (1956) [E xii]   22, 48

CHORAL ORCHESTRAL

23 Spanish Serenade (Stars of the summer night) [arr. of partsong], SATB, small orch, 1892; cond. Rev. J. Hampton, Hereford, 7 April 1893

25 The Black Knight (L. Uhland, trans. Longfellow), sym. for chorus and orch, 1889–92; Worcester Festival Choral Society, cond. Elgar, 18 April 1893   7, 8, 26–7, 28

26 The Snow; Fly, singing bird [arr. of partsongs with chamber acc.], SSA, orch, 1903; London, Queen's Hall, 12 March 1904

27 Scenes from the Bavarian Highlands (C. A. Elgar, after Bavarian trad.), chorus, orch, 1895: 1 The Dance, 2 False Love, 3 Lullaby, 4 Aspiration, 5 On the Alm, 6 The Marksman; Worcester Festival Choral Society, cond. Elgar, Worcester, 21 April 1896

29 The Light of Life (Lux Christi) (E. Capel-Cure, after Bible), short oratorio, S, A, T, B, chorus, orch, 1896; A. Williams, J. King, E. Lloyd, W. Mills, cond. Elgar, Worcester, 10 Sept 1896   8, 26, 28

30 Scenes from the Saga of King Olaf (Longfellow, H. A. Acworth), cantata, S, T, B, chorus, orch, 1894–6; M. Henson, E. Lloyd, D. Ffrangcon-Davies, cond. Elgar, Hanley, Staffs., 30 Oct 1896   8, 12, 26–7, 28, 30, 32

33 The Banner of St George (S. Wensley) ballad, 1896–7, St Cuthbert's Hall Choral Society, cond. C. Miller, London, 18 May 1897

34 Te Deum, Benedictus, chorus, org, orch, 1897; cond. G. R. Sinclair, Hereford, 12 Sept 1897; also version with org alone

35 Caractacus (Acworth), cantata, S, T, Bar, B, chorus, orch, 1898, some 1887 sketches; M. Henson, E. Lloyd, A. Black, J. Browning, cond. Elgar, Leeds, 5 Oct 1898; E v   8, 10, 12, 26, 27, 28, 37

38 The Dream of Gerontius (J. H. Newman), oratorio, Mez, T, B, chorus, orch, 1900; M. Brema, E. Lloyd, H. Plunket Greene, cond. H. Richter, Birmingham Town Hall, 3 Oct 1900; E vi   9, 10, 11, 12-13, 23, 32-3, 35, 43, 181, 228

44 Coronation Ode (A. C. Benson), S, A, T, B, chorus, orch, 1902: 1 Crown the King with Life, 2 Daughter of Ancient Kings [The Queen substituted in 1911], 3 Britain, ask of thyself, 4 Hark upon the hallowed air, 5 Only let the heart be pure, 6 Peace, gentle peace, 7 Land of Hope and Glory [using trio tune of Pomp and Circumstance no.1]; A. Nicholls, M. Foster, J. Coates, D. Ffrangcon-Davies, cond. Elgar, Sheffield, 2 Oct 1902   13

49 The Apostles (Elgar, after Bible), oratorio, S, A, T, 3 B, chorus, orch, 1902-3; E. Albani, M. Foster, J. Coates, K. Rumford, A. Black, D. Ffrangcon-Davies, cond. Elgar, Birmingham Town Hall, 14 Oct 1903; E viii   13, 15, 33, 35-6, 38

51 The Kingdom (Elgar, after Bible), oratorio, S, A, T, B, chorus, orch, 1901-6; A. Nicholls, M. Foster, J. Coates, W. Higley, cond. Elgar, Birmingham Town Hall, 3 Oct 1906; E ix   15, 33, 34, 35, 38, 44

— The Last Judgment [projected title], oratorio, 1906-33, inc.

64 O hearken Thou (Intende voci orationis meae), off, chorus, orch; London, Westminster Abbey, 22 June 1911

67 Great is the Lord, anthem [arr. of 1912 work], 1913

69 The Music Makers (A. O'Shaughnessy), ode, A, chorus, orch, 1912, sketches from 1902; M. Foster, cond. Elgar, Birmingham, 1 Oct 1912; [E x]

74 Give unto the Lord, anthem, SATB, org, orch, 1914; London, St Paul's Cathedral, 30 April 1914

80 The Spirit of England (Binyon), S/T, chorus, orch:
1 The Fourth of August, 1915-17; R. Buckman, cond. A. Matthews, Birmingham, 4 Oct 1917
2 To Women, 1915-16; J. Booth, Leeds Choral Union, cond. Elgar, 3 May 1916
3 For the Fallen, 1915-16; A. Nicholls, Leeds Choral Union, cond. Elgar, 3 May 1916

complete: A. Nicholls, G. Elwes, cond. Elgar Leeds, 31 Oct 1917; [Ex]. With proud thanksgiving, chorus, orch, 1920-21 [reworking of 80/3]; Royal Choral Society, cond. Elgar, London, Royal Albert Hall, 7 May 1921; [E x]   3, 21

ORCHESTRAL

— early works, unpubd: Menuetto (Scherzo), 1878, re-copied 1930; Introductory Overture, inc., and song arrs. for the Christy Minstrels, 1878; Symphony [after Mozart: Sym. no.40], 1878, only 42 bars extant; Intonation no.2, 1878; Minuet (Grazioso), 1879, lost; Air de ballet, 1881; Suite in D: Mazurka, Intermezzo – Sérénade mauresque, Fantasia gavotte, March – pas redoublé, 1882-4 [rev. as op.10]   3, 6

— Dances for Worcester City and County Pauper Lunatic Asylum, Powick: Minuet in g, 1878; sets of 5 quadrilles, La Brunette, Die junge Kokotte, L'Assommoir, 1879; 5 quadrilles, Paris; 5 lancers, The Valentine; polka, Maud, 1880; polkas: Nellie, 1881; La Blonde, 1882; Helcia, 1883; Blumine, 1884   24

1 The Wand of Youth Suites nos.1-2 [incl. rev. of Humoreske Broadheath and early play music]: 1, 1907, cond. H. J. Wood, London, Queen's Hall, 14 Dec 1907; 2, 1908, cond. Elgar, Worcester, 9 Sept 1908   2, 17, 39, 44

3 Cantique [rev. of 1879 Harmony Music 6], arr. small orch, 1912; London, Royal Albert Hall, 15 Dec 1912

— The Lakes, ov., 1883, unpubd, lost

7 Sevillana, 1884, rev. 1889; cond. W. Done, Worcester, 1 May 1884   3, 24

— Scottish Overture, 1885, unpubd, lost

— Three Pieces, str, unpubd, lost; ?rev as op.20; cond. E. Vine Hall, Worcester, 7 May 1888

— Violin Concerto, ?1890, inc., destroyed [possible frag. of slow movt]

10 Three Characteristic Pieces [rev. of Suite, D], 1899; cond. Elgar, New Brighton, 16 July 1899   24-5

11 Sursum corda (Elévation), brass, org, str, timp, 1894 [rev. of 1887 sketch]; cond. H. Blair, Worcester Cathedral, 8 April 1894   26

12 Salut d'amour (Liebesgrüss) [arr. of pf piece], 1889; cond. A. Manns, London, Crystal Palace, 11 Nov 1889   6

15 1 Chanson de nuit, 2 Chanson de matin [arrs. of vn and pf pieces],

19 small orch, 1899; cond. Wood, Queen's Hall, 14 Sept 1901
Froissart, ov.., 1890, rev. 1901; cond. Elgar, Worcester, Public Hall, 10 Sept 1890 — 6, 7, 25, 36

20 Serenade, e, str, 1892 [?rev. of 1888 str pieces]; Worcester Ladies' Orchestral Class, cond. Elgar, 1892; Antwerp, 23 July 1896 — 25-6, 48

21 Minuet [arr. of 1897 pf piece], 1897; cond. Elgar, New Brighton, 16 July 1899

— Three Bavarian Dances [arr. of nos.1, 3 and 6 of Scenes from the Bavarian Highlands, SATB, pf]; cond. Manns, Crystal Palace, 23 Oct 1897

32 Imperial March, 1896-7; cond. Elgar, Crystal Palace, 19 April 1897 — 8, 37

36 Variations on an Original Theme ('Enigma'), 1898-9; cond. H. Richter, London, St James's Hall, 19 June 1899; with rev. finale, cond. Elgar, Worcester, 13 Sept 1899 — 9-10, 12, 17, 25, 28-30, 39

— Sérénade lyrique, small orch, 1899; St James's Hall, 27 Nov 1900 — 13, 37

39 Military Marches (Pomp and Circumstance) nos.1-5: 1, D, 1901 [see also Land of Hope and Glory, song] and 2, a, 1901, cond. A. E. Rodewald, Liverpool, 19 Oct 1901; 3, c, 1904, cond. Elgar, Queen's Hall, 8 March 1905; 4, g, 1907, cond. Elgar, Queen's Hall, 24 Aug 1907; 5, C, 1930, cond. Elgar, London, Kingsway Hall [HMV recording session], 18 Sept 1930

40 Cockaigne (In London Town), ov., 1900-01; cond. Elgar, Queen's Hall, 20 June 1901 — 11, 36

42/2 Funeral March, from Grania and Diarmid, (1901); cond. Wood, Queen's Hall, 18 Jan 1902

43 Dream Children, 2 pieces after C. Lamb, small orch, 1902; cond. A. W. Payne, Queen's Hall, 4 Sept 1902 — 39

47 Introduction and Allegro, str qt, str orch, 1904-5, sketches from 1901; cond. Elgar, Queen's Hall, 8 March 1905 — 15, 36-7, 40, 45

50 In the South (Alassio), ov., 1904; cond. Elgar, London, Covent Garden, 16 March 1904; extract for small orch, cond. G. R. Sinclair, Hereford, 22 Nov 1904; see also 'Solo vocal (with piano)': In Moonlight — 14, 30, 36

55 Symphony no.1, Ab, 1907-8; Hallé Orch, cond. Richter, Manchester, 3 Dec 1908; E xxx — 15, 19, 30, 33, 39-41, 105

58 Elegy, str, 1909; London, Mansion House, 13 July 1909

61 Violin Concerto, b, 1909-10; F. Kreisler, cond. Elgar, Queen's Hall, 10 Nov 1910 — 17, 18, 22, 41-2, 183

62 Romance, bn, orch, 1909-10; E. James, cond. Elgar, Hereford, 16 Feb 1911

63 Symphony no.2, Eb, 1909-11, sketches from 1903; cond. Elgar, Queen's Hall, 24 May 1911; E xxxi — 15, 18, 19, 29, 39-41, 37

65 Coronation March, 1911 [incorporating sketches from 1902 Rabelais ballet]; Westminster Abbey, 22 June 1911

66 Suite, from the Crown of India [nos.1a, 2, 5, 7, 4]; cond. Elgar, Hereford, 11 Sept 1912 — 43

68 Falstaff, c, sym. study with two interludes, 1913, sketches from 1902-3; cond. Elgar, Leeds, 2 Oct 1913 — 18-19, 42, 43

— Carissima, small orch, 1913; cond. Elgar, Hayes, Middlesex [HMV recording session], 21 Jan 1914

70 Sospiri, str, harp, org, 1913-14; cond. Wood, Queen's Hall, 15 Aug 1914

— Rosemary [arr. of 1882 pf piece, Douce Pensée, also 1882 pf trio], 1915

76 Polonia, sym. prelude; cond. Elgar, Queen's Hall, 6 July 1915 — 45

85 Cello Concerto, e, 1919; F. Salmond, cond. Elgar, Queen's Hall, 27 Oct 1919; arr. as va conc. by L. Tertis; Tertis, cond. Elgar, Queen's Hall, 21 March 1930 — 17, 19, 20, 33, 45, 47

— Empire March, 1924; cond. H. Jaxson, Wembley, 21 July 1924 — 37, 48

— Civic Fanfare, 1927, unpubd; cond. Elgar, Hereford, 4 Sept 1927 — 48

— May Song [arr. of 1901 pf piece], 1928

— Minuet, from Beau Brummel (1929)

87 Severn Suite, brass band, 1930, incl. sketches also of 1903: 1 Introduction (Worcester Castle), 2 Toccata (Tournament), 3 Fugue (Cathedral) (1923), 4 Minuet (Commandery) [after early wind qnt pieces], 5 Coda, pubd as scored by H. Geehl; test piece for Brass Band Championship, Crystal Palace, 27 Sept 1930; arr. for orch, 1932, cond. Elgar, London, Abbey Road [HMV recording session], 14 April 1932 — 17, 48

— Nursery Suite, 1931: 1 Aubade [incl. hymn tune of 1878, Drake's Broughton], 2 The Serious Doll, 3 Busy-ness, 4 The Sad Doll, 5 The Wagon Passes, 6 The Merry Doll, 7 Dreaming – Envoy; — 39, 48 cond. Elgar, London, Kingsway Hall [HMV recording session], 23 May 1931

— Mina, small orch, 1933

88 Symphony no.3, 1932–3, inc., unpubd [some sketches pubd in Reed, 1936]; sketches incl. material from other inc. works: The Last Judgment, Callicles, King Arthur, Arden and Piano Concerto   22–3, 48, 49

90 Piano Concerto, sketches 1909–32, inc., unpubd; Poco andante completed and scored for pf, str, by P. M. Young (1950)

— Suite, from The Spanish Lady, str, ed. P. M. Young (1956)

CHORAL   3
(sacred)

— early works, unpubd: Credo [on themes from Beethoven: Syms. nos.5, 7 and 9], 1873; Tantum ergo, 1876; Salve regina, 1876; Credo in e, 1877; hymn tunes in C, G and F, 1878 [in F pubd 1898 as Drake's Broughton, re-used in Nursery Suite]; Brother, for Thee he died, anthem, 1879; Domine salvum fac, motet, 1879; Gloria [arr. of Mozart: Violin Sonata, F, K547: Allegro], 1880; Benedictus sit deus pater, inc., 1882; O salutaris hostia: F, SATB, org, 1880, E♭, SATB, org, 1880, A, lv, org, 1882; Chant for Stabat mater, 1886; litanies etc

— Four Litanies for the Blessed Virgin Mary, 1886

2 1 Ave, verum corpus (Jesu, word of God incarnate) [orig. Pie Jesu], 1887, rev. 1902; 2 Ave Maria (Jesu, Lord of Life and Glory), ?1880s, rev. 1907; 3 Ave maris stella (Jesu, meek and lowly), ?1880s, rev. 1907

— Ecce sacerdos magnus, chorus, org, 1888; Worcester, St George's [with orch, unpubd], 9 Oct 1888   24

34 Te Deum, Benedictus, chorus, org, 1897; also orch version

— Lo, Christ the Lord is born (Wensley) [after Grete Malvern on a Rock, private Christmas card, 1897] carol, SATB (1909)

— O Mightiest of the Mighty (S. Childs Clarke), hymn, 1901; London, Westminster Abbey, 9 Aug 1902

— Two single chants for the Venite, D, G, 1907

— Two double chants for Psalms lxviii and lxxv, D, 1907

52 A Christmas Greeting (C. A. Elgar) carol, 2 S, male chorus ad lib, 2 vn, pf, 1907; Hereford Cathedral, 1 Jan 1908

— They are at rest (Newman), SATB, 1909; Windsor, Frogmore [Royal Mausoleum], 22 Jan 1910

67 Great is the Lord, anthem, SSAATB, org, 1910–12; cond. Frederick Bridge, Westminster Abbey, 16 July 1912; with orch, 1913

— Fear not, O Land, anthem, SATB, org, 1914

— I sing the birth (Jonson) carol, SATB; cond. M. Sargent, London, Royal Albert Hall, 10 Dec 1928

— Goodmorrow (G. Gascoigne) carol, SATB [early hymn tune]; cond. Elgar, Windsor, 9 Dec 1929

(secular)   26

5 A Soldier's Song (C. Flavell Hayward), male chorus, 1884; Worcester Glee Club, 17 March 1884; repubd 1903 as A War Song; Royal Albert Hall, 1 Oct 1903

18 1 O happy eyes (C. A. Elgar), SATB, 1889, rev. 1893, 2 Love (A. Maquarie), SATB, 1907, 3 My love dwelt in a northern land (anon., trans. A. Lang), SATB, 1889; Tenbury Musical Society, 13 Nov 1890

23 Spanish Serenade (Stars of the Summer Night) (Longfellow) SATB, 2 vn, pf, 1892; orchd 1893   26

26 The Snow; Fly, singing bird (C. A. Elgar), SSA 2 vn, pf, 1894; orchd 1903

27 Scenes from the Bavarian Highlands, chorus, pf, 1895; see also 'Choral orchestral'   26

— As torrents in summer [from King Olaf], SATB

— The Sword Song [from Caractacus], SATB

— To her beneath whose steadfast star (F. W. H. Myers), SATB, 1899; Windsor Castle, 24 May 1899

— Weary wind of the west (T. E. Brown) SATB, 1902: Morecambe, 2 May 1903

45 Five Partsongs from the Greek Anthology, TTBB, 1902: 1 Yea, cast me from the heights (anon., trans. A. Strettell), 2 Whether I find thee (anon., trans A. Lang), 3 After many a dusty mile (anon., trans. E. Gosse), 4 It's oh to be a wild wind (anon., trans. W. M. Hardinge), 5 Feasting I watch (Marcus Argentarius, trans. R. Garnett); London Choral Society, cond. A. Fagge, Royal Albert Hall, 25 April 1904   43

— Evening Scene (C. Patmore), SATB, 1905; Morecambe, 12 May 1906

— How calmly the evening (T. Lynch), SATB (1907)

53 Four Choral Songs, SATB, 1907: 1 There is sweet music (Tennyson), 2 Deep in my soul (Byron), 3 O wild west wind (Shelley), 4 Owls, an Epitaph (Elgar) — 43

54 The Reveille (B. Harte), TTBB, 1907; Blackpool, 17 Oct 1908
— Marching Song (Capt. de Courcy Stretton), SATB (1908), Royal Albert Hall, 24 May 1908; arr. as Follow the Colours, 1v, male chorus ad lib, Royal Albert Hall, 10 Oct 1914

56 Angelus (Tuscan), SATB, 1909; Royal Albert Hall, 8 Dec 1910 — 43
57 Go, song of mine (Cavalcanti, trans. D. G. Rossetti), SSAATB, 1909; cond. Elgar, Hereford, 9 Sept 1909
— The Birthright (G. A. Stocks), SATB (1914); also arr. boys' chorus, bugles, drums

71 Two Choral Songs (Vaughan), SATB, 1913–14: The Shower, The Fountain
72 Death on the hills (Maykov, trans. Newmarch), SATB, 1914
73 Two Choral Songs (Maykov, trans. Newmarch), SATB, 1914: Love's Tempest, Serenade
— The Windlass (W. Allingham), SATB, c1914
— The Wanderer (Elgar, after Wit and Drollery, 1661), TTBB (1923); De Reszke Singers, London, Wigmore Hall, 13 Nov 1923
— Zut! Zut! Zut! (Richard Mardon [Elgar]), TTBB, 1923; De Reszke Singers, Wigmore Hall, 13 Nov 1923
— The Herald (A. Smith), TTBB, 1925
— The Prince of Sleep (de la Mare), SATB, 1925
— The Rapid Stream; When Swallows Fly (C. Mackay), unison vv, 1931
— So many true princesses who have gone (Masefield), chorus, military band, 1932; London, Marlborough House, 9 June 1932
— The Woodland Stream (Mackay), unison vv, 1933; Worcester, 18 May 1933

SOLO VOCAL
(with orchestra) — 42

37 Sea Pictures, A, orch: 1 Sea Slumber Song (R. Noel), 2 In Haven (Capri) (C. A. Elgar), 3 Sabbath Morning at Sea (E. B. Browning), 4 Where corals lie (R. Garnett), 5 The Swimmer (A. L. Gordon), 1899 [except no.2, which is rev. of song with pf, Love alone will stay, 1897]; C. Butt, cond. Elgar, Norwich, 5 Oct 1899 — 10, 30

42/3 There are seven that pull the thread (Yeats) [from Grania and Diarmid], 1v, small orch, 1901

— Land of Hope and Glory (Benson) A, chorus, orch, carillon obbl ad lib [arr. from Coronation Ode]; C. Butt, London, June 1902 — 19

48 Pleading (A. L. Salmon) [arr. of song with pf], 1v, orch, 1908
59 Song Cycle (G. Parker), 1v, orch, 1909–10: 3 Oh, soft was the song, 5 Was it some golden star?, 6 Twilight [1, 2, and 4 not composed]; M. Foster, cond. Elgar, London, Queen's Hall, 24 Jan 1910

60 The Torch, The River [arr. of 1909–10 songs with pf], 1v, orch, 1912; M. Foster, cond. G. R. Sinclair, Hereford, 11 Sept 1912

75 Carillon (E. Cammaerts), reciter, orch, 1914; T. Brand, cond. Elgar, Queen's Hall, 7 Dec 1914; text rev. Binyon, 1942 — 19, 45

77 Une voix dans le désert (Cammaerts), reciter, orch, 1915, incl. song Quand nos bourgeons se rouvriront, S, orch; C. Liten, O. Lynn, cond. Elgar, London, Shaftesbury Theatre, 29 Jan 1916 — 45

79 Le drapeau belge (Cammaerts), reciter, orch, 1917; C. Liten, cond. H. Harty, Queen's Hall, 14 April 1917 — 45
See also 'Stage': The Starlight Express

(with piano)
— The Language of Flowers (Percival), 1872, unpubd
— If she love me (Temple Bar Rondeau), acc. inc, unpubd
16/2 Through the long days (J. Hay), 1885; C. Phillips, London, St James's Hall, 25 Feb 1897; see also op.16 below
— Is she not passing fair? (d'Orléans, trans. L. S. Costello), 1886, rev. 1908
— As I laye a-thynkynge ('Thomas Ingoldsby' [R. H. Barham]), 1887
— The Wind at Dawn (C. A. Roberts), 1888; orchd 1912
— Queen Mary's Song (Lute Song) (Tennyson), 1887, rev. 1889
— A Spear; A Sword (C. A. Elgar), 1892, both lost
— Two Mill-wheel Songs (C. A. Elgar), 1892, unpubd [?absorbed in King Olaf]
— Like to the damask rose (S. Wastell), 1892; C. Phillips, St James's Hall, 25 Feb 1897
— The Poet's Life (E. Bourroughs), 1892
— A Song of Autumn (A. L. Gordon), 1892
16 1 Shepherd's Song (B. Pain), ?1894, 2 Through the long days (J. Hay), 1885 (see above), 3 Rondel (Longfellow, from Froissart), 1894; St James's Hall, 7 Dec 1897
31 After (P. B. Marston), 1895; A Song of Flight (C. Rossetti), 1900; H. Plunket Greene, St James's Hall, 2 March 1900

— Rondel (The little eyes that never knew light) (Swinburne), unpubd; G. Walker, Elgar, Worcester Musical Union, 26 April 1897

— Love alone will stay (Lute Song) (C. A. Elgar), 1897; rev. as no.2 Sea Pictures

— Dry those fair, those crystal eyes (H. King); London, Royal Albert Hall, 21 June 1899

— Pipes of Pan (A. Ross) 1899, orchd 1902; London, Crystal Palace, 30 April 1900

— Always and Everywhere (Krasinski, trans. F. Fortey), 1901

— Come, gentle night (C. Bingham), 1901

41 In the Dawn; Speak, Music (A. C. Benson), 1902

— Speak, my heart (Benson), 1902

— In Moonlight (Shelley) [arr. of Canto popolare from In the South], 1904

48 Pleading (A. Salmon), 1908; orchd 1908

— A Child Asleep (E. B. Browning), 1909

— The King's Way (C. A. Elgar) 1909; C. Butt, Crystal Palace, 15 Jan 1910

60 The Torch; The River (Pietro d'Alba [Elgar], after East European trad.), 1909–10, orchd 1912

— The Merry-go-round (F. C. Fox), c1914

— The Brook (E. Soule), c1914

— Arabian Serenade (M. Lawrence), 1914

— The Chariots of the Lord (J. Brownlie); Royal Albert Hall, 28 June 1914

— Soldier's Song (H. Begbie), 1914; C. Butt, Oct 1914; unpubd, withdrawn

— Fight for Right (W. Morris), 1916

— Ozymandias (Shelley), 1917, inc.

— Big Steamers (Kipling), 1918

— It isnae me (S. Holmes), 1930; J. Elwes, Dumfries, Oct 1930

— Modest and Fair; Still to be neat (Jonson) [both for The Spanish Lady]; ed. P. M. Young (1955)

CHAMBER AND INSTRUMENTAL   3, 6, 19, 24

— early works: Reminiscences, vn, pf, 1877; Study for Strengthening the Third Finger, vn, 1878, recopied 1920; Allegro, ob qt, 1878, inc.; Fantasia, vn, pf, 1878, inc.; Str Qt, d, 1878, inc.; Str Qt, Bb, 1878, inc.; Str Trio, C, 1878, inc.; Trio, 2 vn, pf, 1878, inc.; Etude caprice, vn, 1878; Sonata, C, vn, pf, 1878, inc.; Two Polonaises, d, F, vn, pf, 1879, inc.; 2nd study for vn unacc., 1879; Fantasia on Irish Airs, vn, pf, 1881, inc.; Fugue, f#, inc., 1881 [recopied for The Spanish Lady]; Menuetto and Trio, G, vn, vc, pf, 1882 [Trio also as Douce Pensée for pf]; Fugue, d, ob, vn, 1883; Pf Trio, 1886, frag.

— wind qnt music: 3, 24

Peckham March, 1877, unpubd

Harmony Music 1–4 [no.3 inc.], 1878; ed. R. McNicol (1976)

Promenades 1–6, 1878: 1 Moderato e molto maestoso, 2 Moderato 'Madame Taussaud's', 3 Presto, 4 Andante 'Sommiferous', 5 Allegro molto [rev. for scherzando in Minuet, Severn Suite, 1930], 6 Allegro maestoso 'Hell and Tommy'; ed. McNicol (1976)

Andante con variazioni 'Evesham Andante', 1878; ed. McNicol (1977)

Adagio cantabile 'Mrs Winslow's Soothing Syrup', 1878; ed. McNicol (1977)

Intermezzos 1–5, 1879: 1 Allegro moderato 'The Farmyard', 2 Adagio, 3 Allegretto 'Nancy', 4 Andante con moto, 5 Allegretto; ed. McNicol (1977)

Four Dances: Menuetto, 1878, Gavotte 'The Alphonsa', 1879, Sarabande (Largo), 1879 [recopied 1933 for The Spanish Lady], Gigue, 1879; ed. McNicol (1977)

Harmony Music 5, 1879: 1 Allegro moderato 'The Mission', 2 Menuetto [rev. for Minuet of Severn Suite] and Trio, 3 Andante 'Noah's Ark', 4 Finale; ed McNicol (1977)

Harmony Music 6, 1879: 1 Allegro molto, 2 Andante arioso [rev. for 1912 Cantique], unpubd

Harmony Music 7, 1881, unpubd

1 Romance, vn, pf, 1885; Worcester, 20 Oct 1885

4 Idyll, 1884; Pastourelle, ?1883; Virelai, ?1883; vn, pf

— Gavotte, vn, pf, 1885

— Allegretto on G–E–D–G–E, vn, pf, 1885

— Duett, trbn, db, 1887; ed. R. Slatford (1970)

8 String Quartet, 1887, destroyed

9 Violin Sonata, 1887, destroyed

— String Quartet, d, 1888, inc; 3rd movt Intermezzo arr. for org as no.3 of Eleven Vesper Voluntaries

12 Salut d'amour (Liebesgrüss), vn, pf; see also piano and orch pieces   6, 24
13 Mot d'amour (Liebesahnung), Bizarrerie, vn, pf, 1889
15 1 Chanson de nuit, vn, pf, 1897, orchd 1899; 2 Chanson de matin, vn, pf, 1899 [rev. of earlier sketch], orchd 1899
17 La capricieuse, vn, pf, 1891
22 Very Easy Melodious Exercises in the First Position, vn, pf (1892)
24 Etudes caractéristiques, vn (1892) [probably all earlier]
— Offertoire (Andante religioso), vn, pf, 1893
— May Song, vn, pf; see also piano and orch pieces
— Andantino, vn, mand, gui, 1907, inc., unpubd
82 Sonata, e, vn, pf, 1918; W. H. Reed, Landon Ronald, London, Aeolian Hall, 21 March 1919   45
83 String quartet, e, 1918; A. Sammons, W. H. Reed, R. Jeremy, F. Salmond, London, Wigmore Hall, 21 May 1919   20, 45
84 Piano Quintet, a, 1918–19; A. Sammons, W. H. Reed, R. Jeremy, F. Salmond, W. Murdoch, Wigmore Hall, 21 May 1919   15, 20, 45, 47
— March, pf trio [sketch for Empire March], 1924, unpubd

KEYBOARD
(piano)

— Chantant, c, 1872, unpubd
— Hungarian (Melody), 1879, unpubd
— Douce pensée, 1882; orchd 1915 as Rosemary
— March, D. 1883, unpubd
— Griffinesque, 1884
— Enina Valse, 1886, unpubd
— Laura Valse, 1887, unpubd
12 Salut d'amour (Liebesgrüss), 1888; see also 'Chamber and instrumental' and 'Orchestral'
— Presto, 1889
— Sonatine, 1889, rev. 1931
— Minuet, 1897; orchd as op. 21, 1897
— May Song, 1901, also vn, pf; orchd 1928
— Skizze, 1901; ed. J. N. Moore (1976)
46 Concert Allegro, 1901; F. Davies, London, St James's Hall, 2 Dec 1901; (1982)
43 Dream Children; see also 'Orchestral'
— In Smyrna, 1905; ed. J. N. Moore (1976)
— Falstaff: Two Interludes [from orch work] (1914)
— Echo's Dance [from The Sanguine Fan] (1917)
— Adieu (1932)
— Serenade (1932)

(organ)
— Fugue, g, 1870s, inc.; pubd in The Music Student (Aug 1916); [E xxxvi]
3 Cantique [rev. of 1879 Harmony Music 6]; [E xxxvi]; see also 'Orchestral'
14 Eleven Vesper Voluntaries, 1889 [no.3 rev. from 1888 Str Qt]; [E xxxvi]
28 Sonata, G, 1895; H. Blair, Worcester Cathedral, 8 July 1895; [E xxxvi]
— Cadenza for C. H. Lloyd: Organ Concerto, f; G. R. Sinclair, Gloucester, 1904; [E xxxvi]
— Piece for Dot's Nuns, 1906, unpubd; [E xxxvi]
87a Sonata [arr. I. Atkins, from Severn Suite]; [E xxxvi]
— Frags. [E xxxvi]

(carillon)
— Memorial Chime, 1923, unpubd; Loughborough War Memorial Carillon, 22 July 1923; arr. org; [E xxxvi]   47

ARRANGEMENTS
(choral orchestral)

3, 21

The Holly and the Ivy, 1898, unpubd
A. H. Brewer: Emmaus, 1901
God Save the King, S, chorus, orch, 1902
J. S. Bach: St Matthew Passion, performing edn. (1911), collab. I. Atkins
H. Parry: Jerusalem, c1922
J. Battishill: O Lord, Look down from Heaven, 1923
S. S. Wesley: Let us Lift up our Hearts, 1923
H. Purcell: Jehova, quam multi sunt hostes mei, 1929

(orchestral)
anthem, str, 1874, with orig. introduction, unpubd
Adeste fideles, 1878, unpubd
G. F. Handel: Ariodante: Overture, small orch, 1878, unpubd
R. Wagner: Parsifal: Good Friday Music, small orch, 1894, unpubd
J. S. Bach: St Matthew Passion: Two Chorales, brass, 1911, unpubd; Worcester, 14 Sept 1911
J. S. Bach: Fantasy and Fugue, C, bwv537, Elgar's op.86, 1922, 1921; Fugue, cond. E. Goossens, London, Queen's Hall, 27 Oct 1921; Fantasy, LSO, cond. Elgar, Gloucester, 7 Sept 1922.   47
G. F. Handel: Overture, d (from Chandos Anthem no. 2), 1923; LSO, cond. Elgar, Worcester, 2 Sept 1923   47

F. Chopin: Piano Sonata, b♭; Funeral March, 1933; BBC SO, cond. A. Boult, EMI studio, 30 May 1932   47

(solo vocal)

C. M. von Weber: Oberon: O 'tis a Glorious Sight, 1v, pf, 1878, unpubd
M. V. White: Absent and Present, vc obbl, 1885, unpubd
C. H. Dolby: Out on the Rocks, vc obbl, 1885, unpubd
Clapham Town End, folksong arr., 1v, pf, 1890, unpubd

(chamber and instrumental)

L. van Beethoven: Violin Sonata, op.23: Finale, wind qnt, 1878, unpubd
A. Corelli: Concerto X, wind qnt. 1878, unpubd
C. W. Buck: Melody, pf acc., 1885, unpubd
V. Berard: Berceuse – Petite reine, vn, pf, 1907, unpubd

(piano)

R. Schumann: Overture, Scherzo and Finale: Scherzo, c1880, unpubd
R. Wagner: Tannhäuser: Entry of the Minstrels, 1883, unpubd

Principal publishers: Boosey & Hawkes, Novello
MSS in *GB-Lbm*, Elgar Birthplace Museum; smaller collections in several other libraries and in private hands

WRITINGS

Notes for first performances of Enigma Variations, 1899, Introduction and Allegro, 1905, repr. in Powell (1937), 121, 68
Programme notes for Worcestershire Philharmonic Society, 1898–1904

Preface [1904] to D. Ffrangcon-Davies: *The Singing of the Future* (London, 1906)
'Falstaff', *MT*, liv (1913), 575 [historical and analytical note]; pubd separately (London, 1913)
'Musical Notation', *MT*, lxi (1920), 513; also as preface to H. E. Button: *System in Musical Notation* (London, 1920)
'Gray, Walpole, West and Ashton, the Quadruple Alliance', letter to *Times Literary Supplement* (4 Sept 1919); repr. in Young (1956), 253
Letter to *ML*, i (1920), 165 [on Parry, in reply to Shaw's article in previous issue]; repr. in Redwood (1982)
'Scott and Shakespeare', letter to *Times Literary Supplement* (21 July 1921); repr. in Young (1956), 270
'A Poet as Critic', letter to *Daily Telegraph* (12 April 1919)
'A Frisk', letter to *Times Literary Supplement* (6 Aug 1925)
My Friends Pictured Within (London, ?1927) [notes for pianola rolls]
The Wand of Youth: a Note by the Composer (London, 1929) [for HMV Album 80]; repr. from draft, with minor variations, in Moore (1974)
Foreword to H. A. Leicester: *Forgotten Worcester* (Worcester, 1930); repr. in Young (1956), 303
'A Christmas Fable' ('God Made a Puppy') [Elgar's Christmas card in 1932]; repr. in Young (1956), 313
'A Visit to Delius', *Daily Telegraph* (1 July 1933), 5
'An Essay on the Gramophone', *Recorded Sound*, ii/9 (1963), p.iv
ed. P. M. Young: *A Future for English Music and Other Lectures* (London, 1968) [Birmingham University lectures of 1905–6]

BIBLIOGRAPHY

CATALOGUES AND SOURCE MATERIAL

P. M. Young, ed.: *Letters of Edward Elgar and Other Writings* (London, 1956) [incl. letters of G. B. Shaw to Elgar]

J. N. Moore: 'An Elgar Discography', *Recorded Sound*, ii/9 (1963); pubd separately, rev. (London, 1963)

P. M. Young, ed.: *Letters to Nimrod: Edward Elgar to August Jaeger, 1897–1908* (London, 1965)

R. L. E. Foreman: 'Elgar', *The British Musical Renaissance: a Guide to Research* (diss., Library Association Fellowship, London, 1972)

J. N. Moore: *Elgar: a Life in Photographs* (London, 1972)

K. Thompson: *A Dictionary of Twentieth-century Composers (1911–1971)* (London, 1973)

The Elgar Society Newsletter (1973–) [renamed *The Elgar Society Journal*, 1979]

J. N. Moore: *Elgar on Record: the Composer and the Gramophone* (London, 1974) [incl. list of items in Elgar's record collection]

J. Knowles: *Elgar's Interpreters on Record: an Elgar Discography* (London, 1977, rev. 1986)

C. Kent: *Edward Elgar, a Composer at Work: a Study of his Creative Process as seen through his Sketches and Proof Corrections* (diss., U. of London, 1978)

R. Anderson, C. Kent and J. N. Moore, eds.: Prefaces and commentaries to *The Elgar Complete Edition* (London, 1981–)

E. Wulstan Atkins: *The Elgar-Atkins Friendship* (London, 1984)

P. Willetts: 'The Elgar Sketch-books', *British Library Journal*, xi/1 (1985), 25

MONOGRAPHS

R. J. Buckley: *Sir Edward Elgar* (London, 1905, 2/1912)

E. Newman: *Elgar* (London, 1906/R1977, 2/1922)

J. F. Porte: *Sir Edward Elgar* (London, 1921, 2/1970)

F. H. Shera: *Elgar: Instrumental Works* (London, 1931)

A. J. Sheldon: *Edward Elgar* (London, 1932)

B. Maine: *Elgar: his Life and Works* (London, 1933, 2/1973)

J. F. Porte: *Elgar and his Music* (London, 1933)

E. Jose: *The Significance of Elgar* (London, 1934)

W. H. Reed: *Elgar as I Knew him* (London, 1936, 2/1973) [incl. facs. of Sym. no.3]

D. M. Powell ['Dorabella']: *Edward Elgar: Memories of a Variation* (London, 1937, rev. 3/1949)

T. F. Dunhill: *Sir Edward Elgar* (London, 1938)

W. H. Reed: *Elgar* (London, 1939, rev. 3/1949 with chap. by E. Blom)

W. R. Anderson: *Introduction to the Music of Elgar* (London, 1949)

D. M. McVeagh: *Edward Elgar: his Life and Music* (London, 1955)

P. M. Young: *Elgar O. M.: a Study of a Musician* (London, 1955, rev 2/1973)

M. Kennedy: *Portrait of Elgar* (London, 1968, 2/1973, rev. 1983)

M. Hurd: *Elgar* (London, 1969)

I. Parrott: *Elgar* (London, 1971)

R. Burley and F. C. Carruthers: *Edward Elgar: the Record of a Friendship* (London, 1972) [Burley's typescript completed 1948]

R. Fanselau: *Die Orgel im Werk Edward Elgars* (Göttingen, 1974)

S. Mundy: *Elgar, his Life and Times* (Tunbridge Wells, 1980)

M. De-la-Noy: *Elgar: the Man* (London, 1983)

J. N. Moore: *Edward Elgar: a Creative Life* (Oxford, 1984)

——: *Spirit of England: Edward Elgar in his World* (London, 1984)

COLLECTIONS OF ARTICLES

Music Student, viii/12 (1916) [special issue] [P. Scholes: 'Sir Edward Elgar'; T. F. Dunhill: 'Choral Music'; P. Scholes: 'Sir Edward Elgar at Home' (repr. in Redwood, 1982); E. C. Bairstow: 'Songs'; W. Wells-Harrison: 'Symphonies and Shorter Orchestral Works'; P. Scholes: 'Elgar and the War'; N. Kilburn: 'A Personal Note'; G. S. Talbot: 'Church Anthems'; W. W. Cobbett: 'Violin Concerto', 'Shorter Violin Works'; E. J. Bellerby: 'Organ Sonata'; photographs etc]

MT, lxxv (1934), April [special issue] [incl. obituary by Harvey Grace and W. McNaught, notice of Worcester Cathedral memorial service and list of articles in earlier issues of *MT*]

ML, xvi/1 (1935) [special issue] [D. F. Tovey: 'Elgar, Master of Music' (repr. in *Essays and Lectures on Music*, London, 1949); H. J. Foss: 'Elgar and his Age'; † R. Vaughan Williams: 'What have we Learnt from Elgar?; A. E. Brent Smith: 'The Humour of Elgar'; † F. Howes: 'The Two Elgars'; †W. H. Reed: 'The Violin Concerto'] [†– repr. in Redwood, 1982]

H. A. Chambers, ed.: *Edward Elgar Centenary Sketches* (London, 1957) [J. Barbirolli: 'Forty Years with Elgar's Music'; C. Elgar Blake: 'A Family Retrospect'; A. C. Boult: 'Composer as Conductor'; H. A. Chambers: 'Publishing Office Memories'; B. Herrman: 'An American Voice'; A. J. Kirby: 'The Apostles and The Kingdom'; Y. Menuhin: 'Impressions – Musical and Personal'; D. M. Powell: 'The Music Maker'; S. Robinson: 'Elgar's Light Music'; D. Willcocks: 'A Modern View'; P. M. Young: 'Elgar as a Man of Letters']

MT, xcviii (1957), June [special issue] [Elgar Today: a Symposium in which Prominent Musicians give their Personal Views]

Bibliography

WRITINGS ON PARTICULAR WORKS

(*stage*)

B. Jackson: 'Elgar's "Spanish Lady"', *ML*, xxiv (1943), 1; repr. in Redwood (1982)

A. E. Keeton: 'Elgar's Music for the "Starlight Express"', *ML*, xxvi (1945), 43; repr. in Redwood (1982)

R. Crichton: 'Elgar and the Theatre', *Financial Times* (30 Dec 1968)

J. N. Moore: 'The Sanguine Fan', ASD 2970 [disc notes]

——: 'The Starlight Express', SLS 5036 [disc notes]

(*choral*)

J. Bennett: *Scenes from the Saga of King Olaf: Book of Words, with Analytical Notes* (London, 1899)

H. Thompson: *Caractacus: Book of Words, with Analytical Notes* (London, 1900)

A. J. Jaeger: *The Dream of Gerontius: Book of Words, with Analytical and Descriptive Notes* (London, 1901, 2/1974)

C. V. Gorton: *The Apostles: an Interpretation of the Libretto* (London, 1903)

A. J. Jaeger: *The Apostles: Book of Words with Analytical and Descriptive Notes* (London, 1903)

——: *The Kingdom: Book of Words with Analytical and Descriptive Notes* (London, 1906)

C. V. Gorton: *The Kingdom: an Interpretation of the Libretto* (London 1907)

E. Newman: ' "The Music Makers" by Edward Elgar', *MT*, liii (1912), 566

——: ' "The Spirit of England": Edward Elgar's New Choral Work', *MT*, lvii (1916), 235

——: 'Elgar's "Fourth of August" ', *MT*, lviii (1917), 295

R. [D. M.] Powell: 'The Words of "The Apostles" and "The Kingdom" ', *MT*, lxxxix (1948), 201; xc (1949), 149

D. M. Powell: 'The First Performances of "The Apostles" and "The Kingdom" ', *MT*, ci (1960), 21

A. Payne: 'Gerontius Apart', *Music and Musicians*, xiii/4 (1964–5), 25

E. Day: 'Interpreting Gerontius', *MT*, cx (1969), 607; see also letters, pp. 833, 1039, 1138

L. Foreman: 'The Revival of Elgar's Choral Music', *MO*, xcviii (1974–5), 239, 243

C. Kent: 'Elgar's Music for St George's Church, Worcester', *Annual Report* [Church-Music Society], no.77 [1982–3] (London, 1983), 12

——: 'Elgar's Queen Alexandra Memorial Ode', *Elgar Society Journal*, iii/1 (1983), 8

R. Anderson: 'Elgar and some Apostolic Problems', *MT*, cxxv (1984), 13

D. Bury: 'In Pursuit of a Forgotten Obbligato', *Elgar Society Journal*, iii/5 (1984), 11

(*orchestral*)

P. Pitt and A. Kalisch: *In the South: Analytical and Descriptive Notes* (London, 1904)

H. C. Colles: 'Sir Edward Elgar's Symphony', *MT*, xlix (1908), 778

E. Newman: 'Elgar's Violin Concerto', *MT*, li (1910), 631

——: 'Elgar's Second Symphony', *MT*, liii (1912), 566

H. C. Colles: 'Elgar's Violoncello Concerto', *MT*, lxi (1920), 84

R. C. Powell: 'Elgar's "Enigma"', *ML*, xv (1934), 203; see also reply by A. H. Fox Strangways, *ML*, xvi (1935), 37; repr. in Redwood (1982)

C. Barber: 'Enigma Variations–the Original Finale,' *ML*, xvi (1935), 137

E. Newman: 'Elgar's Third Symphony', *Sunday Times* (22 Sept, 20 Oct and 27 Oct 1935)

W. H. Reed: 'Elgar's Third Symphony', *The Listener* (28 Aug 1935)

E. Newman: 'Elgar and his Enigma', *Sunday Times* (16, 23, 30 April, 7 May 1939); also article on the Violin Concerto (21 May 1939)

D. F. Tovey: *Essays in Musical Analysis* (Oxford, 1935–9)

——: *Some English Symphonists* (London, 1941)

B. Maine: 'Elgar's Sketches in Relation to Musicology', *Basil Maine on Music* (London, 1945), 31 [on Sym. no.3]

F. Bonavia: 'Edward Elgar', *The Symphony*, ed. R. Hill (London, 1949, 2/1956), 313

B. Shore: 'Elgar's Second Symphony', *Sixteen Symphonies* (London, 1949), 263

H. Byard: 'Edward Elgar', *The Concerto*, ed. R. Hill (London, 1952), 252

J. Harrison: *Elgar, Master of the Orchestra* (Worcester, 1957)

J. N. Moore: 'An Approach to Elgar's Enigma', *MR*, xx (1959), 38

J. A. Westrup: 'Elgar's Enigma', *PRMA*, lxxxvi (1959–60), 79; repr. in Redwood (1982)

D. Cox: 'Edward Elgar', *The Symphony*, ii, ed. R. Simpson (Harmondsworth, 1967), 15

R. Fiske: 'The Enigma: a Solution', *MT*, cx (1969), 1124; repr. in Redwood (1982)

M. Kennedy: *Elgar Orchestral Music* (London, 1970)

E. Sams: 'Variations on an Original Theme (Enigma)', *MT*, cxi (1970), 258

——: 'Elgar's Enigmas: a Past Script and a Postscript', *MT*, cxi (1970), 692

I. Parrott: 'Elgar's Two-fold Enigma: a Religious Sequel', *ML*, liv (1973), 57

Bibliography

T. van Houten: ' "You of All People": Elgar's Enigma', *MR*, xxxvii (1976), 130

C. Kent: 'A View of Elgar's Methods of Composition through the Sketches of the Symphony no. 2 in E♭ (op. 63)', *PRMA*, ciii (1976–7)

H. Burton: 'Elgar and the BBC with Particular Reference to the Unfinished Third Symphony', *Journal of the Royal Society of Arts*, cxxvii (1979), 224

C. Kent: 'Elgar's Third Symphony: the Sketches Reconsidered', *MT*, cxxiii (1982), 532

D. Hudson: 'Elgar's Enigma; the Trail of Evidence', *MT*, cxxv (1984), 636

V. Jones: 'Helen Weaver, the "Soul" of Elgar's Violin Concerto', *R.A.M. Magazine* (1985), no. 237, p. 328

D. McVeagh: ' "Moriah" and the "Introduction and Allegro" ', *Elgar Society Journal*, iv/4 (1986), 23

(chamber and instrumental)

H. C. Colles: 'Elgar's Quintet for Pianoforte and Strings (Op. 84)', *MT*, lx (1919), 596

W. H. Reed: 'Elgar', *Cobbett's Cyclopaedic Survey of Chamber Music* (London, 1929, rev. 2/1963 by C. Mason), 372

D. McVeagh: 'Elgar's Concert Allegro', *MT*, cx (1969), 135

M. Pope: Foreword to miniature score of the Piano Quintet (London, 1971)

GENERAL

[F. G. Edwards]: 'Edward Elgar', *MT*, xli (1900), 641; repr. in Redwood (1982)

W. C. Stockley: *Fifty Years of Music in Birmingham, 1850–1900* (Birmingham, 1900)

R. de Cordova: 'Dr Elgar', *Strand Magazine* (1904), May, 538 [interview]; repr. in Redwood (1982)

A. Johnstone: *Musical Criticisms* (Manchester, 1905)

G. Cumberland: 'Elgar', *Set Down in Malice* (London, 1918), 79; repr. in Redwood (1982)

G. B. Shaw: 'Sir Edward Elgar', *ML*, i (1920), 7; repr. in Redwood (1982)

C. Gray: 'Edward Elgar', *A Survey of Contemporary Music* (London, 1924), 78

S. Langford: *Musical Criticisms*, ed. N. Cardus (London, 1929)

E. J. Dent: 'Modern English Music', in G. Adler: *Handbuch der Musikgeschichte* (Frankfurt am Main, 2/1930/R 1961)

A. Herbert Brewer: *Memories of Choirs and Cloisters* (London, 1931)

C. Lambert: *Music Ho!* (London, 1934, 3/1966)

A. H. Fox Strangways: 'Elgar', *ML*, xv (1934), 109

E. Newman: 'Elgar: some Aspects of the Man in his Music', *Sunday Times* (25 Feb 1934); repr. in Redwood (1982)

H. P. Greene: *Charles Villiers Stanford* (London, 1935)

M. Anderson de Navarro: *A Few More Memories* (London, 1936)

E. Speyer: *My Life and Friends* (London, 1937)

M. G. Dann: 'Elgar's Use of the Sequence', *ML*, xix (1938), 255

H. J. Wood: *My Life of Music* (London, 1938)

J. A. Westrup: 'Elgar and Joseph Bennett', *Sharps and Flats* (London, 1940), 90

A. Bax: *Farewell, my Youth* (London, 1943)

F. W. Gaisberg: *Music on Record* (New York, 1943, 2/1946)

R. Nettel: 'Elgar', *Music in the Five Towns, 1840–1914* (London, 1944), 86

N. Cardus: 'Elgar', *Ten Composers* (London, 1945, 4/1952), 123; repr. in *A Composers' Eleven* (London, 1958)

R. Nettel: *Ordeal by Music* (London, 1945)

W. McNaught: 'Elgar's Birthplace', *MT*, lxxxviii (1947), 185

E. Goossens: *Overture and Beginners* (London, 1951)

F. Howes: 'Edward Elgar', *The Heritage of Music*, iii, ed. H. J. Foss (London, 1951), 138

H. W. Shaw: *The Three Choirs Festival* (Worcester, 1954)

E. Newman: 'Stately Sorrow', *The Listener*, li (1954), 421; repr. in *Essays on Music* (London, 1967)

D. M. McVeagh: *Elgar: an Appreciation* (Worcester, 1955)

E. Newman: [Elgar Memories], *Sunday Times* (30 Oct, 6 Nov, 13 Nov 1955; 18 Nov, 25 Nov, 2 Dec 1956)

C. Elgar Blake: 'My Memories of my Father', *Music and Musicians*, v/10 (1957), 11; repr. in Redwood (1982)

H. Keller: 'Elgar the Progressive', *Music Review*, xviii (1957), 294

B. Maine: *Twang with our Music* (London, 1957)

D. Mitchell: 'Elgar and the English Oratorio', *The Listener*, lvii (1957), 361

——: 'Some Thoughts on Elgar (1857–1934)', *ML*, xxxviii (1957), 113; repr. in Redwood (1982)

D. M. McVeagh: 'Elgar's Birthplace', *MT*, xcviii (1957), 308

W. Atkins: 'Music in the Provinces: the Elgar–Atkins Letters', *PRMA*, lxxxiv (1957–8), 27

J. N. Moore: 'Elgar as a University Professor', *MT*, ci (1960), 630, 690

H. Keller: 'Elgar', *The Listener*, lxix (1963), 441

A. Payne: 'A New Look at Elgar', *The Listener*, lxxii (1964), 694

A. Whittall: 'Elgar's Last Judgement', *MR*, xxvi (1965), 23

J. Connolly: 'Edward Elgar: Fantasies and Realities', *Composer* (1968), no.28, p.3

Bibliography

D. McVeagh: 'Ashton's Enigma Ballet', *MT*, cix (1968), 1129

H. Cohen: *A Bundle of Time* (London, 1969)

J. MacLeod: *The Sisters d'Aranyi* (London, 1969)

E. Sams: 'Elgar's Cipher Letter to Dorabella', *MT*, cxi (1970), 151

R. Stevenson: 'Whimsy and Spleen', *The Listener*, lxxxv (1971), 730

P. J. Pirie: 'The Personality of Elgar', *Music and Musicians*, xxi/8 (1972–3), 32

J. Buttrey: 'Elgar and Lady Mary Lygon', *ML*, liv (1973), 122, 382

J. Rushton: 'Edward Elgar', *Music and Musicians*, xxii/6 (1973–4), 18

Y. Menuhin: *Sir Edward Elgar: my Musical Grandfather* (London, 1976)

M. Kennedy: 'Elgar and the Festivals', *Two Hundred and Fifty Years of the Three Choirs Festivals*, ed. B. Still (Gloucester, 1977)

P. M. Young: *Alice Elgar: Enigma of a Victorian Lady* (London, 1978)

K. Alldritt: *Elgar on the Journey to Hanley* (London, 1979) [a novel]

G. Hamilton: 'Elgar and the Baker Family', *MT*, cxx (1979), 121

G. Hodgkins: *Providence and Art: a Study of Elgar's Religious Beliefs* (London, 1979)

J. C. Phillips: 'The Elgar Statue', *MT*, cxxi (1980), 440

B. Collett: *Elgar Country* (London, 1981) [guide-book]

P. Collett: *Elgar Lived Here* (London, 1981) [guide-book]

M. Kennedy: *Edward Elgar of Worcester; the Man and the Musician* (Worcester, 2 June 1981) [concert brochure]

N. Temperley, ed.: *The Romantic Age, 1800–1914*, Athlone History of Music in Britain, v (London, 1981)

C. Redwood, ed.: *An Elgar Companion* (Ashbourne, Derbys., 1982)

P. Collett: *An Elgar Travelogue* (London, 1983) [guide-book]

R. Anderson: 'Gertrude Walker: an Elgarian Friendship', *MT*, cxxv (1984), 698

D. Bury: *Elgar and the Two Mezzos* (London, 1984)

J. C. Dibble: 'Parry and Elgar: a New Perspective', *MT*, cxxv (1984), 639

M. Kennedy: 'The Elgar Sound', *Music and Musicians* (1984), Feb, 8
——: 'Lady Elgar', *Music and Musicians* (1984), Sept, 7

C. Kent: 'Elgar's Evolution', *The Listener*, cxi (23 Feb 1984), 36

D. McVeagh: 'Mrs Edward Elgar', *MT*, cxxv (1984), 76

J. N. Moore: 'Elgar's Letters to his Publishers', *MT*, cxxv (1984), 16

R. Philip: 'The Recordings of Edward Elgar (1857–1934): Authenticity and Performance Practice', *Early Music*, xii (1984), 481

N. Reed: 'Elgar's Enigmatic Inamorata', *MT*, cxxv (1984), 430

K. E. L. and M. Simmons: *The Elgars of Worcester* (London, 1984)

B. Trowell: 'Elgar's Marginalia', *MT*, cxxv (1984), 139

P. Dennison: 'Elgar and Wagner', *ML*, lxvii (1985), 93

65

FREDERICK DELIUS

Anthony Payne

CHAPTER ONE

Life

Frederick (baptized Fritz) Theodore Albert Delius was born in Bradford, Yorkshire, on 29 January 1862. His parents, naturalized British citizens, had been born and brought up in Germany. His stern father, who had established a successful wool business in Bradford, did not consider music a fit profession for his children. But amateur music-making was not frowned upon: Delius played the piano from an early age and was allowed to take violin lessons. Formative experiences included an acquaintance with Chopin's Waltz in E minor op. posth. and a visit to Covent Garden when he was 13 to hear *Lohengrin*. He studied at Bradford Grammar School, and then was sent to the International College in Isleworth, from where he was able to make frequent visits to London for concert and opera performances. On leaving school he bowed to his father's wishes and entered the family wool company. He proved headstrong and unreliable, but he was able to visit Norway and Paris on the firm's business, so forming ties which were to last throughout his life.

At last in 1884 he managed to persuade his father to set him up as an orange grower in Florida. This gave him longed-for freedom and enabled him to start serious composition. He settled at Solana Grove near Jacksonville on the St John's River, neglected oranges and acquired a friend and music tutor in Thomas Ward, a

7. *Nina and Edvard Grieg, Johan Halvorsen, Frederick Delius and Christian Sinding at a card party in Leipzig, winter 1887–8*

70

gifted musician living in Jacksonville. For six months Ward gave him lessons in musical technique, and Delius later stated that these were the only lessons from which he gained worthwhile knowledge. At the same time, his sense of solitude amid luxuriant natural surroundings and his immersion in the music of the plantation negroes were experiences decisive to his artistic development.

After further months in Danville, Virginia, where he supported himself by teaching and playing the organ, Delius learnt that his father had agreed to maintain him for an 18-month course at the Leipzig Conservatory. He enrolled there in August 1886 and studied with Sitt, Reinecke and Jadassohn. Although he gained no great benefit from these studies, he made his first tentative attempts at composition and met Grieg, who befriended and encouraged him. It was Grieg who induced Delius's father to let his son continue composing when the Leipzig course ended, and, supported by his father, Delius went to live in Paris, where he moved in artistic and bohemian circles, numbering Gauguin, Strindberg and Munch among his friends. He contracted syphilis in 1895.

By the mid-1890s Delius had completed the operas *Irmelin* and *The Magic Fountain*, together with many songs and instrumental pieces, and he had started work on *Koanga*. In 1896 he met a young student painter, Jelka Rosen, who was later to become his wife. During this period he was a man of bohemian habits, attracted by and attractive to women, but in 1897 – after a brief return to Florida, where he hoped to lease Solana Grove for the cultivation of tobacco or other crops and so improve his financial position – Delius settled with Jelka at Grez-sur-Loing, a village 65 km outside Paris, not far from Fontainebleau. He clearly saw that a more peaceful existence was required for his work: he did not marry Jelka until 1903 and still indulged in forays into Paris, but his life now became increasingly a matter of recording his spiritual experience in music.

With the opera *A Village Romeo and Juliet* (1899–1901) Delius at last found himself completely. The final version of *Appalachia* followed in 1903, *Sea Drift* was finished in 1904 and *A Mass of Life* in 1905. As yet, however, his music was almost unknown in England: apart from a concert which he himself promoted in 1899, no major work was played in his native country until performances of the Piano Concerto and *Appalachia* were given in 1907. At this time Beecham met Delius and became his most devoted interpreter; in Germany, Fritz Cassirer, Hans Haym and Julius Buths had already been championing his work.

Apart from the upheaval of World War I (spent largely at Grez, but with significant excursions to England and Norway), when he suffered greatly from the loss of German royalties, Delius's life was becoming less outwardly eventful. After returning to Grez at the end of the war, he slowly succumbed to illness, developing in the mid-1920s a blindness and paralysis which numerous specialists were unable to cure. Two events stand out from these final years. Eric Fenby, a young Yorkshireman who had heard Delius's music in 1928 and learnt of his physical disability, offered his services as amanuensis. After a taxing apprenticeship he was able to notate a series of works, including the important *Songs of Farewell*, under circumstances related by Fenby in *Delius as I knew him*. Secondly, there was Beecham's Delius Festival of 1929 which the composer attended, an emaciated, other-worldly figure in his bath-chair. This last visit to England brought him wider renown. In the same year he was created a Companion of Honour, and in 1932 received the freedom of Bradford. He had already been awarded the gold medal of the Royal Philharmonic Society, in 1925.

Throughout his final years at Grez, Delius received many visitors, among them distinguished musicians (who would play to him) and composers such as Grainger, Balfour Gardiner, Bax and Elgar; and he heard his works over the radio and on record. But his life was generally that of a recluse, suffering severe pain with impressive fortitude. On his death (10 June 1934) he was buried temporarily in Grez cemetery; almost a year later his remains were removed to Limpsfield in Surrey. French law made it impossible to carry out his original wish to be interred in his garden.

CHAPTER TWO

Works

Delius's musical style was a long time in development. His first masterpiece, *Paris*, was not completed
until he was 37, and his individual genius did not
become evident until *A Village Romeo and Juliet* and
Sea Drift were composed. He grew intensely aware of
the transience of things – an overriding preoccupation for the rest of his life – and this ephemerality
being mitigated only by nature's 'eternal renewing'.
Often the experience is ecstatically embraced, as in *The
Song of the High Hills*; at other times, as in *Sea Drift*, it
is poignantly accepted; but this feeling remains the burden of his total output, and it is a mark of Delius's
imagination that in almost every mature work he viewed
its restricted emotional area from a different perspective.

The technique which enabled Delius to articulate this
highly personal vision slowly matured throughout the
1890s. It was based to a large extent on Wagner, whose
endless flow and harmonic aura Delius attempted to
emulate, and on Grieg, whose airy texture and non-
developing use of chromaticism showed him how to
lighten the Wagnerian load. During this period there
was a steady increase in the number of passages where
the fusion of these elements sounds characteristically
Delian, reaching a peak in the opera *Koanga* (1895–7)

which sets a text by Charles Keary drawn from an episode in *The Grandissimes*, a novel by George Washington Cable. Its tragic story of the deep south, in which an African voodoo prince is sold into slavery, enabled Delius to draw comprehensively on his Florida experiences. Although the dramatic conception is at first stiff, the second act (which includes the well-known 'La Calinda') and the third move impressively to their climaxes. More importantly, the death of the prince Koanga drew from Delius the most personal music that he had yet written. The opera was not heard until the Elberfeld Stadttheater staged it in 1904 under Cassirer; by then Delius had completed *Paris* (1899), in which an almost Straussian orchestral virtuosity, never again to be found appropriate, clothes an already typical harmonic scheme. *Paris* received its première under Haym in 1901, also in Elberfeld.

With his next work, *A Village Romeo and Juliet* (1899–1901), Delius approached complete maturity: the harmonic manner is quite distinctive and the characteristic themes of transitoriness, sumptuous natural beauty and romantic purity reached a new intensity. The opera is based on the novella *Romeo und Julia auf dem Dorfe* from Gottfried Keller's *Die Leute von Seldwyla* and tells of two young lovers who, unable to make a life together because of family feuds and local gossip, spend one day with each other and then end their lives. Abandoning the more conventional *verismo* manner of *Koanga*, Delius cast the work in a series of short scenes. Traditional dramatic features are not totally discarded, but each scene is more concerned with presenting a spiritual state. The close contains some of the most exquisite music written for the stage, and ends with Delius's own conception of a 'Liebestod' as the lovers float away on an old hay barge which they then scuttle. The impossibility of realizing youthful dreams of perfect emotion is expressed with a poignancy most typical of Delius. Cassirer conducted the première at the Komische Oper in Berlin in 1907, and Beecham gave the first performance in England three years later. The opera was revived with some success in 1920, 1927 and 1934, and the centenary celebrations of 1962 included performances in Bradford and at Sadler's Wells Theatre in London. After the completion of this opera, Delius embarked on a further dramatic project, the one-act *Margot la Rouge*, a piece of *verismo* tailored to win the International Melodrama Competition organized by Sonzogno. It failed to win, and was not staged in Delius's lifetime, but the best of the music was salvaged with Fenby's aid some 30 years later to form the *Idyll*, with words from Whitman chosen by Robert Nichols.

During the following three years Delius completed three of his finest works for his favoured forces: soloists, chorus and orchestra. First he rewrote *Appalachia* (1903), a work originally composed in simpler form in 1896, which was another exploration of his experience of the American south. These variations on an old plantation song, first performed in 1904 under Haym, cover a wider range of styles than Delius was later willing to admit. The harmony is always recognizably his own, but there is still a considerable reliance on conventional melodic developments and counterpoints; regular phrase patterns are as much in evidence as the subtle flights of harmony which point forward to his maturity.

The second of these works, *Sea Drift* (1903–4) for baritone, chorus and orchestra, is considered by many to be his greatest achievement. Whitman's treatment of a boy's sorrow at a seabird's loss of its mate is matched by Delius with profound insight. The work's formal structure partly follows that of the text, but its expressive power transcends the poem. There is a seamless flow between the choral commentaries and the baritone narrator's recitatives, from which he breaks away only in the drama's poignant aftermath at 'O past! O happy life!. . . . We two together no more'. The range of choral expression encompasses the hedonistic joy of 'Shine! shine! shine! Pour down your warmth, great sun!' and the still, sad voice of 'O rising stars!', but the various shades of feeling are fused into one great formal arch. Traditional devices of development and recapitulation are largely missing: Delius presents a stream of spiritual experience with a flow of chromatic harmony whose intensity is never broken, and variety of colour and pace is achieved almost imperceptibly, yet with utmost directness. *Sea Drift* was first performed in Essen in 1906 and its success firmly established Delius on the Continent.

Finally Delius embarked on what was to be his grandest project, *A Mass of Life* (1904–5), which sets texts from Nietzsche's *Also sprach Zarathustra* and is scored for four soloists, chorus and orchestra. At his first reading of *Also sprach Zarathustra*, Delius recognized that Nietzsche spoke for him, and he later stated that reading this book was one of the most important events in his life. *A Mass of Life* embodies Delius's philosophy that each man should stand fearlessly alone in the face of ultimate death, should realize his potentialities, whatever the cost, and immerse himself wholeheartedly in life. A broad musical span relates man's spiritual development to the passing of a day, rising to the 'glorious noontide' of maturity and then progressing to the midnight bell of death's call. Delius responded to Nietzsche's rich poetry in some of his most virile and exultant music, as well as in passages of a profoundly hypnotic and static calm. Beecham conducted the first complete performance in London in 1909.

After this colossal undertaking Delius worked on smaller pieces for the next few years; in the *Songs of Sunset* (1906–7), *Brigg Fair* (1907) and *In a Summer Garden* (1908) his art reached a peak of sensuous sweetness and lyrical concentration. This phase was followed by a development towards more sharply defined orchestral sounds (often Nordic in atmosphere), greater formal concision and a more radical juxtaposition of unrelated chords: there is a suggestion of autumn after the summer of the previous works. *An Arabesk* (1911), a setting of a poem by J. P. Jacobsen for baritone, chorus and orchestra, exhibits the new manner, as does *The Song of the High Hills* (1911–12) for wordless chorus and orchestra. The comparative neglect of the music of this time – which includes two of his finest works in *North Country Sketches* (1913–14) and *Eventyr* (1917) – has led to an underestimation of Delius's range.

His final opera, *Fennimore and Gerda* (1908–10), initiated this later style. Based on an episode from Jacobsen's novel *Niels Lyhne*, the work is – like *A Village Romeo and Juliet* – constructed as a series of tableaux, but Delius was here attempting something new: a contemporary conversation piece. Niels, a young poet, is in love with his best friend's wife, Fennimore, who at first returns his love, but then rejects him when

8. *Title-page, designed by Jelka Delius, of the first edition of the vocal score of Delius's 'Fennimore and Gerda' (1919)*

she learns of her husband's death. In the final two scenes, Niels, now a farmer, finds happiness with the young Gerda. Just as *Koanga* was the product of Delius's Florida impressions, so this last opera draws on his love for Scandinavia, and the drama proceeds against the backdrop of the northern seasons. Its première was at Frankfurt in 1919, but it was not produced in England until the Hammersmith Municipal Opera performances of 1968. The music is finely sustained and the atmosphere is evoked swiftly yet tellingly, particularly in the erotic outbursts of the central love scene. The period ushered in by this opera did not see a complete abandonment of Delius's more intimate sensuousness: his best-known orchestral tone poem, *On Hearing the First Cuckoo in Spring* (1912), epitomizes his sweet nostalgia, while the softly clashing lines of its companion-piece, *Summer Night on the River* (1911), produce one of his few impressionist pieces.

A quite unpredictable phase opened in 1914 with the completion of the First Violin Sonata, which he had begun ten years previously (an earlier sonata has been published posthumously). This was followed by a succession of works which attempted, not always successfully, to come to terms with conventional forms. Their structural articulation is sometimes a little stiff, but in the finest work of the group, the Violin Concerto (1916), the beauty of individual sections offsets formal weaknesses. Delius was not the composer to organize the subtle interplay of forces essential to the concerto form, and this is even more obvious in the Double Concerto for violin, cello and orchestra. He was clearly unsure of what to do with his soloists at times, and invented some perfunctory passage-work. Cluttered solo writing also mars parts of the Cello Concerto (1921), even when the editorial alterations of the published score are used. Linear melody was not one of Delius's strong points and the concertos emphasize this deficiency, but the Cello Sonata (1916) has long, expansive lines which are exceptionally resourceful and flexible, continuing throughout the work except for two short pauses. The String Quartet, also written in 1916, begins with three movements of a fluidity characteristic of Delius's finest music, but the work ends with a repetitive and short-winded finale.

While working in these conventional genres, Delius completed what for a considerable time remained the least known of his large choral works, the Requiem (1913–14) for soprano, baritone, chorus and orchestra. The original German text, by Heinrich Simon, expresses Delius's long-held pantheistic beliefs, preaching courage in the sight of death and finding consolation in nature's never ending cycles. A harmonic style which is sometimes starkly dissonant, together with thicker instrumental doubling, produce music which is unique in Delius's oeuvre for its lack of vibrancy, suggesting a certain self-denial. The Requiem marks Delius's attempt to extend his expressive compass, but the results are rather dry and only in the magnificent final section does the music spring to life as chorus and soloist hymn 'Springtime, Summer, Fall and Winter, and then new Springtime'. Discreet bitonal touches in the coda – fanfares in B against a tonality of D – also show a new departure. The work was first heard in 1922 in London (under Albert Coates) and in Frankfurt: no performances followed until 1950 (New York) and 1965 (Liverpool, conducted by Groves).

Delius's next choral and orchestral work was written to a commission from Basil Dean in 1920 for incidental music to Flecker's *Hassan*, which was scheduled for production in the following year at His Majesty's Theatre. This was the last music that Delius was able to write in his own hand, but his creative powers remained unaffected by his illness, and the atmospheric choruses and interludes contain some of his best work, including the Serenade, which quickly became a popular favourite. After postponements the play with Delius's music was staged in Darmstadt in 1923; the first English production followed in the same year.

The Second Violin Sonata was completed with the aid of Jelka as copyist, but then Delius's composing almost came to a halt. Blind and paralysed, it would have been impossible for him to write any further major work had it not been for Fenby's intervention. Fenby set in order and completed two pieces for the 1929 Delius Festival: *Cynara*, originally intended for the *Songs of Sunset*, and *A Late Lark*. As the rapport between composer and amanuensis developed, more ambitious projects became possible. *A Song of Summer* was composed by using material from *A Poem of Life and Love* (1918) and the Third Violin Sonata was completed. Then came the *Songs of Farewell*, the crowning point of the Delius–Fenby collaboration. These powerfully concentrated and exultant Whitman settings for eight-part chorus and orchestra exhibit a new freshness and clarity of style. Sargent conducted the première in 1932. There followed a sequence of smaller pieces: the Caprice and Elegy, the *Fantastic Dance*, the delightful *Irmelin Prelude* (reworked from the opera) and the *Idyll* (1932) for soprano, baritone and orchestra. Delius now composed no more, but these final works were a glorious and remarkable achievement.

After Delius's death his music continued to be promoted by Beecham, most notably in the second Delius Festival of 1946 and in the centenary celebrations which Beecham helped to plan, but did not live to direct. There were fears that Delius's music would die with its most determined advocate, but other conductors have taken it up and its permanent place appears to be assured.

The strength of Delius's personality is most evident in a harmonic style which sounds quite unlike the work of any other. His chordal vocabulary never strays beyond late Romantic practice, relying on triads, secondary 7ths and dominant discords, with a comparatively narrow range of chromatic alterations and diatonic discords. But the syntax is entirely individual. The rate of harmonic change is extremely flexible, sometimes so fast as to border on atonality, at other times hypnotically slow. The more chromatic harmonies can wind sinuously downward, or they may be abruptly juxtaposed, as in his later music, without any traditional linking relationship. Forms are built from a stream of these harmonies: Fenby (1971) likened the method to a 'prose' (i.e. rhythmically pliable) melody of chords. Even when Delius employed varied harmonic supports for repetitions of a simply phrased melody, it is the irregular ebb and flow of the harmony that is the prime structural factor, belying the melodic simplicity. Indeed Delius's melodies are rarely complex and usually seem to be stitched into the texture merely to point the harmony.

Delius's structural thinking is most readily examined

in those works which are based neither on texts nor on obvious variation forms, as is the case with *Brigg Fair* and the *Dance Rhapsody* no.1. *In a Summer Garden* may be taken as perhaps the most refined example of the way in which Delius seems to improvise a structure, generating a harmonic flight. Yet the word improvisation misrepresents the tautness of the form. The structural profile is etched in terms of harmonic tensions, set up by the extent to which positive key references or cadences are avoided, and the speed with which implied areas of tonality pass by. *In a Summer Garden* respects none of the traditional formal types, although there are vestiges of sonata and ternary structures. Precedents for its freely evolving processes can be found in the *Siegfried Idyll* and the *Prélude à l'après-midi d'un faune*; but the sonata form is much stronger in the *Siegfried Idyll*, and the Debussy, although closer in incidental phraseology, is a more orthodox ternary form. In any case, the *Prélude* was unknown to Delius at the time of composing *In a Summer Garden*, according to a letter the composer wrote to Bantock.

The opening section fluctuates capriciously between drowsy, static sequences and short bursts of activity, the changes of mood and texture achieved with extraordinary speed and concentration. The texture consists of a mosaic of tiny motifs and chordal sequences which continually evolve and regroup. The next section is more settled and exposes a broad melody which constitutes the only self-contained music in the work. The mosaic particles then return but with more determination develop into a climactic melodic passage of considerable grandeur. The lyrical intensity is then gradually dispersed with the emergence of further new

9. *Frederick Delius: portrait (1912) by Jelka Delius (with Paul Gauguin's painting 'Nevermore' in the background)*

textural offshoots, and this process is marvellously combined with hints of recapitulation and coda. The whole structure shows Delius's remarkable ability to prolong a sensuous moment by purely harmonic means without monotony and move elliptically into subtly contrasted areas.

A particularly fine example of Delius's large-scale form exists in *The Song of the High Hills*. Gone are the sensitive fluctuations, the continuous play of light and shade and the pointillist orchestration of *In a Summer Garden*. The flood of harmony is much steadier, and the areas of tension, which sometimes passed in a bar or two in the shorter work are now vastly stretched out sometimes with the aid of long pedal points. The form is simply ternary in outline, with an expansive interlude in the first section that foreshadows the intense contemplation of the central portion of the work. There is a strongly marked point of recapitulation and more obvious repetition of material. Delius's harmonic subtlety is now exclusively employed in sustaining unwavering levels of tension for long periods. The middle section, sub-titled 'The wide far distance – the great solitude', breaks down into no more than three or four of these harmonic spans, which makes the moments of transition crucially important. Music which has become firmly entrenched in one area of contemplation has to be eased on to another static plane without disrupting the hypnotic mood. Unpredictably this is not done by imperceptible changes but by comparatively bald juxtaposition of texture. The timing, however, is judged to a nicety as is the harmonic character, and the whole episode, apparently sectional to the score-reading eye, becomes an unbroken flow in performance.

Finally the strength of Delius's character is too evident in a less purely musical way. His egotism enabled him to give an overriding value to his sensual responses, and it is perhaps this that is the secret of his vision. Delius's music deals with the pristine romance of his formative experiences – the sound of negro songs over the still air of Solana Grove, his first knowledge of total love (an affair that came to nothing according to Fenby (1936)). Such things are obsessively relived in his music; it may be that his style matured only when he recognized the impossibility of recapturing them in reality.

WORKS

Numbers in right-hand margins denote references in the text.

STAGE

Zanoni (incidental music, Bulwer Lytton), draft pf score, 1888, inc.

Irmelin (opera, 3, Delius), 1890–92; E. Graham, T. Round, RPO, cond. T. Beecham, Oxford, New Theatre, 4 May 1953 — 71

The Magic Fountain (lyric drama, 3, Delius), 1893–5: K. Pring, J. Mitchinson, BBC Concert Orch, cond. N. Del Mar, BBC, 20 Nov 1977 — 71

Koanga (lyric drama, 3, C. F. Keary after G. W. Cable), 1895–7; C. Whitehill, R. Kaiser, cond. F. Cassirer, Elberfeld, Stadttheater, 30 March 1904 — 71, 74–5, 80

Folkeraadet (incidental music, G. Heiberg), 1897; cond. P. Winge, Oslo, Christiania Theater, 18 Oct 1897

A Village Romeo and Juliet (lyric drama in 6 pictures, Delius after G. Keller), 1899–1901; W. Merkel, L. Artót de Padilla, cond. Cassirer, Berlin, Komische Oper, 21 Feb 1907 — 72, 74, 75–6, 78

Margot la Rouge (lyric drama, 1, B. Gaston-Danville [Rosenvall]), 1902; M. Sonnenberg, J. Anderson, cond. E. Fenby, Opera Theatre of Saint Louis, Missouri, 8 June 1983 — 76

Fennimore and Gerda (opera in 11 pictures, Delius after J. P. Jacobsen), 1908–10; R. van Scheidt, E. Holt, cond. G. Brecher, Frankfurt am Main, Opernhaus, 21 Oct 1919 — 78, 79, 80

Hassan (incidental music, J. E. Flecker), 1920–23; cond. J. Rosenstock, Darmstadt, Hessische Landes-Theater, 1 June 1923; full version cond. E. Goossens, London, His Majesty's Theatre, 20 Sept 1923 — 82

ORCHESTRA

Florida, suite, 1887, rev. 1889; cond. H. Sitt, Leipzig, Rosenthal, early 1888

Hiawatha, tone poem, 1888, inc.; excerpt NRK [Norwegian Broadcasting] Orch, cond. S. Bruland, Norwegian Television, 13 Jan 1984

Suite, vn, orch, 1888; R. Holmes, BBC Scottish SO, cond. V. Handley, BBC, 28 Feb 1984

Rhapsodic Variations, 1888, inc.

Idylle de Printemps, 1889

Suite d'orchestre, 1889, incl. Marche caprice, rev. 1890; Marche caprice, RPO, cond. Beecham, Westminster, Central Hall, 21 Nov 1946

Three Small Tone Poems: Summer Evening, Winter Night [Sleigh Ride], Spring Morning, 1889–90; RPO, cond. R. Austin, Westminster, Central Hall, 18 Nov 1946

Légendes (Sagen), pf, orch, 1890, inc.

Petite suite d'orchestre, small orch, 1890; Beauchamp Sinfonietta, cond. D. Tall, Stratford-on-Avon, 13 May 1978

Paa Vidderne (On the Heights), sym. poem after Ibsen, 1890–92; Christiania Music Society, cond. I. Holter, Oslo, 10 Oct 1891

Légende, vn, orch, ?1895; J. Dunn, cond. A. Hertz, London, St James's Hall, 30 May 1899

Over the Hills and Far Away, fantasy ov., 1895–7; Elberfeld Concert Society, cond. H. Haym, Elberfeld, Stadthalle, 13 Nov 1897

Appalachia: American Rhapsody, orch, 1896; see 'Choral and Vocal' — 76

Piano Concerto, c.3 movts, 1897; J. Buths, Elberfeld Concert Society, cond. Haym, Elberfeld, Stadthalle, 24 Oct 1904; rev. 1 movt, 1906; Theodor Szántó, Queen's Hall Orch, cond. H. Wood, London, Queen's Hall, 22 Oct 1907 — 72

La ronde se déroule, sym. poem after H. Rode, 1899; cond. Hertz, St James's Hall, 30 May 1899; rev. 1901 as Lebenstanz [Life's dance], cond. Buths, Düsseldorf, 21 Jan 1904; rev. 1912, Berlin PO, cond. O. Fried, Berlin, 15 Nov 1912

Paris: A Nocturne (The Song of a Great City), 1899; Elberfeld Concert Society, cond. Haym, Elberfeld, 14 Dec 1901 — 74, 75

Brigg Fair: An English Rhapsody, 1907; Liverpool Orchestral Society, cond. G. Bantock, Liverpool, 18 Jan 1908 — 78, 84

In a Summer Garden, rhapsody, 1908; Philharmonic Society of London, cond. Delius, Queen's Hall, 11 Dec 1908; rev. version, Boston SO, cond. M. Fiedler, Boston, 19 April 1912 — 78, 84, 86

A Dance Rhapsody, no.1, 1908; LSO, cond. Delius, Hereford, Shire Hall, 8 Sept 1909 — 84

Two Pieces for Small Orchestra: On Hearing the First Cuckoo in Spring, 1912, Summer Night on the River, 1911; cond. A. Nikisch, Leipzig, Gewandhaus, 23 Oct 1913 — 80

North Country Sketches, 1913–14; LSO, cond. Beecham, Queen's Hall, 10 May 1915 ... 78

Air and Dance, str, 1915; cond. Beecham, London 1915 (private perf.)

Double Concerto, vn, vc, orch, 1915–16; M. and B. Harrison, New Queen's Hall Orch, cond. Wood, Queen's Hall, 21 Feb 1920 ... 80

Violin Concerto, 1916; A. Sammons, Royal Philharmonic Society, cond. A. Boult, Queen's Hall, 30 Jan 1919 ... 80

A Dance Rhapsody, no.2, 1916; New Queen's Hall Orch, cond. Wood, Queen's Hall, 20 Oct 1923

Eventyr (Once upon a time), ballad after Asbjørnsen, 1917; Queen's Hall Orch, cond. Wood, Queen's Hall, 11 Jan 1919 ... 78

A Song before Sunrise, small orch, 1918; New Queen's Hall Orch, cond. Wood, Queen's Hall, 19 Sept 1923

Poem of Life and Love, 1918; see 'A Song of Summer' below

Cello Concerto, 1920–21; A. Barjansky, cond. F. Löwe, Vienna, 31 Jan 1923 ... 82

A Song of Summer [from Poem of Life and Love], 1929–30; BBC Orch, cond. Wood, Queen's Hall, 17 Sept 1931 ... 81

Caprice and Elegy, vc, chamber orch, 1930; B. Harrison, USA, 1930 ... 82

Irmelin Prelude, 1931; LPO, cond. Beecham, Covent Garden, 23 Sept 1935 ... 82

Fantastic Dance, 1931; BBC SO, cond. Boult, Queen's Hall, 12 Jan 1934 ... 82

CHORAL AND VOCAL

Six German Partsongs: Lorelei (Heine), Oh! Sonnenschein (R. Reinick), Durch den Wald (von Schreck), Ave Maria (?), Sonnenscheinlied (Bjørnsjerne Bjørnson), Frühlingsanbruch (?), SATB, 1885–7; nos. 3, 5, Linden Singers, cond. I. Humphris, London, St John's, Smith Square, 11 Jan 1974

Paa Vidderne (Ibsen), reciter, orch, 1888; S. S. Hungnes, Oslo PO, cond. C. Farncombe, Norwegian Television broadcast, 17 May 1983

Sakuntala (H. Drachmann), T, orch, 1889

Twilight Fancies (Bjørnson), 1v, pf, 1889, orchd 1908; O. Wood, Queen's Hall Orch, cond. H. Wood, Liverpool, 21 March 1908 ... 78

The Bird's Story (Ibsen), 1v, pf, 1889, orchd 1908; O. Wood, Queen's Hall Orch, cond. H. Wood, Liverpool, 21 March 1908 ... 74, 78, 86

Maud (Tennyson), 5 songs, T, orch, 1891

Two Songs (Verlaine), 1v, pf, 1895, later orchd; Il pleure dans mon cœur, J. Waterston, London, Grafton Galleries, 25 Jan 1915 ... 78

Seven Danish Songs (J. P. Jacobsen, H. Drachmann), 1v, orch/pf, 1897; 5 songs, C. Andray, cond. Hertz, St James's Hall, 30 March 1899; 2 songs, Andray, cond. V. d'Indy, Paris, Société Nationale de Musique, 16 March 1901

Mitternachtslied Zarathustras (Nietzsche), Bar, male chorus, orch, 1898; D. Powell, cond. Hertz, St James's Hall, 30 May 1899

The Violet (L. Holstein), 1v, pf, 1900, orchd 1908; O. Wood, Queen's Hall Orch, cond. H. Wood, Liverpool, 21 March 1908

Summer Landscape (Drachmann), 1v, pf, 1902, orchd 1903 ... 72, 76

Appalachia: Variations on an Old Slave Song (trad.), Bar, chorus, orch, 1902–3 [rev. of Appalachia: American Rhapsody]; Elberfeld Choral and Orchestral Societies, cond. Haym, Elberfeld, Stadthalle, 15 Oct 1904 ... 72, 74, 76–7, 228

Sea Drift (W. Whitman), Bar, chorus, orch, 1903–4; J. Loritz, cond. G. Witte, Essen, 24 May 1906 ... 72, 76

A Mass of Life (Nietzsche), S, A, T, Bar, chorus, orch, 1904–5; Part I, 2, and Part II, inc.: M. van Lammen, O. von Welden, B. Hébert, R. Gmür, Munich Choral Society, Munich Hofkapelle, cond. L. Hess, Munich, 4 June 1908: complete, C. Gleeson White, M. G. Grainger-Kerr, W. Millar, C. Clark, North Staffordshire District Choral Society, Beecham Orch, cond. Beecham, Queen's Hall, 7 June 1909 ... 72, 77–8

Songs of Sunset (E. Dowson), Mez, Bar, chorus, orch, 1906–7; J. Culp, T. Bates, Edward Mason Choir, Beecham Orch, cond. Beecham, Queen's Hall, 16 June 1911 ... 78, 82

On Craig Ddu (A. Symons), SATTBB, 1907; Blackpool, 1910

Wanderer's Song (Symons), TTBB, 1908

Midsummer Song (?Delius), SSAATTBB, 1908; Whitley Bay and District Choral Society, cond. W. G. Whittaker, 1910

La lune blanche (Verlaine), 1v, orch/pf, 1910; J. Waterston, cond. Beecham, Grafton Galleries, 25 Jan 1915

An Arabesque [An Arabesk] (Jacobsen), Bar, chorus, orch, 1911; P. Heming, Welsh Musical Festival Choral Society, LSO, cond. A. E. Sims, Newport, Monmouthshire, 28 May 1920 ... 78

The Song of the High Hills (textless), chorus, orch, 1911–12; Philharmonic Choir, Royal Philharmonic Society, cond. A. Coates, Queen's Hall, 26 Feb 1920 ... 74, 78, 86

Two Songs for Children: Little Birdie (Tennyson), unison, pf, The Streamlet's Slumber Song, 2-part, pf, 1913

I-Brasil (W. Sharp [F. Macleod]), 1v, orch/pf, 1913; M. Thomas, Westminster, Central Hall, 21 November 1946

Requiem (H. Simon), S, Bar, chorus, orch, 1913–14; A. Evans, N. Williams, Philharmonic Choir, Royal Philharmonic Society, cond. Coates, Queen's Hall, 23 March 1922   81

To be sung of a Summer Night on the Water (textless), 2 songs, SATTBB (T solo in no.2), 1917; Oriana Madrigal Society, cond. C. K. Scott, London, Aeolian Hall, 28 June 1921

The splendour falls on castle walls (Tennyson), chorus, 1923; Oriana Madrigal Society, cond. Scott, Aeolian Hall, 17 June 1924

A Late Lark (W. E. Henley), T, orch, 1924/29; H. Nash, Orchestra of the Columbia Graphophone Company, cond. Beecham, Queen's Hall, 12 Oct 1929   82

Cynara (E. Dowson), Bar, orch, 1907/29; J. Goss, BBC SO, cond. Beecham, Queen's Hall, 18 Oct 1929   82

Songs of Farewell (Whitman), chorus, orch, ?1920/1930; Philharmonic Choir, LSO, cond. M. Sargent, 21 March 1932   72, 82

Idyll: Once I passed through a populous city (Whitman) [from Margot la Rouge], S, Bar, orch, 1932; D. Labbette, R. Henderson, BBC SO, cond. Wood, Queen's Hall, 3 Oct 1933   76, 82

CHAMBER AND INSTRUMENTAL

Zum Carnival Polka, pf, 1885
Pensées mélodieuses, pf, 1885
String Quartet, 1888, inc.
Romance, vn, pf, 1889
2 pieces, pf, Valse, Rêverie (inc.), 1889–90
Violin Sonata, B, 1892; Paris, 1893 (private perf.)   80
Badinage, pf, ?c1895
Romance, vc, pf, 1896; J. L. Webber, T. Mikkila, Helsinki, 22 June 1976
Violin Sonata no.1, 1905/14; A. Catterall, R. J. Forbes, Manchester, Houldsworth Hall, 24 Feb 1915   80
Cello Sonata, 1916; B. Harrison, H. Harty, London, Wigmore Hall, 31 Oct 1918   81

String Quartet, 1916; orig. version, 3 movts, London Qt, Aeolian Hall, 17 Nov 1916; rev. version, 4 movts, London Qt, Aeolian Hall, 1 Feb 1919   81
Dance, hpd, 1919
Five Pieces, pf, 1922–3
Three Preludes, pf, 1923; E. Howard-Jones, London, 4 Sept 1924   82
Violin Sonata no.2, 1923; A. Sammons, E. Howard-Jones, London, 7 Oct 1924   82
Violin Sonata no.3, 1930; M. Harrison, A. Bax, Wigmore Hall, 6 Nov 1930   82

SONGS

Over the Mountains High (Bjørnson), 1885
Zwei braune Augen (H. C. Andersen), 1885
Der Fichtenbaum (Heine), 1886
Five Songs from the Norwegian: Slumber Song (Bjørnson), The Nightingale (J. S. C. Welhaven), Summer Eve (J. Paulsen), Longing (T. Kjerulf), Sunset (A. Munch), 1888
Hochgebirgsleben (Ibsen), 1888
O schneller, mein Ross (E. Geibel), 1888
Chanson de Fortunio (A. de Musset), 1889
Seven Songs from the Norwegian: Cradle Song (Ibsen), The Homeward Journey (A. O. Vinje), Evening Voices (Twilight Fancies) (Bjørnson), Sweet Venevil (Bjørnson), Minstrel (Ibsen), Love concealed (Bjørnson), The Bird's Story (Ibsen), 1889–90; nos.3, 7, also orchd
Skogen gir susende, langsom besked (Bjørnson), 1890/91
Four Songs (Heine): Mit deinen blauen Augen, Ein schöner Stern, Hör' ich das Liedchen klingen, Aus deinen Augen, 1890–91
Three Songs (Shelley): Indian Love Song, Love's Philosophy, To the Queen of my Heart, 1891
Lyse Naetter (Drachmann), 1891
Jeg havde en nyskaaren Seljefløjte (V. Krag), 1892/3.
Nuages, (J. Richepin), 1893
Two Songs (Verlaine): Il pleure dans mon coeur, Le ciel est, par-dessus le toit, 1895; also orchd
The page sat in the lofty tower (Jacobsen), ?1895

Seven Danish Songs: Summer Nights (Drachmann), Through long, long years (Jacobsen), Wine Roses (Jacobsen), Let Springtime Come (Jacobsen), Irmelin Rose (Jacobsen), In the Seraglio Garden (Jacobsen), Silken Shoes (Jacobsen), 1896–7; also orchd
Traum Rosen (M. Heinitz), c1898
Im Glück wir lachend gingen (Drachmann), c1898
Four Songs (Nietzsche): Nach neuen Meeren, Der Wanderer, Der Einsame, Der Wanderer und sein Schatten, 1898
The Violet (Holstein), 1900, also orchd
Autumn (Holstein), 1900
Black Roses (E. Josephson), 1901
Jeg hører i Natten (Drachmann), 1901
Summer Landscape (Drachmann), 1902, also orchd
The nightingale has a lyre of gold (Henley), 1910
La lune blanche (Verlaine), 1910, also orchd
Chanson d'automne (Verlaine), 1911

I-Brasil (W. Sharp [F. Macleod]), 1913, also orchd
Four Old English Lyrics: It was a lover and his lass (Shakespeare), So white, so soft, so sweet is she (B. Jonson), Spring, the sweet spring (T. Nashe), To Daffodils (R. Herrick), 1915–16
Avant que tu ne t'en ailles (Verlaine), 1919/32

Principal publishers: Boosey & Hawkes, Leuckart, Oxford University Press, Stainer & Bell, Universal

WRITINGS
with Papus [pseud. of Gérard Encausse]: *Anatomie et physiologie de l'orchestre* (Paris, 1894)
'Musik in England im Kriege', *Musikblätter des Anbruch*, i (1919), 18
'At the Cross-Roads', *The Sackbut*, i (1920), 205
'Recollections of Strindberg', *The Sackbut*, i (1920), 353

BIBLIOGRAPHY
BOOKS

M. Chop: *Frederick Delius* (Berlin, 1907)

H. Haym: *Delius, A Mass of Life: Introduction to the Words and Music* (Leipzig and Vienna, 1913; Eng. trans., 1925)

P. Heseltine: *Frederick Delius* (London, 1923, rev. 2/1952/*R*1974)

R. H. Hull: *Delius* (London, 1928)

C. Delius: *Frederick Delius: Memories of my Brother* (London, 1935)

E. Fenby: *Delius as I knew him* (London, 1936, 2/1948/*R*1975, 4/1981)

A. Hutchings: *Delius* (London, 1948)

A. K. Holland: *The Songs of Delius* (London, 1951) [articles repr. from *MO*, lx (1936–7)]

T. Beecham: *Frederick Delius* (London, 1959, rev. 2/1975)

A. Bottomley, ed.: *Frederick Delius 1862–1962* (Bradford, 1962) [programme book for the Delius Centenary Festival]

Frederick Delius: Centenary Festival Exhibition (London, 1962)

G. Jahoda: *The Road to Samarkand: Frederick Delius and his Music* (New York, 1969)

M. Walker and S. Upton: *Frederick Delius: a Discography* (London, 1969) [*Delius Society Newsletter*, no.24]

E. Fenby: *Delius* (London, 1971)

L. Carley and R. Threlfall: *Delius and America* (London, 1972) [exhibition catalogue]

A. Jefferson: *Delius* (London, 1972)

R. Lowe: *Frederick Delius 1862–1934: a Catalogue of the Music Archive of the Delius Trust, London* (London, 1974)

L. Carley: *Delius: the Paris Years* (London, 1975)

C. Palmer: *Delius: Portrait of a Cosmopolitan* (London, 1976)

C. Redwood, ed.: *A Delius Companion* (London, 1976, 2/1980)

F. Tomlinson: *Warlock and Delius* (London, 1976)

L. Carley and R. Threlfall: *Delius: a Life in Pictures* (London, 1977, 2/1984)

R. Threlfall: *Frederick Delius (1862–1934): a Catalogue of the Compositions* (London, 1977)

D. Redwood: *Flecker and Delius: the Making of 'Hassan'* (London, 1978)

A. Eggum and S. Biørnstad, eds.: *Frederick Delius og Edvard Munch* (Oslo, 1979) [exhibition catalogue; Eng. and Norwegian text]

S. Banfield, ed.: *The Fourth Delius Festival: 8–14 March 1982* (Keele, 1982) [programme book]

L. Carley: *Delius: a Life in Letters*, i: *1862–1908* (London, 1983; Cambridge, Mass., 1984) [ii, in preparation]

Bibliography

J. B. Smith: *Frederick Delius and Edvard Munch: their Friendship and their Correspondence* (Rickmansworth, 1983)

Delius 1862–1934, compiled by The Delius Trust (London, 1984) [50th anniversary brochure]

R. Threlfall: *Frederick Delius: a Supplementary Catalogue* (London, 1986)

M. Walker: *Delius on Record: an Annotated Discography* (London, in preparation)

OTHER LITERATURE

R. A. Streatfeild: *Musiciens anglais contemporains* (Paris, 1913)

H. Brian: 'The Art of Delius', *MO*, xlvii (1923–4), 598, 700, 799, 906, 1002, 1098, 1194; xlviii (1924–5), 49

G. Abraham: 'Delius and his Literary Sources', *ML*, x (1929), 182; repr. in *Slavonic and Romantic Music* (London, 1968), 332ff

C. Gray: *Peter Warlock: a Memoir of Philip Heseltine* (London, 1934)

A. K. Holland: 'The Songs of Delius', *MO*, lx (1936–7), 19, 118, 306, 403, 592, 695, 783; repr. (London, 1951)

T. Beecham: *A Mingled Chime* (New York, 1943, London, 1944)

R. Nettel: *Music in the Five Towns 1840–1914* (London, 1944)

D. Hudson: *Norman O'Neill: a Life of Music* (London, 1945)

Tempo, no.26 (1952–3) [Delius issue]

N. Cardus: *A Composers' Eleven* (London, 1958)

A. Payne: 'Delius's Stylistic Development', *Tempo*, no.60 (1961–2), 6

D. Cooke: 'Delius and Form: a Vindication), *MT*, ciii (1962), 392, 460

Delius Society Newsletter (1962–) [renamed *Delius Society Journal*, July 1974; quarterly]

R. Lowe: 'Delius's First Performance', *MT*, cvi (1965), 190

J. B. Smith: 'Portrait of a Friendship: Edvard Munch and Frederick Delius', *Apollo* (1966), 38

G. Jahoda: *The Other Florida* (New York, 1967)

J. van Ackere: 'Un musicien méconnu: Frederick Delius, coloriste', *Revue générale belge*, v (1968), 75

I. A. Copley: 'Warlock and Delius: a Catalogue', *ML*, xlix (1968), 213

L. Carley: 'Jelka Rosen Delius: Artist, Admirer and Friend of Rodin: the Correspondence 1900–1914', *Nottingham French Studies*, ix (1970), 16, 81

C. Palmer: 'Delius and Poetic Realism', *ML*, li (1970), 404

P. J. Pirie: 'Delius the Unknown', *Music and Musicians*, xix/11 (1970–71), 34

W. Randel: 'Frederick Delius in America', *Virginia Magazine of History and Biography*, lxxix (1971), 349

——: ' "Koanga" and its Libretto', *ML*, lii (1971), 141

J. G. Brennan: 'Delius and Whitman', *Walt Whitman Review*, xviii/3 (1972), 90

R. Lowe-Dugmore: 'Frederick Delius and Norway', *SMA*, vi (1972), 27; see also vii (1973), 98

L. Carley: 'Hans Haym: Delius's Prophet and Pioneer', *ML*, liv (1973), 1

R. Lowe: 'The Music Archive of the Delius Trust', *MR*, xxxiv (1973), 294

R. Threlfall: 'Delius Music Manuscripts in Australia', *SMA*, vii (1973), 69

R. Lowe-Dugmore: 'Delius and Elgar: a Postscript', *SMA*, viii (1974), 92

C. Redwood: 'Delius and Strindberg', *ML*, lvi (1975), 364

J. Bird: *Percy Grainger* (London, 1976)

R. Threlfall: 'Delius in Eric Fenby's MSS', *Composer*, no.57 (1976), 33

C. Redwood: 'Delius's "Magic Fountain" ', *MT*, cxviii (1977), 909

R. Threlfall: 'Delius's Unknown Opera: The Magic Fountain', *SMA*, xi (1977), 60

R. Lowe-Dugmore: 'Documenting Delius', *SMA*, xii (1978), 114; xiii (1979), 44

P. Jones: 'The Delius Birthplace', *MT*, cxx (1979), 990

L. Foreman, ed.: *The Percy Grainger Companion* (London, 1981)

A. J. Boyle: '*A Mass of Life* and its "Bell-motif" ', *MR*, xliii (1982), 44

J. van Ackere: 'Frederick Delius of de Wellust van de Klank', *Academiae analecta*, xliv (1983), 59

C. Redwood, ed.: *An Elgar Companion* (Ashbourne, Derbys., 1983)

S. Lloyd: *H. Balfour Gardiner* (Cambridge, 1984)

RALPH VAUGHAN WILLIAMS

Hugh Ottaway

followed a period of two years at the Royal College of Music, London, then three at Trinity College, Cambridge (MusB 1894, BA in history 1895), and a further year or so at the RCM: a substantial period of study, during which his teachers of composition were Parry, Wood and Stanford.

Even as a schoolboy, he had been drawn increasingly to composition, and on going up to Cambridge he knew very well what he wanted to become. But progress was slow; Wood did not believe he would ever make a composer, and a Darwin cousin, Gwen Raverat, writing of her Cambridge childhood, recalled 'overhearing scraps of conversation about "that foolish young man, Ralph Vaughan Williams", who *would* go on working at music when "he was so hopelessly bad at it" '. In later years the composer himself remarked on his 'amateurish technique', which he said had dogged him all his life; but his early groping had much to do with a deep dissatisfaction with the English musical scene and an inability to see his own path. He knew that he must strive for the highest professional standards; hence his return to the RCM and his subsequent studying with Bruch in Berlin (1897) and Ravel in Paris (1908). At the same time he recognized that, creatively, salvation would be found, not in imitating foreign models, but in a regenerative use of native resources. This led him to English folksong, to Elizabethan and Jacobean music, and to a philosophy of musical citizenship, which he both practised and preached (see especially his essay 'Who Wants the English Composer?' and *National Music*). These interests and ideals he shared with Holst, whom he met at the RCM in 1895. The close friendship that at once developed is notable because the two composers subjected their work in progress to each other's criticism. These 'field-days', as they called them, lasted until Holst's death in 1934.

It is a part of Vaughan Williams's strength and importance that he cannot be adequately discussed in narrowly musical terms. His outlook was human and social. He never forgot that music was for people; he was interested in every situation, however humble, for which music was needed; and his feeling for genuinely popular traditions amounted to a reverence that was almost religious: the most obvious comparison is with Bartók and Kodály in Hungary. Two points immediately follow: throughout a public life of more than 60 years, Vaughan Williams engaged in a wide range of musical activities, sometimes of a kind that many lesser composers would have considered beneath them; and at every stage in his development the extensive list of works shows different levels of composition, from the simplest occasional pieces to the most visionary personal expressions.

'Visionary' is a word much used in discussing Vaughan Williams's music, and it has often been assumed that the vision is theistic and specifically Christian. The reality is more complex. 'He was an atheist during his later years at Charterhouse and at Cambridge,' wrote Ursula Vaughan Williams, 'though he later drifted into a cheerful agnosticism: he was never a professing Christian'. He was a first-generation atheist with a profound, not to say visionary, sense of the past, which means a disappointed theist. Moreover, in the popular traditions of the English church, as in folksong, he was aware of the common aspirations of generations of ordinary men with whom he felt a deep, contemplative sympathy. And so there is in his work a fundamental tension between traditional concepts of belief and morality and a spiritual anguish which is also visionary.

It was not until 1909–10 that a personal voice fully emerged in Vaughan Williams's music: *On Wenlock Edge* and the Fantasia on a Theme by Thomas Tallis are reliable points of reference. By then he had gained experience in a number of directions; he had worked as a church organist – perhaps the only appointment he was glad to give up – had taken the FRCO and MusD, and had launched out as writer, lecturer, music editor and folksong collector. He was editing *Welcome Songs* for the Purcell Society, but far more important was his selecting of the tunes for *The English Hymnal* (1906), a task to which he devoted many months, rediscovering old tunes and weeding out Victoriana. Some tunes, including the justly celebrated *Sine nomine* ('For all the saints'), he wrote himself; he adapted 35 to 40 from folksongs. Since collecting his first folksong, *Bushes and Briars*, in 1903, he had become one of the foremost activists in the movement, notably in Norfolk, Essex and Sussex. In all he collected over 800 songs and variants. Another important development was the Leith Hill Musical Festival: from its inception in 1905 until 1953 Vaughan Williams was principal conductor, and his performances of Bach, particularly of the *St Matthew Passion*, became national events. His Bach was noted for its dramatic and spiritual qualities; he had little time for the school of 'authenticity'.

By 1914 he had behind him a considerable body of work, including two symphonies, and a growing reputation for independence and strength of character.

Although nearly 42, he felt bound to involve himself in the war. He served as a wagon orderly with the Royal Army Medical Corps in France and on the Salonica front, and later returned to France as an artillery officer. Soon after the armistice he was made director of music for the First Army of the British Expeditionary Force, with responsibility for organizing amateur music-making among the troops. The impact of the war on his imagination was deep and lasting but did not express itself in an obvious protest or change of style; rather is it felt in a more intense inwardness.

II   The years after World War I

After Vaughan Williams was demobilized in 1919, he became a member of the teaching staff of the RCM. He was conductor of the Bach Choir in 1920–28, for a short time conducted the Handel Society, and he did much to revive and expand the Leith Hill Festival. The English Folk Dance Society and other bodies made demands on his time, which he gave freely, still managing to revise pre-war compositions – *A London Symphony*, *The Lark Ascending*, *Hugh the Drover* – and to write new ones. This capacity for reconciling all manner of musical activity – practical, educational, administrative, advisory – with his own creative work lasted into old age. So did his capacity for friendship, which became particularly marked in the 1920s as he found himself thrust into prominence in many branches of musical life. One new friend was the young conductor Adrian Boult, who in 1922 gave the first performance of the *Pastoral Symphony*. Boult soon emerged – and was to continue – as Vaughan Williams's foremost interpreter. The *Pastoral Symphony* was also played (under Boult

101

again) at one of the ISCM festivals: works by Vaughan Williams were given at Salzburg (1924), Venice (1925), Prague (1925), Geneva (1929) and London (1931).

As a teacher of composition, Vaughan Williams had something of Parry's gift for encouraging his pupils to be themselves. He expected them to do as he did – seek the best advice but use their own judgment. Where there was strength of character as well as some talent, he succeeded, and often a lasting relationship resulted, as with Gordon Jacob and Elizabeth Maconchy. He also taught, and conducted, at summer schools of the English Folk Dance and Song Society, of which he was elected president in 1932. In the same year he lectured on national music at Bryn Mawr College, Pennsylvania. From the 1920s onwards, he was increasingly in demand as composer–conductor, a role in which he often distinguished himself, particularly in performances of *A London Symphony*. His 1937 recording of the Fourth Symphony is not only 'historic' but an outstanding performance in its own right.

The Fourth Symphony, first performed in 1935, is another notable landmark; for many this confirmed Vaughan Williams's leadership of 'the English school' and his lasting capacity for self-renewal. In the same year, having previously refused a knighthood and other honours, he accepted the OM. Many years later he wrote to Rutland Boughton: 'I have always refused all honours and appointments which involved obligation to anyone in authority – the OM involved no such obligation'. Purely musical honours, which had effectively begun in 1919 with an honorary DMus at Oxford, included at least five more doctorates from British universities, the Cobbett Medal (1930), the Gold Medal

10. *Ralph Vaughan Williams (right) and Gustav Holst on a walking tour of the Malvern Hills in September 1921*

of the Royal Philharmonic Society (1930), the Collard Life Fellowship (1934, in succession to Elgar), the Shakespeare Prize (University of Hamburg, 1937) and the Albert Medal of the Royal Society of Arts (1955).

The Hamburg award troubled him, and before accepting he stated bluntly that he belonged to 'more than one English society whose object is to combat all that the present German *régime* stands for'. Politically he was in the tradition of the 19th-century free-thinking radical who devoted his energies to particular causes. For Vaughan Williams the plight of the German refugees was just such a cause, and his activity on their behalf led in 1939 to his music being banned by the Nazis. During the war years he directed the work of the Home Office Committee for the Release of Interned Alien Musicians, helped to organize the lunchtime concerts at the National Gallery and did much for the Council for the Encouragement of Music and the Arts (now the Arts Council of Great Britain) and other bodies engaged in promoting music. A new interest, beginning with *49th Parallel* (1940–41), was music for films, which was almost the only medium that he had not explored, and he found it stimulating. But his principal wartime composition was the Fifth Symphony, 'music imbued with what one can only call greatness of soul' (Mellers); first played in 1943, this met with a response of deep gratitude, even from many who had not known that Vaughan Williams mattered to them.

In the postwar years he learnt to his dismay that he had become an almost patriarchal figure and that critics were attributing prophetic intentions (and concrete meanings) to the Symphonies nos.4–6. A reaction to the latter, almost certainly, was his writing of semi-facetious

programme notes, particularly for the first performances of the Sixth and Ninth symphonies. He denied
that the Sixth was a 'war symphony'; but this disturbing
work, first played in 1948, accorded so well with the
postwar disillusionment that within a little over two
years it had received 100 performances – a record
exceeded by only one English symphony, Elgar's First.
Once again, though not with intent, he had done the
unpredictable and challenged comfortable opinion.

The 1950s brought important changes in Vaughan
Williams's personal life, his music and the critical
climate. In 1951 his wife Adeline (née Fisher), whom he
had married in 1897, died at the age of 80, having been
an invalid for many years; and in the same year he
suffered 'the bitterest disappointment of his musical life'
(Douglas), the inept production at Covent Garden of the
morality *The Pilgrim's Progress*, on which he had been
working, intermittently, for up to 40 years: Bunyan, like
Blake and Whitman, had long been embedded in his
personal mythology. In 1953 he married Ursula Wood,
a close family friend, and left Dorking, where he had
been living since 1929, for central London. Apart from
deafness, he was in good health; London's cultural life
was paradise regained, and he travelled abroad more
than he had done for decades. In 1954 he visited the
USA again, lecturing at Cornell and other universities,
conducting *A London Symphony* and touring exten-
sively. Throughout these years he was not only a
familiar presence at London concerts, the Cheltenham
Festival and the Three Choirs Festival, but was active
in public controversy – for example, over the intended
organ for the Festival Hall (1950) and the threat to the
BBC Third Programme (1958) – and wrote a great deal

Vaughan Williams

of music, including the last three symphonies.

To a new generation of critics Vaughan Williams, like Sibelius, tended to symbolize resistance to central Europe in general and the Second Viennese School in particular. His own references to 'amateurish technique' were taken up and misapplied, the principal works of his last years were said to be laboured and repetitive, and it was even hinted that he was no longer doing his own scoring. This last was based on the fact that, from the Sixth Symphony onwards, fair copies of the full scores (his own handwriting was anything but fair) had been produced by Roy Douglas, whose task it was to achieve legibility and, in consultation with the composer, to correct discrepancies and oversights. What made the hint ironical, but perhaps plausible to the unsuspecting, was Vaughan Williams's renewed interest in colour and texture, the outward sign of far deeper changes in the music of the last ten years, beginning with the film score of 1948 for *Scott of the Antarctic* (see below and Ottaway, *MT*, 1972).

The new critical climate may well have contributed in the period following his death to the marked reduction in the number of performances of his major works; but a surer guide to public interest was the continuing demand for new recordings and the readiness of companies to provide them. When he died many English music-lovers felt a sense of loss that was personal no less than musical. This 'extraordinary, ordinary man' (Kennedy, 1964) had not only become an institution; he had also, as Parry said of Elgar, reached the hearts of the people.

Vaughan Williams died in London on 26 August 1958. On 19 September, before a crowded assembly, his ashes were interred in the north choir aisle of Westminster Abbey, near the burial places of Purcell and Stanford; the first music that was played was his *Five Variants of 'Dives and Lazarus'*, on a tune that he had known and loved since 1893.

Works

Although the variety within Vaughan Williams's extensive output would seem to favour discussion of the
works according to genre, the development through
60 years presents an overriding case for division into
periods. The five periods chosen here are neither arbi-
trary nor absolute: up to 1908, 1909–14, 1919–34,
1935–44 and 1945–58. Each has its distinguishing
character, or characters; equally striking, however, at
least from the second period onwards, is the recurrence
of earlier modes of expression. Few major composers
have kept open so many avenues for so long, which is a
reflection of that unusual blend of outward- and inward-
looking qualities which characterized the man. Because
he was an intuitive artist, little disposed to theorize,
except about the human and social aspects of music, he
was never inhibited by fears of inconsistency, stylistic or
otherwise. Some unlikely works appear side by side,
particularly in the third period: for instance, *Job* and
The Poisoned Kiss, the Fourth Symphony and the Suite
for viola and small orchestra. If there was a streak of
clumsiness in his make-up, he was also 'a perfectionist,
though he might not have thought of himself as such'
(Douglas). This shows clearly in his revisions of some of
the works that meant most to him. As late as 1950 he
made some changes in the scoring of the *Pastoral*

Symphony (1921), and the much revised *Hugh the Drover* (1910–14) did not take its final form until 1956.

I Early works

The first period, that of Vaughan Williams's long 'apprenticeship', culminated in *A Sea Symphony* (1903–9), which stands at the brink of the first period of maturity. The main emphasis throughout is on vocal music, but with the orchestra becoming increasingly important in the last five or six years. Although there are songs and partsongs dating from the 1890s, the earliest composition that is widely known is *Linden Lea* (1901). This setting for voice and piano of words by the Dorset dialect poet William Barnes is not without significance: sub-titled 'a Dorset folksong' (which it is not), it has an open-air freshness and an attachment to simple things, but is also related to the domestic (drawing-room) song forms of the time. This vein is extended and broadened in the *Songs of Travel* (Stevenson, 1901–4), which have likewise retained their early popularity. These have a moving eloquence and afford many insights into the composer's temperament, particularly 'The Infinite Shining Heavens' and 'Bright is the Ring of Words'; but there is also a received Romanticism of a kind that disappeared under the impact of folksong and of Elizabethan music. This is also marked in the rather less sharply focussed Rossetti cycle *The House of Life* (1903), from which 'Silent Noon' has remained popular. However remote they may seem from the composer of 20 years later, these early songs are among the finest written in England around 1900 and are as notable for strength of purpose as for sensitive word-setting. Their achievement is underlined by the fact that at no other stage did Vaughan Williams give much attention to the solo song with piano accompaniment.

Choral music, with and without orchestra, is prominent throughout his development. *Toward the Unknown Region* (Whitman, 1905–6), 'a song for chorus and orchestra', was the first work to make a major impact on critics and public alike. Despite the choral debt to Parry and some residual chromaticism, there is much that is individual, particularly in the harmonic language and the scoring. Noteworthy too is the first four-note phrase (ex.1), a melodic fingerprint that persisted into old age.

Ex.1

Grave ma non troppo

p sostenuto

The crucial years for *A Sea Symphony* (Whitman) were 1906–8. Beginning as 'songs of the sea' in emulation of Stanford, this became a fully choral symphony, a triumph of instinct over environment. The tone is optimistic, Whitman's emphasis on the unity of being and the brotherhood of man comes through strongly, and the vitality of the best things in it has proved enduring. Whatever the indebtedness to Parry and Stanford, and in the finale to Elgar, there is no mistaking the physical exhilaration or the visionary rapture. Melodic invention mingling duplets and triplets, harmonic images such as ex.2, the quasi-epilogue with its

110

alternating chords and *niente* close, these are among the features that are fundamental Vaughan Williams.

Ex.2

The unpublished works include two or three for orchestra showing an earlier and more significant interest in the medium than has sometimes been suggested, notably the *Bucolic Suite* (1900) and *Harnham Down* (1904–7). The composer thought well enough of *In the Fen Country* (1904) to revise the scoring in 1935; it contains elements of his mature pastoral style as well as an alien chromaticism. The first folksong works are the three *Norfolk Rhapsodies* (1905–6), of which the second and third were withdrawn: no.1 has a distinctive tone poetry, atmospheric and pure in expression, and points clearly to the next period. Two folksongs are quoted, briefly, in the scherzo of *A Sea Symphony*, but these are incidental in a work whose style has a different ancestry. Whitman's liberating thought and the music of English villagers had still to make common cause.

In general, Vaughan Williams did not use folksongs in orchestral and instrumental works, but he so absorbed the folksong idiom that his melodic writing was profoundly conditioned and freed from impurities. Certain tunes, notably *Searching for Lambs* and *Dives and Lazarus*, are often felt to be almost within earshot, so much a part of him did their turns of phrase become. From the 30 years 1905–35 there are many folksong arrangements, for voice and piano and for unaccompanied chorus, and as late as 1949 he wrote *Folksongs of the Four Seasons* for women's voices and orchestra. The harmonization is always idiomatic: even in his later student years he was drawn to the modes; indeed, he once presented Stanford with a modal waltz.

II Towards 'A London Symphony' 1909–14

This period extends from the G minor String Quartet and *On Wenlock Edge* – the immediate beneficiaries of Vaughan Williams's studying with Ravel – to *Hugh the Drover*, *A London Symphony* and *The Lark Ascending*, all substantially complete in 1914. The common ground is the assimilation of folksong, the confident use of a distinctive body of imagery, at once national and personal, and the achievement of a unified style. In most works, but not the Fantasia on a Theme by Thomas Tallis, there are traces of former ways, usually involving a chromatic expressiveness: only in the G minor Quartet (1908–9) and the *Five Mystical Songs* (Herbert, 1911) are these a serious handicap. At least five works from this period are among those that have proved most durable, and their popularity is not unconnected with their emotional background, which is stable and secure, however anguished the foreground. This 'security', though in part a reflection of the composer's growing self-confidence, has much to do with the pre-war climate of Liberal optimism and the sense of community inherent in it. The most anguished foreground is in the finale of *A London Symphony*, but at the close, after a climax of harrowing intensity, the vision is 'contained' by a warm G major chord throughout the orchestra. Similarly, the romance for violin and orchestra *The*

Lark Ascending is wholly idyllic, and therefore different in feeling from the postwar pastoral works. The boisterous good humour of the suite from *The Wasps* (incidental music to Aristophanes' comedy, 1909) is a more extrovert reflection of the same stable background. All these works are rich in expressions basic to Vaughan Williams's maturity.

The achievement that most clearly transcends this period ambience is the Fantasia on a Theme by Thomas Tallis for double string orchestra (1910, rev. 1919). This is perhaps the first unqualified masterpiece; it is also the work that has travelled most widely, which challenges the view that the composer's 'Englishness' necessarily limits his appreciation abroad. He was drawn to Tallis's Phrygian tune when researching for *The English Hymnal* (see no.92) and found in it a grandeur and an intimacy which crystallized something essential to his own musical style: this way of writing for strings, though many times modified, may be traced as far as the Ninth Symphony. There is a new massiveness and exaltation, a quiet deliberation, and always a sense of wonder: comparison of the opening (ex.3) with ex.1 shows a

Ex.3

notable difference in harmonic movement, the progression in ex.3 being entirely by common chords and coloured by the 'false relations' of Elizabethan music.

113

Although less concentrated, and less pure in expression, the Housman song cycle *On Wenlock Edge* for tenor, piano and string quartet (1908–9) is more broadly representative of the works of this period. It is also an outstanding contribution to English song, more ambitious than the great majority of Housman settings and sounding greater depths. (A comparison of 'Bredon Hill' and 'Is my team ploughing?' with the slightly later settings by Butterworth can only emphasize Vaughan Williams's dramatic sense and the scale of his intentions.) Essentially a cycle, framed by songs that give a cosmic dimension to human suffering, *On Wenlock Edge* has plenty of vital ideas and marks the first clear emergence of the 'disappointed theist'. In the opening song, which gives its title to the whole, there is a new chromaticism, anguished and free from Rossetti-like associations (cf the finale of *A London Symphony*) and in 'From far, from eve and morning' and 'Clun' consecutive triads form awesome, yet disarmingly simple, images of eternity. The vocal part, too, is generally simple (also demanding), but is less close to folksong than some have suggested. Early in the 1920s the composer made a version for tenor and orchestra, but it is the original that has achieved classic status.

In their separate ways the most ambitious works from this period are *A London Symphony* (1912–13, with substantial postwar revisions) and *Hugh the Drover* (1910–14, also much revised). The former, Vaughan Williams's first purely orchestral symphony, stands in much the same relation to the Germanic mainstream as do the later symphonies of Dvořák: the form is traditional, the expression personal and national. A striking innovation is the matching introduction and epilogue, visionary in tone. Also used by Bax, the epilogue is Vaughan Williams's most personal contribution to symphonic form (cf all his symphonies except the *Pastoral*, where the finale has its own introduction and epilogue, and nos.8 and 9). Although the *London* was originally to have been a symphonic poem and has been described as 'a misplaced opera' – a tribute to its vivid imagery – the composer rightly insisted that it was 'self-expressive, and must stand or fall as "absolute" music'; the use made of the Westminster chimes and other London sounds does not amount to a programme. Lambert heard the opening of *La mer* in the introduction: certainly the experience of Debussy's music was important at this stage, both in its purely sensuous aspect and in confirming the instinct to move chords freely, bodily, from point to point ('block chording').

Hugh the Drover, or Love in the Stocks, was ambitious in attempting, almost unconcernedly, to break through the barrier of English taste that stood in the way of native opera, and in this it had some success, becoming the best-known example between the revival of *Dido and Aeneas* in 1895 and *Peter Grimes* (1945). Some, including Czechs, have seen it as an English equivalent of *The Bartered Bride*, but the libretto is artificial, presenting a picture-postcard view of Cotswold village life in the 19th century, and the music ranges in style from the *Songs of Travel* to *A London Symphony*. Although stagy, it is also stageworthy, and in a good performance holds the attention with its picturesque action, including a boxing-match, and its sense of musical enjoyment. About ten traditional tunes are

115

incorporated: the term 'ballad opera', used by the composer though strictly misapplied, is appropriate in spirit. For *Hugh the Drover* is above all an entertainment.

III   The interwar works 1919–34
The third creative period was bounded by the next symphonies, the *Pastoral* and the F minor. This was a period of immense vigour and variety in which three trends are particularly striking: a deepening of the visionary aspect; an extending of the expressive range, embracing new forms of imagery; and a simultaneous working on markedly different levels. This last puzzled some of Vaughan Williams's admirers, especially those who had set their own limits to the kind of composer he was. Folksong arrangements, occasional and 'serviceable' church music, competition partsongs and simple, popular expressions such as the unison song *Let us now praise famous men*, these are found side by side with some of his most penetrating masterpieces. There are important achievements in almost every field except chamber music.

Ideas for the *Pastoral Symphony* had begun to form as early as 1916, when Vaughan Williams was in France with the Royal Army Medical Corps, and of this the 'bugle call' for a natural trumpet in the slow movement is direct evidence. More thought-provoking pointers are the tensions experienced beneath the seemingly tranquil surface of the music and the sudden impassioned upsurges which challenge the prevailing quietude. For all its indifference to the things commonly held to make a symphony 'go', notably contrasts in tempo, dynamics and basic material, the *Pastoral* is a dramatic work; it is also the expression of a man thrown

mainly to words from *Revelation*, is prefaced by a quotation from Plato concerning the immortality of the soul. This is the most visionary of these works; its expression is plainer, more severe, in a way that anticipates aspects of *Job*, and a less 'churchy' oratorio would be hard to imagine. Although the deepest of Vaughan Williams's choral and orchestral works, it has not achieved the prominence of Holst's *Hymn of Jesus*, with which it has a close spiritual affinity.

The exploratory nature of this period is also revealed in a group of works employing a solo instrument. The Concerto for violin and strings (1924–5), formerly called *Concerto accademico*, is Vaughan Williams's nearest approach to a Bachian 'neo-classicism' and was probably written in response to Holst's Fugal Concerto. The Piano Concerto (1926–31), in which the toccata-like manner of the first movement invites comparison with Bartók, is an interesting transition to the Fourth Symphony, but it was conceived piecemeal and cannot be considered wholly successful. There is also a version by Joseph Cooper for two pianos and orchestra (1946), which overcomes some problems of balance – but not, of course, those of unity. The outstanding work in this group is *Flos campi* (1925), a suite for solo viola, small chorus (wordless) and small orchestra, each movement of which is headed by a Latin quotation from the *Song of Songs*. Rapt, intense, yet ultimately serene, this is among Vaughan Williams's most imaginative achievements. The often quoted bitonal opening is a natural development from the *Pastoral Symphony* and *Sancta civitas*, and the diatonic polyphony of the final number points to the close of the Fifth Symphony. There is also much that reaches out through *Riders to the Sea* to the

Sixth Symphony and beyond. The Suite (1934) for viola and small orchestra, written, like *Flos campi*, for Tertis, is a comparatively low-pressure work in eight short movements, some of which are excellent examples of the composer's treatment of folksong-like material. Perhaps the finest actual folksong work from this period is the Six Studies in English Folksong (1926) for cello and piano.

The three operas written between 1924, when *Hugh the Drover* was first performed, and 1932 are remarkable evidence of Vaughan Williams's working on different levels. The first, *Sir John in Love* (1924–8), is a natural successor to *Hugh* without any of the immaturities. Based on *The Merry Wives of Windsor*, it is an opera in four acts requiring 20 soloists and elaborate staging; musically, however, it represents a relaxation from the visionary vein, an enjoyment of traditional cakes and ale. The one-act *Riders to the Sea* (1925–32), an almost complete setting of Synge's play, is both a theatrical tour de force and a visionary masterpiece; moreover, in its response to the theme of man defeated by nature – a far cry from the *Pastoral Symphony* – and in the comprehensiveness of its musical imagery, it seems to reach to the brink of the final period: even the characteristic chord relationship from the end of the Sixth Symphony makes its first appearance here (ex.5).

Ex.5
(a) *Riders to the Sea* (b) Sixth Symphony

Very different from both these operas is *The Poisoned*

119

11. Scene from the first production of Vaughan William's 'Job' (London, 1931), choreographed by Ninette de Valois, with Anton Dolin (centre) as Satan

Kiss (1927–9), a 'romantic extravaganza' with spoken dialogue based on a story by R. Garnett. Here a sense of fun prevails, and a delight in doing something different, without obligations; significantly, this is one of the few compositions not shown to Holst while in progress.

Holst's influence outlived his death in 1934 (in, for instance, the Sixth Symphony) but is most marked in this period. Particular evidence may be found in the Violin Concerto, the *Magnificat* for contralto solo, women's choir, solo flute and orchestra, the ballet *Job* and the Fourth Symphony. This in no way limits the individuality of these works, of which the last two would have to be included in any reckoning of Vaughan Williams's most important creations. *Job*, 'a masque for dancing' (1927–30), brings together a number of the basic types of imagery from the preceding years and in the music for Satan introduces new ones: so potent are the ingredients, and so high the imaginative level, that the Symphonies nos.4–6, utterly different from each other though they are, are all indebted to this seminal score. The scenario by Keynes and Raverat based on Blake's *Illustrations to the Book of Job* failed to interest Dyagilev, for whom it was intended, and Vaughan Williams completed his score as a concert work in nine scenes, in which form it was first given. The ballet was mounted by the Camargo Society in 1931 and has entered the repertory of the British Royal Ballet (see fig.11).

The Fourth Symphony, in F minor (1931–4), renews the angular, Satanic element in *Job*, turns away from modal 'blessedness' and achieves a structural power that is intellectually and emotionally challenging in a way quite new to Vaughan Williams's music. Two basic motifs (ex.6) unite the four movements and dominate the musical imagery. Their extreme terseness, their discordant harmonic implications and the tension arising from their immediate juxtaposition go far to account for the essential violence of this work. Together with

Ex.6

Riders to the Sea, the Fourth may be held to represent a response to experience so different from that of the *Pastoral* and its 'religious' satellites as to constitute an opposite pole.

IV   The World War II period 1935–44

The many who, unlike the composer, interpreted the Fourth Symphony as 'ancestral voices prophesying war' thought they saw corroborative evidence in *Dona nobis pacem* (1936), a cantata for soloists, chorus and orchestra using texts from various sources, with Whitman well to the fore. There is some related imagery – not least the falling semitone on 'dona' – but this work ranges widely in point of style, successfully incorporating a setting of Whitman's 'Dirge for Two Veterans' made before World War I, and ending optimistically in a serviceable, popular manner found in works from all periods. Although less than a masterpiece, *Dona nobis pacem* deserves a permanent place among the musical works written against war. *Five Tudor Portraits* (1935), a Skelton suite for soloists, chorus and orchestra, is by the composer of *Sir John in Love* and the Suite for viola and small orchestra; it is music of relaxed enjoyment, with many characteristic niceties of expression.

Neither of these works is particularly representative of this fourth period, but in their broader lyricism and warmth of manner they may be said to point the way. Disappointed expectations based on the 'modernity' of the Fourth Symphony gave rise to the view that, after Holst's death, Vaughan Williams reverted to a more traditional style. The cause remains speculative, but it is true that for a number of years he concentrated on a more benign, euphonious manner which was regarded by many as definitive. Reversion is too crude a description; a drawing-out and interweaving of threads going back through *Job* to the Tallis Fantasia would be more accurate. A sense of spiritual security is conveyed by a modal–diatonic norm of expression, offset but seldom undermined by contrary elements. The sentiments made explicit in the *Serenade to Music* (1938), a setting for 16 soloists and orchestra of words from *The Merchant of Venice*, are basic to this period. Written for Wood's golden jubilee as a conductor, the *Serenade* is best in its original version but may be given by only four soloists, with chorus, or with all the vocal parts treated chorally. There is also an orchestral version. In a similar vein is *The Bridal Day* (1938–9, rev. 1952–3), a masque with a text by Ursula Wood (later the composer's wife) after Spenser's *Epithalamion*. Originally intended for the English Folk Dance and Song Society, this was not performed until 1953, when it was presented by BBC television.

The commanding landmark in this period is the Fifth Symphony (1938–43, rev. 1951), written after some sustained work on *The Pilgrim's Progress* but apparently in the belief that the morality (opera) would not be completed. Three principal themes and some subsidiary material are therefore 'borrowed' but are treated independently with few, if any, programmatic overtones. This Symphony in D is concerned with the evolution of mode and key as well as of the thematic stuff. The first movement opens and closes in a deeply modal region with the flattened 7th (C♮) much emphasized, but in the themes of the finale the 7ths are consistently 'sharpened', and the symphony ends in the purest, and serenest, D major. Making its affirmations in spite of the Fourth, with which it has in common only its mastery of means, the Fifth marks the climax of Vaughan Williams's traditional (religious) responses.

Like the *Pastoral Symphony*, the Fifth has a number of 'satellites' or associated works. These include the *Five Variants of 'Dives and Lazarus'* (1939) for strings and harp(s), which is perhaps the most personal of all the folksong compositions, the String Quartet in A minor (1942–4) and the Concerto for oboe and strings (1944). Written for Goossens, the Concerto is at once capricious, lyrical and nostalgic, and is the composer's most successful essay in this form. The A minor Quartet, easily the finest of the handful of chamber works, ends in D in the spirit of the Fifth Symphony, but the other movements, which are either agitated or joyless, make the dominant impression. Here, and in some of the music for the war film *The Story of a Flemish Farm* (1943), are the first intimations of the ferment that was to produce the Sixth Symphony. Not that anyone could have foreseen the Sixth, still less the richness of the period that followed.

12. *Autograph MS from the first movement of Vaughan Williams's Symphony no.5 in D, composed 1938–43, with the revisions of 1951; the violin and viola notes, most of the clefs, and the crossed out portions are not in the composer's hand*

V   The final period

After its many early performances, Foss remarked on 'the flood of explanatory prose which the [Sixth] Symphony has unloosed'. There had been few other works in the post-Romantic era that had so compelled their admirers to ask what the music meant; for the Sixth, in E minor (1944–7), was experienced by many as a spiritual negation of the Fifth, which it was felt to supplant as a definitive statement. The composer denied that he had written a 'war symphony', but later cited Prospero's words 'We are such stuff as dreams are made on, and our little life is rounded with a sleep' as a verbal indication of 'the substance of my last movement' (Kennedy, 1964). This movement, Epilogue, presents the ethos of the work in its most acute form and with the emphasis of an unrelieved *pianissimo* (*senza crescendo*). Essentially it is a meditation on a single theme, which 'drifts about contrapuntally' and finally disintegrates, leaving only the chords of E♭ major and E minor alternating in a void. An equivalent chord relationship, though less decisively used, has been noted in *Riders to the Sea* (ex.5), which of the earlier works is the one that has most in common with the imagery of the Sixth. Both these works bear directly on the film score for *Scott of the Antarctic* (1948).

It was a stroke of artistic good fortune that Vaughan Williams was asked for that particular score precisely at this juncture. The spiritual desolation of the Sixth found its physical counterpart in the polar wastes, and the sense of challenge and endurance was re-engaged by the story of Scott's last expedition. Moreover, the human values represented – heroic endeavour, loyalty, dedication, personal warmth – were a timely corrective to the

126

'ultimate nihilism' (Cooke) of the symphony. He soon knew that what he was writing was no ordinary film score and that an Antarctic symphony might well come of it. In fact, he was achieving a reconciliation that would produce not one but three more symphonies and would affect almost everything he wrote in the very active ten years remaining to him. This is partly a matter of colour – he was fascinated by his new Antarctic sounds, 'the 'phones and 'spiels' (tuned percussion) particularly – but basically it concerns the fusion and transformation of hitherto opposed worlds of feeling: the 'blessedness' of the Fifth and the nihilistic vision of the Sixth were resolved in a tragic but resilient humanism. Thus the last three symphonies share the same stylistic and philosophical orientation and have a wider range of imagery than any of the others since *A London Symphony*. It does not follow that they are greater symphonies; however, experience has shown that the late works are more likely to be under- than overrated.

The *Sinfonia antartica* (no.7) was begun in 1949 but proved troublesome and other works supervened. The same year saw the completion of *The Pilgrim's Progress*, which really belongs to the two preceding periods. Both the dramatic conception – effectively, a series of tableaux – and the musical realization have been adversely criticized, but a minority holds that this morality in four acts is one of his supreme achievements: a distinguished Cambridge production by Dennis Arundell in 1954 is cited as supporting evidence. The most penetrating critical point is both musical and dramatic: that *The Pilgrim's Progress* is 'an aftermath' (Richard Capell, in the *Daily Telegraph*

127

of 28 April 1951), the composer's Bunyanesque vision having already found its most intense expression in the middle symphonies. But it remains a deeply individual work and will always have its advocates. No less individual are two smaller-scale works from 1949. One of these, *An Oxford Elegy* for speaker, small chorus and small orchestra, uses another text long thought of by Vaughan Williams as a possible basis for an opera libretto – Arnold's *The Scholar Gipsy*, parts of which are combined here with some lines from *Thyrsis*. This is an unusually successful melodrama and, although broadly pastoral in manner, belongs unequivocally to the final period: like the Cavatina in the Eighth Symphony and many pages from the Ninth, it makes a unique contribution to the music of old age. The other work is in an equally problematical genre, that initiated by Beethoven's Choral Fantasia: the *Fantasia on the Old 104th* for solo piano, chorus and orchestra, which is a paean of praise in the composer's 'serviceable' manner but also contains his most distinguished piano writing. Since the piano was in general unsympathetic to him, its use here might almost be included among the instances of unlikely instruments featured in this period. There is a Romance in D♭ for harmonica, strings and piano (1951) – a markedly post-*Scott* piece written for Larry Adler – and a Concerto in F minor for bass tuba and orchestra (1954), notable for its warmly lyrical slow movement. This instrumental interest was by no means limited to soloistic possibilities; in the Eighth Symphony there is an important part for vibraphone, and the Ninth has a flugelhorn and three saxophones.

The *Sinfonia antartica* was completed in 1952. It is arguably neither sufficiently symphonic nor sufficiently

13. Ralph Vaughan Williams

programmatic, and for that reason the least successful of the mature symphonies, but is capable of making a deep impression. The opening theme, which is a kind of 'motto', reveals a synthesis of the harmonic feeling of the Sixth Symphony and the melodic aspiration of the Fifth and is thus a microcosm of the most characteristic music of the last years. In the Eighth (1953–5, rev. 1956) and Ninth (1956–7, rev. 1958) the post-*Scott* orientation achieves unambiguous symphonic form. The Eighth, in D minor, has a comparative lightness of heart and a capacity for humour, but these qualities are shot through with sadness and anxiety, even in the rumbustious finale. The Ninth, in E minor, is a more sombre work, at once heroic and contemplative, defiant and wistfully absorbed, and largely visionary in tone. The opening movement, which is not really in sonata form, is one of Vaughan Williams's deepest utterances, particularly rich in his feeling for tonal and harmonic contradictions. The flat inflections in the opening theme, which is rendered 'more minor than minor', afford further insights into the language of this final period. Formally, too, there is much evidence of a new orientation: neither of these symphonies has an epilogue, the opening movement of the Eighth is in variation form, that of the Ninth engages in an elusive interpenetration of themes, and there are examples of construction based on the blunt juxtaposing of sharply contrasting ideas – a technique derived from the *Antartica*.

Of the other late works, the following are of special interest: the *Three Shakespeare Songs* (1951) for unaccompanied chorus, of which the second, 'The Cloud-capp'd Towers', is a memorable setting of the words associated with the Epilogue of the Sixth Symphony; *Hodie* (1953–4), a Christmas cantata (various texts) for soloists, chorus, boys' voices and orchestra, which looks back over many years but could only have been written in the 1950s; the Sonata in A minor (1954) for violin and piano; and, supremely, the *Ten Blake Songs* (1957) for voice and oboe, a masterpiece of economy and precision written for the film *The Vision of William Blake*. In his last years Vaughan Williams showed more interest in the solo song than at any time since the first decade of the century; he had planned two song cycles for voice and piano, to poems by his wife, and of these the completed items were published posthumously as *Four Last Songs*.

Works: final period

All assessments of Vaughan Williams have emphasized his Englishness. This is a matter of temperament and character no less than of musical style and may be felt to have permeated everything he did. In the long run, however, more attention will be given to the specific content of his music: that is, to individuality rather than nationality. That he re-created an English musical vernacular, thereby enabling the next generation to take their nationality for granted, and did much to establish the symphony as a form of central significance for the English revival is historically important; but his illumination of the human condition, especially though not exclusively in those works commonly regarded as visionary, is a unique contribution.

WORKS

Numbers in right-hand margins denote references in the text.

STAGE

The Shepherds of the Delectable Mountains (pastoral episode, 1, Vaughan Williams, after Bunyan), 1921; cond. A. Bliss, London, RCM, 11 July 1922; incl. in The Pilgrim's Progress — 117, 202

Old King Cole (ballet, chorus and orch, 1923; cond. B. Ord, Cambridge, Trinity College, 5 June 1923

Hugh the Drover, or Love in the Stocks (romantic ballad opera, 2, H. Child), 1910–14, last rev. 1956; cond. M. Sargent, London, His Majesty's, 14 July 1924 — 101, 109, 112, 114, 115–16, 119

On Christmas Night (masque with dancing, singing and miming, A. Bolm, Vaughan Williams, after Dickens), 1926; cond. E. Delamarter, Chicago, Eighth Street, 26 Dec 1926

Sir John in Love (opera, 4, Vaughan Williams, after Shakespeare), 1924–8; cond. Sargent, London, RCM, 21 March 1929 — 119, 122

Job (masque for dancing, G. Keynes, G. Raverat, after Blake), 1927–30; cond. C. Lambert, London, Cambridge, 5 July 1931 — 108, 118, 120, 121, 123

The Poisoned Kiss (romantic extravaganza, 3, E. Sharp, after R. Garnett), 1927–9, last rev. 1956–7; cond. C. B. Rootham, Cambridge, Arts, 12 May 1936 — 108, 119, 121

Riders to the Sea (opera, 1, Vaughan Williams, after Synge), 1925–32; cond. Sargent, London, RCM, 1 Dec 1937 — 118, 119, 122, 126

The Bridal Day (masque, U. Wood, after Spenser), 1938–9, rev. 1952–3; cond. S. Robinson, BBC television, 5 June 1953 — 123

The Pilgrim's Progress (morality, 4, Vaughan Williams, after Bunyan, etc), completed 1949, rev. 1951–2; cond. L. Hancock, London, Covent Garden, 26 April 1951 — 105, 117, 124, 127, 128

ORCHESTRAL AND BAND
(for orchestra unless otherwise stated)

Bucolic Suite, 1900, unpubd; cond. D. Godfrey, 10 March 1902 — 111

The Solent, impression, 1903

In the Fen Country, sym. impression, 1904, last rev. 1935; Beecham Orch, cond. T. Beecham, London, Queen's Hall, 22 Feb 1909 — 111

Harnham Down, no.1 of Two Impressions for Orchestra, 1904–7, unpubd; cond. E. von Reznicek, Queen's Hall, 12 Nov 1907 — 111

Norfolk Rhapsody no.1, 1905–6; cond. H. Wood, Queen's Hall, 23 Aug 1906 — 111

Norfolk Rhapsody no.2, 1906, unpubd; cond. Vaughan Williams, Cardiff, 27 Sept 1907 — 111

Norfolk Rhapsody no.3, 1906, unpubd; cond. Vaughan Williams, Cardiff, 27 Sept 1907 — 111

The Wasps, Aristophanic suite [from incidental music], incl. ov., 1909; New SO, cond. Vaughan Williams, Queen's Hall, 23 July 1912

Fantasia on a Theme by Thomas Tallis, 2 str orch, 1910, last rev. 1919; LSO, cond. Vaughan Williams, Gloucester Cathedral, 6 Sept 1910 — 100, 112, 113, 123

A London Symphony (no.2), 1912–13, main rev. 1920, last rev. 1933; Queen's Hall Orch, cond. G. Toye, Queen's Hall, 27 March 1914 — 100, 101, 102, 105, 112, 114–15, 127

The Lark Ascending, romance, vn, orch, 1914, rev. 1920; M. Hall, British SO, cond. A. Boult, Queen's Hall, 14 June 1921 — 101, 112, 113

Pastoral Symphony (no.3), completed 1921; Royal Philharmonic Society Orch, cond. Boult, Queen's Hall, 26 Jan 1922 — 101–2, 108–9, 115, 116–17, 118, 119, 122, 124

English Folk Song Suite, military band, 1923; Royal Military School of Music Band, cond. H. E. Adkins, Twickenham, Kneller Hall, 4 July 1923

Sea Songs, march, military/brass band, 1923; Wembley, April 1924 — 118, 119

Toccata marziale, military band, 1924; Royal Military School of Music Band, cond. Adkins, Wembley, 1924 — 118, 121

Flos campi, suite, va, small SATB chorus, small orch, 1925; L. Tertis, Queen's Hall Orch, cond. Wood, Queen's Hall, 10 Oct 1925

Concerto (Concerto accademico), d, vn, str, 1924–5; J. d'Aranyi, London Chamber Orch, cond. A. Barnard, London, Aeolian Hall, 6 Nov 1925

Fantasia on Sussex Folk Tunes, vc, orch, 1929; P. Casals, Royal Philharmonic Society, cond. J. Barbirolli, Queen's Hall, 13 March 1930

Job, concert version of ballet, 1930; Queen's Hall Orch, cond. Vaughan Williams, Norwich, St Andrew's Hall, 23 Oct 1930 — 121

Prelude and Fugue, c, 1930 [arr. of organ work, 1921]; LSO, cond. Vaughan Williams, Hereford Cathedral, 12 Sept 1930

Piano Concerto, C, 1926–31; H. Cohen, BBC SO, cond. Boult, Queen's Hall, 1 Feb 1933 — 118

Henry V, ov., brass band, 1933; University of Miami Wind Ensemble, cond. F. Fennell, University of Miami, 3 Oct 1979

The Running Set, 1933; cond. Vaughan Williams, London, Royal Albert Hall, 6 Jan 1934

Fantasia on Greensleeves [arr. R. Greaves from Sir John in Love], 1/2 fl, harp, str, 1934; BBC SO, cond. Vaughan Williams, Queen's Hall, 27 Sept 1934

Suite, va, small orch, 1934; Tertis, LPO, cond. Sargent, Queen's Hall, 12 Nov 1934 — 108, 119, 122

Symphony no.4, f, 1931–4; BBC SO, cond. Boult, Queen's Hall, 10 April 1935 — 102, 104, 108, 116, 118, 121–2, 123, 124

2 Hymn-tune Preludes, small orch, 1936; LSO, cond. Vaughan Williams, Hereford Cathedral, 8 Sept 1936 — 123

Serenade to Music, arr. orch 1939; LSO, cond. Wood, Queen's Hall, 10 Feb 1940

5 Variants of 'Dives and Lazarus', str, harp(s), 1939; New York Philharmonic Society Orch, cond. Boult, New York, Carnegie Hall, 10 June 1939 — 107, 124

Symphony no.5, D, 1938–43, rev. 1951; LPO, cond. Vaughan Williams, Royal Albert Hall, 24 June 1943 — 104, 118, 121, 123–4, 125, 126, 127, 129

The Story of a Flemish Farm [suite from film], 1943; LSO, cond. Vaughan Williams, Royal Albert Hall, 31 July 1945

Concerto, a, ob, str, 1944; L. Goossens, Liverpool PO, cond. Sargent, Liverpool Philharmonic Hall, 30 Sept 1944 — 124

Symphony no.6, e, 1944–7, rev. 1950; BBC SO, cond. Boult, Royal Albert Hall, 21 April 1948 — 104–5, 106, 119, 121, 124, 126, 127, 129, 130

Partita, 2 str orch [from Double Trio, 1938], 1946–8; BBC SO, cond. Boult, BBC, 20 March 1948

Concerto grosso, str in 3 groups, 1950; Rural Music Schools Association massed orch, cond. Boult, Royal Albert Hall, 18 Nov 1950

Romance, Db, harmonica, str, pf, 1951; L. Adler, Little SO, cond. D. Saidenberg, New York, Town Hall, 3 May 1952 — 128

Sinfonia antartica (no.7), S, small SSA chorus, orch, 1949–52; M. Ritchie, women of Halle Choir, Halle Orch, cond. Barbirolli, Manchester, Free Trade Hall, 14 Jan 1953 — 106, 127, 128–9, 130

Prelude on an Old Carol Tune [adapted from incidental music to The Mayor of Casterbridge], 1953; BBC West of England Light Orchestra cond. R. Redman, BBC, 18 Nov 1952

Bass Tuba Concerto, f, 1954; P. Catelinet, LSO, cond. Barbirolli, London, Royal Festival Hall, 13 June 1954 — 128

Prelude on 3 Welsh Hymn Tunes, brass band, 1955; Salvation Army International Staff Band, cond. B. Adams, BBC, 12 March 1955

Symphony no.8, d, 1953–5, rev. 1956; Halle Orchestra, cond. Barbirolli, Manchester, Free Trade Hall, 2 May 1956 — 106, 115, 127, 128, 129, 130

Variations, brass band, 1957; Royal Albert Hall, 26 Oct 1957

Flourish for Glorious John [Barbirolli], 1957, unpubd; Halle Orch, cond. Barbirolli, Manchester Free Trade Hall, 16 Oct 1957

Symphony no.9, e, 1956–7, rev. 1958; RPO, cond. Sargent, Royal Festival Hall, 2 April 1958 — 105, 106, 113, 115, 127, 128, 129–30

VOCAL ORCHESTRAL

Toward the Unknown Region (Whitman), SATB, orch, 1905–6; Leeds Festival Chorus and Orch, cond. Vaughan Williams, Leeds Town Hall, 10 Oct 1907 — 110

Three Nocturnes (Whitman), Bar, semi-chorus, orch, 1908, unpubd

Willow-wood (D. G. Rossetti), cantata [after version for 1v, pf], Bar/Mez, female chorus, orch, 1908–9; F. Austin (Bar), Liverpool Welsh Choral Union, cond. H. Evans, Liverpool, 25 Sept 1909

A Sea Symphony (no.1) (Whitman), S, Bar, SATB, orch, 1903–9, last rev. 1923; C. Gleeson-White, C. Innes, Leeds Festival Chorus and Orch, cond. Vaughan Williams, Leeds Town Hall, 12 Oct 1910 — 100, 109, 110–11

5 Mystical Songs (Herbert), Bar, SATB, orch, 1911; C. Innes, Three Choirs Festival Chorus, LSO, cond. Vaughan Williams, Worcester Cathedral, 14 Sept 1911 — 112

Fantasia on Christmas Carols, Bar, SATB, orch, 1912; C. Innes, Three Choirs Festival Chorus, LSO, cond. Vaughan Williams, Hereford Cathedral, 12 Sept 1912

Four Hymns (Taylor, Watts, Crashaw, Bridges), T, va, str, 1914; S. Wilson, A. Hobday, LSO, cond. J. Harrison, Cardiff, 26 May 1920

Lord, Thou hast been our Refuge (Ps xc), motet, SATB, semi-chorus, orch/org, 1921

Let us now praise famous men (Ecclesiasticus), unison chorus, pf/org/small orch, 1923 — 116

On Wenlock Edge (Housman), T, orch, arr. 1921–3; J. Booth, cond. Vaughan Williams, London, Queen's Hall, 24 Jan 1924 — 114

Sancta civitas (Revelation), oratorio, T, Bar, SATB, semi-chorus, distant chorus, orch, 1923–5; A. Cranmer, T. Jones, Oxford Bach Choir, Oxford Orchestral Society, cond. H. P. Allan, Oxford, Sheldonian Theatre, 7 May 1926 — 117, 118

Darest thou now, o Soul (Whitman), unison chorus, pf/str, 1925

Te Deum, G, SATB, org/orch, 1928; Canterbury Cathedral and Chapel Royal choirs, C. Palmer (org), cond. W. Davies, Canterbury Cathedral, 4 Dec 1928

Benedicite (Apocrypha, J. Austin), S, SATB, orch, 1929; M. Rees, Leith Hill Festival Chorus (Towns) and Orch, cond. Vaughan Williams, Dorking, Drill Hall, 2 May 1930

Psalm, c, SATB, orch, 1929; Leith Hill Festival Chorus (Division II) and Orchestra, cond. Vaughan Williams, Dorking, Drill Hall, 29 April 1930

Three Choral Hymns (Coverdale), Bar/T, SATB, orch, 1929; I. Glennie (T), Leith Hill Festival Chorus (Division I) and Orch, cond. Vaughan Williams, Dorking, Drill Hall, 30 April 1930

Three Children's Songs for a Spring Festival (Farrer), unison chorus, str, 1929; Leith Hill Festival Children's Choirs, cond. Vaughan Williams, Dorking, Drill Hall, 1 May 1930

In Windsor Forest (Shakespeare), cantata [adapted from Sir John in Love], SATB, orch, 1930; National Provincial Bank Musical Society, cond. H. J. Baggs, Queen's Hall, 14 April 1931 — 121

Magnificat, A, SA, fl, orch, 1932; A. Desmond, women of Three Choirs Festival Chorus, LSO, cond. Vaughan Williams, Worcester Cathedral, 8 Sept 1932

Five Tudor Portraits (Skelton), choral suite, A/Mez, Bar, SATB, orch, 1935; A. Desmond, R. Henderson, Festival Chorus, LPO, cond. Vaughan Williams, Norwich, St Andrew's Hall, 25 Sept 1936 — 122–3

Nothing is here for Tears (Milton), choral song, unison chorus/SATB, pf/org/orch, 1936; BBC Singers, cond. W. Davies, BBC, 26 Jan 1936 — 128

Dona nobis pacem (Whitman, etc), cantata, S, Bar, SATB, orch, 1936; R. Flynn, R. Henderson, Huddersfield Choral Society, Halle Orch, cond. A. Coates, Huddersfield Town Hall, 2 Oct 1936 — 122, 123

Flourish for a Coronation (various), SATB, orch, 1937; Philharmonic Choir, LPO, cond. T. Beecham, Queen's Hall, 1 April 1937

Festival Te Deum, SATB, org/orch, 1937; Coronation Choir and Orch, cond. Boult, Westminster Abbey, 12 May 1937

Serenade to Music (Shakespeare), 4S, 4A, 4T, 4B/S, A, T, B, SATB, orch, 1938; I. Baillie, S. Allen, E. Suddaby, E. Turner, M. Balfour, M. Brunskill, A. Desmond, M. Jarred, P. Jones, H. Nash, F. Titterton, W. Widdop, N. Allin, R. Easton, R. Henderson, H. Williams, BBC SO, LSO, LPO, Queen's Hall Orch, cond. Wood, Royal Albert Hall, 5 Oct 1938 — 123

All Hail the Power, hymn, arr. unison chorus, SATB, org/orch, 1938

Six Choral Songs, to be Sung in Time of War (Shelley), unison chorus, pf/orch, 1940; BBC Chorus, BBC SO, cond. L. Woodgate, BBC, 20 Dec 1940

England, my England (Henley), choral song, Bar, SSAATTBB, unison chorus, orch/pf, 1941; D. Noble, BBC Chorus, BBC SO, cond. Boult, BBC, 16 Nov 1941

A Song of Thanksgiving (various), S, speaker, SATB, orch, 1944; E. Suddaby, V. Dyall, BBC Chorus, Thomas Coram Schools children's choir, G. Thalben-Ball (org), BBC SO, cond. Boult, BBC, 13 May 1945

The Voice out of the Whirlwind (Job), motet, SATB, org/orch, 1947; choirs from Chapels Royal, Canterbury Cathedral, St Paul's Cathedral and Westminster Abbey, W. McKie (org), cond. J. Dykes Bower, London, St Sepulchre, Holborn, 22 Nov 1947 — 112

Folksongs of the Four Seasons, cantata, SSAA, orch, 1949; massed choirs of the National Song Festival of the National Federation of Women's Institutes, LSO, cond. Boult, Royal Albert Hall, 15 June 1950

An Oxford Elegy (Arnold), speaker, small SATB chorus, small orch, 1947–9; S. Wilson, Eglesfield Musical Society, cond. B. Rose, Oxford, Queen's College, 19 June 1952 — 128

Fantasia (quasi variazione) on the Old 104th (Pss), pf, SATB, orch, 1949; M. Mullinar, Three Choirs Festival Chorus, LSO, cond. Vaughan Williams, Gloucester Cathedral, 6 Sept 1950 — 128

The Sons of Light (U. Wood), cantata, SATB, orch, 1950; Schools Music Association massed choirs, LPO, cond. Boult, Royal Albert Hall, 6 May 1951

Sun, Moon, Stars and Man (U. Wood), song-cycle [adapted from The Sons of Light], unison chorus, str/pf, 1950: Birmingham North District Secondary Schools choir, CBSO, cond. D. MacMahon, Birmingham Town Hall, 11 March 1955

The Old Hundredth Psalm Tune, arr. SATB, unison chorus, orch, org, 1953; Coronation Choir and Orch, Kneller Hall trumpeters, cond. W. McKie, Westminster Abbey, 2 June 1953

Hodie (This Day) (various), Christmas cantata, S, T, Bar, SATB, 130 boys' chorus, orch, 1953–4; N. Evans, E. Greene, G. Clinton, Three Choirs Festival Chorus, LSO, cond. Vaughan Williams, Worcester Cathedral, 8 Sept 1954

Epithalamion (Spenser), cantata [after The Bridal Day], Bar, SATB, small orch, 1957; G. Clinton, Goldsmiths' Choral Union Cantata Singers, RPO, cond. R. Austin, Royal Festival Hall, 30 Sept 1957

The First Nowell (Pakenham), nativity play, solo vv, SATB, small orch, 1958, completed Douglas; St Martin-in-the-Fields Concert Orch and Singers, cond. J. Churchill, London, Theatre Royal, Drury Lane, 19 Dec 1958

See 'Orchestral and band' for works with wordless chorus

OTHER CHORAL WORKS

(with org/pf)

Sound Sleep (C. Rossetti), SSA, pf, 1903
O clap your hands (Ps xlvii), motet, SATB, brass, org, 1920
A Farmer's Son so Sweet (trad.), arr. TBB, pf, 1921
The Seeds of Love (trad.), arr. TBB, pf, 1923
Magnificat and Nunc dimittis (The Village Service), SATB, org, 1925 121
An Acre of Land (trad.), arr. TTBB, pf, ?1934
The Ploughman (trad.), arr. TTBB, pf, ?1934
The Pilgrim Pavement (Partridge), hymn, S, SATB, org, 1934
O how amiable (Pss lxxxiv, xc), anthem, SATB, org, 1934
Morning, Communion and Evening Services, d. unison chorus, SATB, org, ?1939
The Airman's Hymn (Lytton), unison chorus, pf/org, 1942

O Taste and See (Pss), motet, SATB, org, 1952; coronation service choristers, cond. W. McKie, Westminster Abbey, 2 June 1953
A Vision of Aeroplanes (Ezekiel), motet, SATB, org, 1956; St Michael's Singers, J. Birch, cond. H. Darke, London, St Michael's, Cornhill, 4 June 1956
A Choral Flourish (Pss), SATB, org/2tpt, 1956; Royal Choral Society, Bach Choir, Croydon Philharmonic Society, St Michael's Singers, cond. R. Jacques, London, Royal Festival Hall, 3 Nov 1956

(unaccompanied)

3 Elizabethan Songs, partsongs, SATB, ?1891–6: Sweet Day (Herbert), The Willow Song, O Mistress mine (Shakespeare)
Come Away Death (Shakespeare), partsong, SSATB, early
Ring out your bells (Sidney), madrigal, SSATB, 1902
Rest (C. Rossetti), partsong, SSATB, 1902
Fain would I change that note (anon.), canzonet, SATB, 1907
Love is a sickness (Daniel), ballet, SATB, 1913
O Praise the Lord of Heaven (Ps cxlviii), anthem, SSAATTBB, semi-chorus, 1913
Mass, g, S, A, T, B, SSAATTBB, 1920–21; City of Birmingham 117 Choir, cond. J. Lewis, Birmingham Town Hall, 6 Dec 1922; 1st liturgical perf., Westminster Cathedral Choir, cond. R. R. Terry, Westminster Cathedral, 12 March 1923
O vos omnes, motet, A, SSAATTBB, 1922
I'll never love thee more (Graham), SATB, 1934
Valiant for Truth (Bunyan), motet, SATB, org/pf ad lib, 1940
A Call to the Free Nations (Briggs), SATB/unison chorus, 1941
The Souls of the Righteous (Solomon), motet, S, T, Bar, SATB, 1947
Prayer to the Father of Heaven (Skelton), motet, SATB, 1948; Oxford Bach Choir (Cantata Section), cond. T. Armstrong, Oxford, Sheldonian Theatre, 12 May 1948
Three Shakespeare Songs, SATB, 1951: Full Fathom Five, The 130 Cloud-capp'd Towers, Over Hill, Over Dale
Silence and Music (U. Vaughan Williams), SATB, 1953; Cambridge University Music Society, Golden Age Singers, cond. B. Ord, Royal Festival Hall, 1 June 1953
Heart's Music (Campion), SATB, 1954
Song for a Spring Festival (U. Vaughan Williams), SATB, 1955

(arrangements of English folksongs unless otherwise stated)   112

Bushes and Briars, TTBB/SATB, 1908
The Jolly Ploughboy, TTBB, 1908
Ward the Pirate, TTBB, 1912
Down Among the Dead Men, TTBB, 1912
Alister McAlpine's Lament (Scottish trad.), SATB, 1912
The Winter is Gone, TTBB, 1912
Mannin Veen (Manx trad.), SATB, 1912
Five English Folksongs, SATB, 1913: The Dark-eyed Sailor, The Springtime of the Year, Just as the Tide was Flowing, The Lover's Ghost, Wassail Song
The Mermaid, S, SATB, 1921
The Farmer's Boy, TTBB, 1921
Loch Lomond (Scottish trad.), Bar, TTBB, 1921
The Old Folks at Home (Foster), Bar, TTBB, 1921
Ca' the Yowes (Scottish trad.), T, SATB, 1922
The Seeds of Love, TTBB, 1923
The Turtle Dove, Bar, SSATB, ?1924
An Acre of Land, SATB, ?1934
John Dory, SATB, ?1934
The world it went well with me then, TTBB, ?1934
Tobacco's but an Indian weed, TTBB, ?1934
Dives and Lazarus, T, Bar/B, TTBB, ?1942
The Unquiet Grave, SSA, 1950
Early in the Spring, SSA, 1950
In Bethlehem City, SSA, 1950
Three Gaelic Songs, SATB, 1954: Dawn on the hills, Come let us gather cockles, Wake and rise
God bless the master of this house, SATB, 1956

(hymn tunes)   100

Down Ampney (Come down, O Love Divine), c1905
Randolph (God be with you till we meet again), c1905
Salve festa dies (Hail thee, festival day), c1905
Sine nomine (For all the saints), c1905
Cumnor (Servants of God, or sons), 1925
Guildford (England, arise the long, long night is over), 1925
Magda (Saviour, again to Thy dear name), 1925
Oakley (The night is come like to the day), 1925

King's Weston (At the name of Jesus), 1925
Abinger (I vow to thee my country), 1931
Mantegna (Into the woods my master went), 1931
Marathon (Servants of the great adventure), 1931
White Gates (Fierce raged the tempest), 1931
Little Cloister (As the disciples, when Thy Son had left them), 1935
Also many arrs. from folksong tunes; see The English Hymnal and Songs of Praise

(carols)

8 Traditional English Carols, arr. SATB/1v, pf, 1919: On Christmas Day, On Christmas Night, The Twelve Apostles, Down in yon forest, May-day Carol, The truth sent from above, The Birth of the Saviour, Wassail Song
12 Traditional Carols from Herefordshire, arr. SATB/1v, pf, 1920: The Holy Well (2 versions), Christmas now is drawing near at hand, Joseph and Mary, The Angel Gabriel, God Rest you Merry, Gentlemen, New Year's Carol, On Christmas Day, Dives and Lazarus, The Miraculous Harvest, The Saviour's Love, The Seven Virgins
9 Carols, arr. Bar, TTBB, ?1942: God Rest you Merry, Gentlemen, As Joseph was a-walking, Mummers' Carol, The First Nowell, The Lord at first, Coventry Carol, I saw three ships, A Virgin most pure, Dives and Lazarus
2 Carols, arr. SATB, 1945: Come love we God, There is a flower
Also contributions to The Oxford Book of Carols (London, 1928), incl. four originals: The Golden Carol (trad.), Wither's Rocking Hymn (Wither), Snow in the Street (Morris), Blake's Cradle Song (Blake)

SONGS

(for 1v, pf unless otherwise stated)

A Cradle Song (Coleridge), ?1894
How can the tree but wither? (Vaux), ?1896
Claribel (Tennyson), ?1896
The Splendour Falls (Tennyson), ?1896
Dreamland (C. Rossetti), ?1898
Linden Lea (W. Barnes), 1901; J. Milner, Hooten Roberts Musical Union, nr Rotherham, 4 Sept 1902   109
Orpheus with his Lute (Shakespeare), ?1901

Boy Johnny (C. Rossetti), ?1902
If I were a Queen (C. Rossetti), ?1902
Tears, Idle Tears (Tennyson), 1902
Willow-wood (D. G. Rossetti), cantata, 1902–3, unpubd
When I am dead, my dearest (C. Rossetti), ?1903
The Winter's Willow (Barnes), ?1903
The House of Life (D. G. Rossetti), 1903: Love-sight, Silent Noon, 109–10
Love's Minstrels, Heart's Haven, Death in Love, Love's Last Gift
Songs of Travel (Stevenson), no.7 1901, remainder 1904: The 109, 115
Vagabond, Let Beauty Awake, The Roadside Fire, Youth and Love,
In Dreams, The Infinite Shining Heavens, Whither must I Wander?,
Bright is the Ring of Words, I have Trod the Upward and the
Downward Slope
Buonaparty (Hardy), 1908
The Sky above the Roof (Verlaine, trans. M. Dearmer), 1908
On Wenlock Edge (Housman), T, pf, str qt, 1908–9: On Wenlock Edge, 100, 112, 114
From far, from eve and morning, Is my team ploughing?, Oh, when I
was in love with you, Bredon Hill, Clun; G. Elwes, Schwiller Qt, F.
Kiddle, London, Aeolian Hall, 15 Nov 1909
Merciless Beauty (Chaucer), 3 rondels, S/T, 2 vn, vc, 1921: Your eyen
two, So hath your beauty, Since I from love
Dirge for Fidele (Shakespeare), 2 Mez, pf, 1922
4 Poems by Fredegond Shove, c1922: Motion and Stillness, Four
Nights, The New Ghost, The Water Mill
2 Poems by Seumas O'Sullivan, 1925: The Twilight People, A Piper
3 Songs from Shakespeare, 1925: Take, O take those lips away, When
icicles hang by the wall, Orpheus with his Lute (2nd setting)
3 Poems by Walt Whitman, ?1925: Nocturne, A Clear Midnight, Joy,
Shipmate, Joy!
Along the Field (Housman), 1v, vn, 1927, rev. 1954: We'll to the woods
no more, Along the field, The half-moon westers low, In the morning,
The sigh that heaves the grasses, Goodbye, Fancy's Knell, With rue
my heart is laden
7 Songs from The Pilgrim's Progress (Bunyan), before 1951
In the Spring (Barnes), 1952
10 Blake Songs, 1v, ob, 1957: Infant Joy, A Poison Tree, The Piper, 130
London, The Lamb, The Shepherd, Ah! Sunflower, Cruelty has a

human heart, The Divine Image, Eternity; W. Brown, J. Craxton,
BBC, 8 Oct 1958
3 Vocalises, S, cl, 1958; M. Ritchie, K. Puddy, Manchester, Free
Trade Hall, 8 Oct 1958
4 Last Songs (U. Vaughan Williams), 1954–8; Procris, Tired, Hands, 130
eyes and heart, Menelaus; P. Bowden, E. Lush, BBC, 3 Aug 1960

(arrangements of English folksongs unless otherwise stated)
Blackmwore by the Stour (Barnes), 1901 112
Entlaubet ist der Walde (Ger. trad.), 1902
Adieu (Ger. trad., trans. Ferguson), S, Bar, pf, 1903
Think of me (Ger. trad., trans. Ferguson) S, Bar, pf, 1903
Cousin Michael (Ger. trad., trans. Ferguson), S, Bar, pf, 1903
Réveillez-vous, Piccars (Fr. trad., trans. England), 1903
Jean Renaud (Fr. trad., trans. England), 1903
L'amour de moy (Fr. trad., trans. England), 1903
Chanson de quête (Fr. trad.), ?1904
La ballade de Jésus Christ (Fr. trad.), ?1904
Folksongs from the Eastern Counties (ed. Sharp), collected and arr.
1903–6: Bushes and Briars, Tarry Trowsers, A Bold Young Farmer,
The Lost Lady Found, As I Walked Out, The Lark in the Morning,
On Board a Ninety-eight, The Captain's Apprentice, Ward the Pirate,
The Saucy Bold Robber, The Bold Princess Royal, The Lincolnshire
Farmer, The Sheffield Apprentice, Geordie, Harry the Tailor
The Spanish Ladies, 1912
Folksongs for Schools (ed. McNaught), arr. unison vv, pf, 1912: The
Jolly Ploughboy, The Cuckoo and the Nightingale, Servant Man and
Husbandman, The Female Highwayman, The Carter, I will give my
love an apple, My Boy Billy, Down by the Riverside, The Fox,
Farmyard Song, The Painful Plough
Folksongs from Newfoundland (collected and ed. Karpeles), arr. ?1934:
Sweet William's Ghost, The Cruel Mother, The Gypsy Laddie, The
Bloody Gardener, The Maiden's Lament, Proud Nancy, The Morning
Dew, The Bonny Banks of Virgie-o, Earl Brand, Lord Akeman, The
Lover's Ghost, She's like the swallow, Young Floro, The winter's
gone and past, The Cuckoo
2 English Folksongs, 1v, vn, ?1935: Searching for Lambs, The Lawyer

6 English Folksongs, ?1935: Robin Hood and the Pedlar, The Ploughman, One man, two men, The Brewer, Rolling in the dew, King William

CHAMBER AND INSTRUMENTAL

Quintet, c, pf, vn, va, vc, db, 1903, unpubd
Ballade and Scherzo, 2 vn, 2 va, vc, 1904, unpubd
String Quartet, g, 1908–9, rev. 1921; Schwiller Qt, London, Novello's Rooms, 8 Nov 1909 — 112
Phantasy Quintet, 2 vn, 2 va, vc, 1912; London Qt, London, Aeolian Hall, 23 March 1914
2 Pieces, vn, pf, ?1912
Suite de ballet, fl, pf, ?1913
3 Preludes on Welsh Hymn Tunes, org, 1920: Bryn Calfaria, Rhosymedre, Hyfrydol
6 Short Pieces, pf, ?1920
Prelude and Fugue, c, org, 1921, orchd 1930
6 Studies in English Folksong, vc, pf, 1926; M. Muckle, A. Muckle, London, Scala Theatre, 4 June 1926; also arr. vn/va/cl, pf — 119
Hymn Tune Prelude on Song 13 by Orlando Gibbons, pf, 1928; H. Cohen, London, Wigmore Hall, 4 Jan 1930
6 Teaching Pieces, pf, 1934
Double Trio, str sextet, 1938, unpubd
Suite for Pipes, 1939
Household Music, 3 preludes on Welsh hymn tunes, str qt/other insts, 1940–41; Blech Qt, Wigmore Hall, 4 Oct 1941
String Quartet, a, 1942–4; Menges Qt, London, National Gallery, 12 Oct 1944 — 124
Introduction and Fugue, 2 pf, 1945–6; C. Smith, P. Sellick, Wigmore Hall, 23 March 1946
The Lake in the Mountains, pf, 1947
Sonata, a, vn, pf, 1954; F. Grinke, M. Mullinar, BBC, 12 Oct 1954 — 130
Two Preludes on Welsh Folksongs, org, 1956

INCIDENTAL MUSIC

(for the theatre)

Pan's Anniversary (masque, Jonson), Stratford-on-Avon, 24 April 1905
The Wasps (Aristophanes), T, Bar, TTBB, orch, Cambridge, New, 26 Nov 1909 — 113
The Pilgrim's Progress (Bunyan), S, A, SATB, str, Reigate Priory, Dec 1906; London, Imperial, 16 March 1907

The Merry Wives of Windsor (Shakespeare), Stratford-on-Avon, 1913; lost
Richard II (Shakespeare), Stratford-on-Avon, 1913
Henry IV, Part 2 (Shakespeare), Stratford-on-Avon, 1913
Richard III (Shakespeare), Stratford-on-Avon, 1913
Henry V (Shakespeare), Stratford-on-Avon, 1913
The Devil's Disciple (Shaw), Stratford-on-Avon, 1913

(for films)

49th Parallel, 1940–41 — 104
Coastal Command, 1942
The People's Land, 1943 — 124
The Story of a Flemish Farm, 1943
Stricken Peninsula, 1944
The Loves of Joanna Godden, 1946
Scott of the Antarctic, 1948 — 106, 126–7, 128, 129

Dim Little Island, 1949
Bitter Springs, 1950
The England of Elizabeth, 1955
The Vision of William Blake, 1957 — 130

(for radio)

The Pilgrim's Progress (Bunyan), 1942
Richard II (Shakespeare), 1944, lost
The Mayor of Casterbridge (Hardy), 1950

Principal publishers: Curwen, OUP, Stainer & Bell

WRITINGS

'Conducting', 'Fugue', Grove 2
'Who Wants the English Composer?', RCM Magazine, ix (1912), 11; repr. in Foss (1950) — 98
National Music (London, 1934); repr. in National Music and Other Essays — 98
Some Thoughts on Beethoven's Choral Symphony with Writings on other Musical Subjects (London, 1953); repr. in National Music and Other Essays
The Making of Music (Ithaca, NY, 1955); repr. in National Music and Other Essays
Correspondence with Holst and some early articles in Heirs and Rebels, ed. U. Vaughan Williams and I. Holst (London, 1959) — 113
National Music and Other Essays (London, 1963)

BIBLIOGRAPHY

E. Evans: 'English Song and "On Wenlock Edge" ', *MT*, lix (1918), 247
——: 'Modern British Composers: Vaughan Williams', *MT*, lxi (1920), 232, 302, 371

A. H. Fox Strangways: 'Ralph Vaughan Williams', *ML*, i (1920), 78

H. C. Colles: 'The Music of Vaughan Williams', *The Chesterian*, xxi (1922), 129

H. Howells: 'Vaughan Williams's "Pastoral Symphony" ', *ML*, iii (1922), 122

J. Holbrooke: *Contemporary British Composers* (London, 1925), 94

A. E. F. Dickinson: *An Introduction to the Music of R. Vaughan Williams* (London, 1928)

H. Howells: 'Vaughan Williams's "Concerto accademico" ', *The Dominant*, i (1928), 24

H. Ould: 'The Songs of Ralph Vaughan Williams', *English Review*, xlvi (1928), 605

S. A. Bayliss: 'Obsession and Originality', *The Sackbut*, x (1930), 216

F. Toye: 'Studies in English Music: Vaughan Williams and the Folk Music Movement', *The Listener*, v (1931), 1057

E. Rubbra: 'Vaughan Williams, some Technical Characteristics', *MMR*, lxiv (1934), 27

D. F. Tovey: 'Vaughan Williams: Pastoral Symphony', *Essays in Musical Analysis*, ii (London, 1935), 129

R. Terry: ' "Dona nobis pacem" ', *The Listener*, xvi (1936), 879

A. Frank: 'Reincarnating Skelton', *The Listener*, xvii (1937), 141

E. Rubbra: 'The Later Vaughan Williams', *ML*, xviii (1937), 1

S. Goddard: 'The Operas of Vaughan Williams', *The Listener*, xx (1938), 917

W. Kimmel: 'Vaughan Williams's Choice of Words', *ML*, xix (1938), 132

H. Brian: 'The Music of Ralph Vaughan Williams', *MO*, lxiii (1939–40), 345, 391

E. Blom: 'King Solomon and Vaughan Williams', *The Listener*, xxiv (1940), 69

S. Goddard: ' "The Poisoned Kiss" ', *The Listener*, xxvi (1941), 737

W. Kimmel: 'Vaughan Williams's Melodic Style', *MQ*, xxvii (1941), 491

H. J. Foss: 'Vaughan Williams's Symphonic Manner', *The Listener*, xxvii (1942), 317

W. H. Mellers: 'Two Generations of English Music', *Scrutiny*, xii (1944), 261

S. Goddard: 'Ralph Vaughan Williams, O.M.', *British Music of our Time*, ed. A. L. Bacharach (Harmondsworth, 1946), 83

W. H. Mellers: *Music and Society* (London, 1946, rev. 2/1950), 108, 2/160

N. Suckling: 'Vaughan Williams and the Fat Knight', *The Listener*, xxxv (1946), 693

G. N. Long: 'Vaughan Williams's Fourth Symphony: a Study in Interpretation', *MMR*, lxxvii (1947), 116

S. Goddard: 'Ralph Vaughan Williams', in *The Symphony*, ed. R. Hill (Harmondsworth, 1949), 395

G. Keynes: ' "Job" ', *Sadler's Wells Ballet Book*, ed. A. L. Haskell, ii (London, 1949), 35

H. J. Foss: *Ralph Vaughan Williams* (London, 1950)

S. Wilson: ' "Hugh the Drover" ', *Opera*, i (1950), 29

A. Hutchings: 'Vaughan Williams and the Tudor Tradition', *The Listener*, xlv (1951), 276

M. Mullinar: ' "The Pilgrim's Progress" ', *RCM Magazine*, xlvii (1951), 46

H. Murrill: 'Vaughan Williams's Pilgrim', *ML*, xxxii (1951), 324

C. Smith: ' "The Pilgrim's Progress" ', *Opera*, ii (1951), 373

M. Cooper: 'Ralph Vaughan Williams', *The Spectator*, clxxxix (1952), 463

N. Demuth: *Musical Trends in the 20th Century* (London, 1952), 142

E. J. Dent: 'Ralph Vaughan Williams', *MT*, xciii (1952), 443

H. J. Foss: ' "The Pilgrim's Progress" by Vaughan Williams', *Music 1952*, ed. A. Robertson (Harmondsworth, 1952), 38

H. Ottaway: ' "Riders to the Sea" ', *MT*, xciii (1952), 358

——: 'Vaughan Williams: Symphony in D and "The Pilgrim's Progress" ', *MT*, xciv (1953), 456

E. M. Payne: *The Folksong Element in the Music of Vaughan Williams* (diss., U. of Liverpool, 1953)

R. Taylor: 'Vaughan Williams and English National Music', *Cambridge Journal*, vi (1953), 615

J. S. Weissmann: 'The New Vaughan Williams', *MR*, xiv (1953), 148

P. M. Young: *Vaughan Williams* (London, 1953)

F. Howes: *The Music of Ralph Vaughan Williams* (London, 1954)

E. M. Payne: 'Vaughan Williams and Folksong', *MR*, xv (1954), 103

——: 'Vaughan Williams's Orchestral Colourings', *MMR*, lxxxiv (1954), 3

D. Mitchell: 'Contemporary Chronicle: Revaluations: Vaughan Williams', *MO*, lxxviii (1954–5), 409, 471

H. Ottaway: 'Vaughan Williams and the Symphonic Epilogue', *MO*, lxxix (1955–6), 145

J. D. Bergsagel: *The National Aspects of the Music of Ralph Vaughan Williams* (diss., Cornell U., 1957)

H. Ottaway: 'Vaughan Williams's Eighth Symphony', *ML*, xxxviii (1957), 213

S. Pakenham: *Ralph Vaughan Williams: a Discovery of his Music* (London, 1957)

Bibliography

A. Bliss and others: 'Tributes to Vaughan Williams', *MT*, xcix (1958), 535

M. Karpeles: 'Ralph Vaughan Williams, O.M.', *JEFDSS*, viii (1958), 121

V. D. Konen: *Ralf' Vorn Yuillyams* (Moscow, 1958)

O. Neighbour: 'Ralph Vaughan Williams, 1872–1958', *The Score*, no.24 (1958), 7

J. Warrack: 'Vaughan Williams and Opera', *Opera*, ix (1958), 698

E. Benbow, ed.: 'Ralph Vaughan Williams, 1872–1958', *RCM Magazine*, lv (1959) [special issue]

D. Cooke: 'Symphony No.6 in E minor, by Vaughan Williams', *The Language of Music* (London, 1959), 252

D. Brown: 'Vaughan Williams's Symphonies: some Judgments Reviewed', *MMR*, xc (1960), 44

S. Finkelstein: *Composer and Nation: the Folk Heritage of Music* (London, 1960), 228

J. Day: *Vaughan Williams* (London, 1961, rev. 2/1975)

P. J. Willetts: 'The Ralph Vaughan Williams Collection', *British Museum Quarterly*, xxiv (1961), 3

A. E. F. Dickinson: 'The Vaughan Williams Manuscripts', *MR*, xxiii (1962), 177

——: *Vaughan Williams* (London, 1963)

M. Kennedy: *The Works of Ralph Vaughan Williams* (London, 1964, rev. 2/1980)

H. Ottaway: 'VW5 – A New Analysis', *MT*, cv (1964), 354

E. S. Schwartz: *The Symphonies of Ralph Vaughan Williams* (Amherst, 1964)

U. Vaughan Williams: *R.V.W.: a Biography* (London, 1964/R1985)

H. Ottaway: *Vaughan Williams* (London, 1966)

D. Cox: 'Ralph Vaughan Williams', *The Symphony*, ed. R. Simpson, ii (Harmondsworth, 1967), 114

P. R. Starbuck: *Ralph Vaughan Williams, O.M., 1872–1958: a Bibliography of his Literary Writings and Criticism of his Musical Works* (diss., Library Association, 1967)

M. Hurd: *Vaughan Williams* (London, 1970)

J. E. Lunn and U. Vaughan Williams: *Ralph Vaughan Williams: a Pictorial Biography* (London, 1971)

U. Vaughan Williams: 'Vaughan Williams and Opera', *Composer*, no.41 (1971), 25

A. C. Boult: 'Vaughan Williams and his Interpreters', *MT*, cxiii (1972), 957

R. Douglas: *Working with R.V.W.* (London, 1972)

L. Foreman: 'VW: a Bibliography of Dissertations', *MT*, cxiii (1972), 962

H. Ottaway: *Vaughan Williams Symphonies* (London, 1972)

141

——: 'Scott and After: the Final Phase', *MT*, cxiii (1972), 959

U. Vaughan Williams: 'The VW Centenary', *MT*, cxiii (1972), 955

M. Kennedy: 'The Unknown Vaughan Williams', *PRMA*, xcix (1972–3), 31

U. Vaughan Williams: 'Ralph Vaughan Williams and his Choice of Words for Music', *PRMA*, xcix (1972–3), 81

M. Kennedy: 'Ralph Vaughan Williams in the First Centenary of his Birth', *Studi musicali*, ii (1973), 175

H. Ottaway: 'Misplaced Symphony?', *MT*, cxiv (1973), 1143

D. M. Foraud: 'Vaughan Williams at Reigate Priory', *Composer*, no.54 (1975), 15

U. Vaughan Williams: 'Pupil and Friend: Ralph Vaughan Williams and Ravel', *Adam*, xli (1978), 26

G. Bush: 'Hugh the Drover Rides Again', *Records and Recordings*, xxii/9 (1978–9), 12

H. Cole: 'Vaughan Williams Remembered', *Composer*, no.68 (1979–80), 25

Vaughan Williams in Dorking: a Collection of Personal Reminiscences of the Composer Dr Ralph Vaughan Williams, OM, Dorking and Leith Hill District Preservation Society (Dorking, 1979)

M. Kennedy: *A Catalogue of the Works of Ralph Vaughan Williams* (London, 1982)

M. Campbell: 'British Additions to the Cello Repertory', *The Strad*, xciii (1982–3), 810

R. Palmer, ed.: *Folk Songs Collected by Ralph Vaughan Williams* (London, 1983)

J. McKay Martin: 'Recollections of RVW', *MO*, cvii (1983–4), 303

L. Pike: 'Tallis – Vaughan Williams – Howells: Reflections on Mode Three', *Tempo*, no.149 (1984), 2

GUSTAV HOLST

Imogen Holst

CHAPTER ONE

Life

I Early life and teaching

Gustav Holst – originally Gustavus Theodore von Holst – was born in Cheltenham on 21 September 1874. His great-grandfather Matthias (1769–1854), a composer of insignificant piano pieces, left Riga in Latvia for England in the early years of the 19th century; he had German ancestors and a Russian wife. Matthias's son Gustavus Valentine (1799–1870), brother of the painter Theodor von Holst, was the first of the family to marry an Englishwoman. He settled in Cheltenham, where he taught the harp and piano. His son Adolph (1846–1901) was an outstanding pianist and organist; in 1871 he married Clara Lediard, a piano pupil, and Gustav was their first child. From an early age Gustav practised the piano every day under his father's stern supervision. As a child he suffered from asthma and short sight, and found it difficult to keep pace with his energetic younger brother Emil (who became a film actor, and took the name Ernest Cossart). His mother died suddenly when he was seven; a few years later his father married another pupil, who was a theosophist.

Holst began composing while he was at Cheltenham Grammar School. His father gave him little encouragement, but he learnt what he could from reading Berlioz's treatise on instrumentation, and at the age of 17 he had the practical experience of conducting village choirs near Cheltenham. He already suffered from the neuritis in his right arm which was to trouble him, intermittently, for the rest of his life. Adolph soon realized that it would be impossible for Gustav to become a solo pianist, and allowed him to have several months in Oxford learning counterpoint, before sending him to London to study composition under Stanford.

Holst failed to win a scholarship when he entered the Royal College of Music in 1893, and it was not until two years later that he succeeded. Stanford found him hardworking but not at all brilliant. The lessons were often frustrating, though Holst was grateful to Stanford for helping him to be self-critical. The music he was writing was saturated with imitations of Wagner: he used to queue for standing room in the gallery at Covent Garden on Wagner nights, and after the performance he would walk back to his lodgings in a state of feverish excitement. It was in 1895 that he first met his fellow student Vaughan Williams. They at once became friends and formed what was to be a lifelong habit of playing the sketches of their newest compositions to each other while they were working at them.

When still a student, Holst was invited to conduct the Hammersmith Socialist Choir in William Morris's house. He taught them Morley madrigals and Purcell partsongs, and he fell in love with his youngest soprano, Isobel Harrison. They became engaged, knowing that they would have to wait years before they could afford to be married. It was possibly at Morris's house that Holst learnt about Hindu literature and philosophy. He wanted to set some of the poems to music, but the translations were so unsatisfactory that he decided to learn Sanskrit. He had lessons at University College,

London, and although he never became fluent in Sanskrit he was able to read stories from the *Ramayana* and the *Mahābharata* and to translate hymns from the *Rig Veda*.

His second study at the RCM was the trombone, and he used to pay for his board and lodging by playing on the pier at Blackpool or Brighton during the summer holidays, and at London theatres during the pantomime season. He also played in the White Viennese Band, wearing a uniform with brass buttons and speaking with an assumed foreign accent. After leaving college in 1898 he joined the Carl Rosa Opera Company, and later he toured with the Scottish Orchestra. This was useful experience which gave him the feel of an orchestra from the inside, and he was always glad to have known what he called the 'impersonality' of orchestral playing. When he married in 1901 it seemed that trombone playing was to be his only way of earning a living, since the few partsongs he had had published brought in very little money. But after two years he realized that touring left no time or energy for composing, and he decided to risk giving up the trombone. There were several anxious months, during which his wife earned their meals by dressmaking, before he was rescued by the offer of a teaching post.

His first teaching appointment was at the James Allen's Girls' School, Dulwich. Two years later, in 1905, he was appointed director of music at St Paul's Girls' School, Hammersmith; this was the only teaching post he kept until the end of his life. He also taught in evening institutes, where he conducted the first performances in England of several Bach cantatas. In 1907 he took charge of the music at Morley College, where the orchestra then consisted of two violins, one flute, three sharp-pitch clarinets, a cornet and a piano; four years later they were giving the first performance since 1697 of Purcell's *The Fairy Queen*.

Holst was an unorthodox teacher. He hated textbooks and examinations. He believed in 'learning by doing', and his elementary harmony pupils were encouraged to make up rounds and to spend the rest of the lesson singing them. He used to invite the members of his amateur choirs and orchestras to meet every Whitsun for three crowded days of music-making. These informal festivals began in 1916 in the church at Thaxted, Essex, the place where he made his home for many years. Everyone was allowed to take part, for he never turned away any inexperienced singer or player who was prepared to work hard at his favourite music.

Teaching took up most of his time. He could only compose at weekends and during August, when he wrote without interruption in his soundproof music room at St Paul's Girls' School. This double life was exhausting. He had to save up his ideas until the end of each week, which is why he took two years to write *The Planets* (1914–16). He was unfit for war service, owing to neuritis and weak sight, but in the autumn of 1918 he was sent to the Middle East as music organizer in the YMCA's army education scheme. (It was because of this activity that he gave up the 'von' in his name.) There were hundreds of pupils among the troops who were waiting to be demobilized, and his concerts of English music in Salonica and Constantinople were triumphs of organization, with singers and players coming from as far away as Baku. His genius for encouraging beginners made an unforgettable impression on those who worked with him. When he returned to England in the summer of 1919, *The Planets* had already had its first (incomplete) public performance.

II Later years

Holst never considered *The Planets* to be his best work. He was bewildered by its sudden success; and when, soon afterwards, *The Hymn of Jesus* was greeted as a masterpiece, he wrote to his friend W. G. Whittaker: 'It made me realize the truth of "Woe to you when all men speak well of you"'. He used to say that every artist ought to pray not to be a success: 'If nobody likes your work, you have to go on just for the sake of the work, and you are in no danger of letting the public make you repeat yourself'. But now, according to *The Times*, he had 'achieved the position, rare for an Englishman, of being a really popular composer'. It was a position that he would gladly have avoided. When audiences 'rose to their feet with tumultuous applause' he gazed at them in blank dismay. He dreaded having to go to parties where he was surrounded by gushing admirers. Press photographers found him unhelpful, and he remained tongue-tied when faced with reporters wanting a story for their gossip columns. Earning more money meant little to him, as he had no use for material possessions. His wife enjoyed having a town house and a country house during the two or three years of their comparative prosperity, but he himself never minded where he lived, as long as he could escape to the silence and solitude that were essential for composing.

After 1920 his working life became more complicated. Publishers were suddenly interested in his hitherto neglected works, which meant that he had to revise his early scores at the same time as correcting proofs of the things he had just written. He was appointed to the staff of the RCM, and of University College, Reading, and had to spend more time in teaching and lecturing. There were many performances that he had to conduct, often with insufficient rehearsal, and he found pre-electric recording sessions particularly exhausting.

In February 1923, while conducting his students at Reading, he slipped from the rostrum and fell on the back of his head. The concussion was not serious, and he seemed to recover during the spring, in time to lecture and conduct at the University of Michigan. But later, when he returned to England, he began to suffer from headaches and sleeplessness. During that difficult autumn his brief popularity as a composer reached its height, and he had more work than ever before. By the end of the year the strain had become too great and his doctor ordered him to cancel all his professional engagements and to live in the country for the whole of 1924. Fortunately he managed to go on composing, and during those solitary months in Thaxted he was able, for the first time, to lead what he called 'the life of a real composer'.

When he came back to London in 1925 he gave up all teaching, except for a little work at St Paul's Girls' School. Life simplified itself in other ways, for he found to his relief that he was no longer a popular composer. Critics complained that his newest works were too stark and 'cerebral'. Audiences, apart from a minority of enthusiasts, were bewildered. Even Vaughan Williams admitted after the first performance of the *Choral Symphony* that he felt only a 'cold admiration' for it, and he hoped they were not going to 'drift apart, musically speaking'. Holst was unperturbed. He had learnt from Hindu philosophy that 'drifting' was occasionally necessary. And he knew that the symphony was as good as anything he had yet written.

From 1927 to 1933 was the best time of his life as a composer. He had more leisure for thinking; and he felt free to take occasional holidays, exploring field paths in Sicily or northern France, and walking over the Gloucestershire hills or through the quiet London streets. He had time for looking at pictures and for reading about the space–time continuum in Jeans's recently published *The Mysterious Universe*. He enjoyed meeting his past pupils at Whitsun festivals and making music with them again. Whenever possible he listened to concerts of contemporary works by young composers.

His own new music continued to disappoint most listeners. Several publishers refused his manuscripts and many critics were indifferent or hostile. He never felt bitter about it: he used to say that the greatest luck an artist could have was to be known and respected by everyone who cared for real art, and ignored by all the rest. The encouragement of those who had faith in his music meant a great deal to him. When Cheltenham organized a Holst Festival in 1927, he referred to it as the most overwhelming event of his life. He had always refused conventional titles and honours (he was made a Fellow of the RCM without being consulted), but he accepted the gold medal of the Royal Philharmonic Society in 1930, and when Yale University gave him the Howland Memorial Prize for distinction in the arts, he felt he had received 'the greatest honour this world can give – the company of honourable men'.

*14. Gustav Holst:
portrait (1911)
by Millicent
Woodforde*

Later years

In 1932 he took up the post of visiting lecturer in composition at Harvard University. He liked working there, and he was looking forward to a concert tour during the spring. However, in March he had a severe attack of haemorrhagic gastritis caused by a duodenal ulcer. He was well enough to return to England later in the summer, but he had to lead 'a restricted life'. He spent the next 18 months in and out of clinics. In spite of frequent pain he was able to go on composing, and was planning to write a symphony. During the Whitsun week of 1934 he had an operation in a London nursing home, and he died two days later on 25 May. At the request of his friend Bishop Bell, his ashes were buried in Chichester Cathedral.

Directness of expression was Holst's chief characteristic, in his life and in his music. He aimed at clear thinking and clear feeling, and he took it for granted that those with whom he was working would be just as objective and as free from selfconsciousness. He hated conventionality, and rejoiced in what he called 'the fantastic unexpectedness of life'. In his single-mindedness he often gave strangers the impression that he was naive, but they were mistaken. He was thoroughly practical in everything he undertook. He had no use for vagueness, and he believed that stupidity was the sin against the Holy Spirit. He was endlessly patient with his amateurs, but with professionals he could be ruthless: 'There is no room in music for the second-rate – it might just as well be the nineteenth-rate'. Lack of rhythm was one of the few things that made him really angry, for rhythm mattered to him more than anything else in life. The painting by Millicent Woodforde in the National Portrait Gallery, London (reproduced opposite) gives a

CHAPTER TWO

Works

I 'Early works

The music that Holst wrote at school and at college
shows the determination of an imaginative but groping
beginner. There are songs and piano pieces influenced
by Mendelssohn, and comic operettas influenced by
Gilbert and Sullivan. Long afterwards, he used to refer
to them as 'early horrors' and this description also
applies to several of the works with opus numbers. His
first attempts at orchestral music are heavily influenced
by Wagner; Grieg and Dvořák are in evidence as well.
Occasionally there are glimpses of the genuine Holst: in
the nobly felt 'Elegy' in memory of William Morris from
the symphony *The Cotswolds*; in the *Suite de ballet*, with
its angular tunes and cross-rhythms; and in *The Mystic
Trumpeter*, where the challenging trumpet-calls of
'Mars' are heard for the first time: the work as a whole
is the most successful of his early attempts to find his
own voice. Even the discarded three-act opera *Sita*,
which he afterwards described as 'good old Wagnerian
bawling', has its rare moments of originality in the
hushed enharmonic changes and the tranquil 7/4
phrases. One of the best works from these early years is
the short *Ave Maria* for eight-part female chorus; the
singable phrases of the flowing counterpoint show that
he was already a practical composer.

Vaughan Williams began collecting English folksongs

in 1903, and when Holst heard them he was so excited that he learnt as much as he could from Cecil Sharp, Lucy Broadwood and other folksong collectors. The tunes transformed his orchestral writing. In *A Somerset Rhapsody* (1906–7), dedicated to Cecil Sharp and founded on traditional songs, the modal harmonies helped to banish the chromaticisms of the previous ten years. In Two Songs without Words (1906), dedicated to Vaughan Williams, the tunes are his own, and the direct style is also unmistakably his own. This directness can be heard in the two suites for military band of 1909 and 1911. It was characteristic of him to write music for bandsmen, who needed a change from 19th-century 'selections'; nearly 20 years later he enjoyed writing *A Moorside Suite* as a test piece for a brass band championship contest.

His love of folksongs also transformed his way of setting words to music. He began searching for what he called 'the musical idiom of the English language', and he aimed at writing tunes that would be 'at one with the words'. Medieval poetry helped him to achieve the simplicity of the Four Old English Carols (1907) and the lyrical freedom of the Four Songs for Voice and Violin (1916–17). Here the music owes a good deal to the freedom of plainsong, which he had learnt about when Vaughan Williams was editing *The English Hymnal*; its influence can be recognized in the unaccompanied declamation of the first of the Two Psalms (1912).

His earliest settings of his own translations of Sanskrit verses are the *Hymns from the Rig Veda* (1907–8) for voice and piano. Never having heard any Indian music, he struggled to find appropriate sounds for the mood of the words. In *Varuna I* ('Sky'), which is the best of these nine songs, there is the sense of space and timelessness characteristic of his later music; a fine example is *Betelgeuse* from the Twelve Songs (1929) with words by Humbert Wolfe. While writing the *Hymns from the Rig Veda* Holst was already at work on his chamber opera *Sāvitri* (1908), for which he had made his own libretto, founded on an episode from the *Mahābharata*. *Sāvitri* is an astonishing achievement. The opening, with its bitonal counterpoint, is as economical as his most mature works; and at the height of the drama, the intensity of the music is strong enough to withstand occasional echoes from a recent Wagnerian past. The four groups of *Choral Hymns from the Rig Veda* (1908–12) are uneven, since he was not yet harmonically secure. The best, however, are well worth hearing; particularly *To the Unknown God* from the first group, with its *sotto voce* chanting and sombre procession; and *To Agni* ('Fire'), with its exciting 5/4 rhythms, from the second (and most original) group. In short hymns such as these he could achieve his aims, but he was unable to sustain the excitement throughout a work as long as the *The Cloud Messenger* (1909–10), where the problems of extended form still defeated him.

II 'The Planets'

Holst was a slow developer, but it is worth remembering that he had a great deal to unlearn. He was nearly 40 when he began writing *The Planets* (1914–16), the first large-scale work in which he was able to express himself fully. The experience of writing his earlier orchestral suite, *Beni Mora* (1909–10), had helped: the oriental tunes, which he had heard while on holiday in Algeria, had offered new possibilities for

157

15. Sketch for the opening bars of Holst's 'The Hymn of Jesus', composed in 1917

exploring unfamiliar sounds. In 1913, when his friend Clifford Bax talked to him about astrology, the clearly defined character of each planet suggested the contrasting moods of a work that was to be unlike anything he had yet written. The first informal performance of *The Planets* on 29 September 1918 was a present to Holst from his friend and patron Balfour Gardiner. Adrian Boult conducted, and the New Queen's Hall Orchestra had one rehearsal, lasting less than two hours, in which to sight-read the hurriedly copied parts. The invited audience at that private performance were astounded to hear such a work by an English composer. Listening to 'Mars', they felt sure that the music was meant to be a description of the war that was still going on, but Holst had finished the movement before August 1914. It was the end of 'Neptune' that made the greatest impression on that first audience, although Holst himself considered 'Saturn' to be the best movement. During the many years since it was written *The Planets* has suffered from being quoted in snippets as background music, but in spite of all unwanted associations it has survived as a masterpiece, owing to the strength of Holst's invention.

III Music for choirs and for amateurs

The Hymn of Jesus, composed in 1917, was Holst's most strikingly original work; it has nothing in common with English oratorio of the 19th century. Holst was as unconventional about religion as he was about anything else. He chose for his text the 'dancing' hymn in the apocryphal Acts of St John, and with the help of a pupil he learnt enough Greek to make his own translation. To audiences of the early 1920s the music was a revelation, with its leaping rhythms and its

159

piercing discords at each passionate outburst of entreaty. It still gives its listeners and its performers a sense of overwhelming religious exultation. The *Ode to Death* (1919), to Whitman's words, is also memorable; the tranquil acceptance in the music expresses Holst's own attitude to death.

His longest choral work, the First Choral Symphony (1923–4), was commissioned for the Leeds Festival. Holst made his own selection of contrasting poems by Keats. The two best movements, the *Ode on a Grecian Urn* and the brilliant Scherzo, can each be performed as a separate work. He had planned a second choral symphony, with poems by Meredith, but he never wrote it: the fragmentary sketches are in the British Library. A Choral Fantasia (1930) was commissioned by the Three Choirs Festival. The words are by Robert Bridges, and Holst dedicated the work to his memory: it is like a requiem for poets and composers. The shorter choral works, apart from those written for amateurs, include the *Dirge for Two Veterans* (1914) with its characteristic 'sad procession', and the eight-part motet *The Evening-watch* (1924), a setting of Henry Vaughan's *Dialogue between the Body and the Soul*.

Throughout his life, Holst wrote music for his pupils to sing and play. When he began teaching there were few worthwhile compositions to be found in publishers' catalogues of school music, and he had to provide his own material: his songs from *The Princess* (1905) were written for the James Allen's Girls' School. His best-known composition for his pupils is the *St Paul's Suite* for strings (1912–13); 20 years later he wrote its companion-piece, the *Brook Green Suite*, for the junior orchestra at the school. In 1916 he wrote several short works for the Thaxted choir, including *This have I done for my true love*, which he considered his best partsong, and the carols *Lullay my liking* and *Bring us in good ale*. It was for the Whitsun festivals at Thaxted that he wrote *Turn back O Man* and other Festival Choruses. For his pupils at Morley College he wrote the *Short Festival Te Deum* (1919); the incidental music for John Masefield's play *The Coming of Christ* (1927), which was produced in Canterbury Cathedral; and *The Golden Goose* (1926), a choral ballet designed for open-air performance with plenty of opportunity for improvisation in the acting and dancing. His second choral ballet, *The Morning of the Year* (1926–7), was written for the English Folk Dance Society: it was the first work to be commissioned by the BBC music department.

It is not always easy to separate his music for amateurs from the works he wrote for concert performances. The Seven Partsongs (1925–6) for female voices and strings and the Six Choruses (1931–2) for male voices and strings were first tried through by his students, but they are too subtle and intricate to be described as music for learners. And although at the end of his life he dedicated his three-key Canons to his pupils, they are difficult enough to be a challenge for any professional singers.

IV Operas

Of Holst's four published operas (including early and unfinished works there are seven others), the earliest, *Sāvitri* (1908), is the most dramatic. The simplicity and economy must have seemed revolutionary at the time when this short chamber opera was written. There is no overture: a stage direction says 'no curtain is necessary', and, without warning, the distant voice of unseen Death is heard in the darkness. In spite of the uneven writing and the occasional weaknesses of the text, it is always a moving experience to hear the work performed. His second opera, *The Perfect Fool* (1918–22), had been in his mind for many years before he wrote it. The brilliantly effective ballet music is often performed, but the opera is seldom revived. Its 19th-century parodies are excellent, but it suffers from Holst's inadequate text, particularly in the spoken dialogue, which should be tossed aside conversationally instead of being declaimed *fortissimo* to the back rows of an opera house. *At the Boar's Head* (1924) is a setting of the tavern scenes from Shakespeare's *Henry IV*. The music is founded on traditional 17th-century English dance-tunes, and it is one of his most skilful works. His last opera, *The Wandering Scholar*, was written in 1929–30. The text by Clifford Bax is founded on an incident in a book by Helen Waddell. The music, with its clear characterization, is Holst at his best in a scherzando frame of mind. The work remained in manuscript for more than 30 years after his death. He was too ill to go to the first performance in 1934, and he left pencil queries in the margins of the unrevised score: Imogen Holst has edited it for publication with the help of Benjamin Britten.

V Later orchestral works

At the beginning of the 1920s Holst told his friends that he was returning to his 'early love of counterpoint'. The Fugal Overture (1922) was intended to be played as an overture to *The Perfect Fool*, although it is a fine concert work in its own right. The Fugal Concerto (1923)

*16. Gustav
Holst, aged 59,
a few months
before his death*

for flute, oboe and strings is nearer to chamber music than
to orchestral writing. (His only successful chamber music
written after 1903 is the three-key *Terzetto* of 1925.)
His first full-scale orchestral work after *The Planets* was
Egdon Heath (1927), written in homage to Thomas
Hardy. The music grew out of a sentence in Hardy's
The Return of the Native, where the heath is described
as 'a place perfectly accordant with man's nature –
neither ghastly, hateful, nor ugly; neither commonplace,
unmeaning, nor tame; but like man, slighted and enduring; and withal singularly colossal and mysterious in its
swarthy monotony'. In spite of its lack of critical

and public success Holst knew that it was his best work. In the Double Concerto (1929) for two violins and orchestra there is a characteristic contrast between the slow interweaving threads of bitonal sound in the Lament and the energetic cross-rhythms of the Variations on a Ground. These contrasting moods are also heard in *Hammersmith* (1930), a BBC commission for military band which Holst later transcribed for orchestra. The music was the result of having worked in Hammersmith for 35 years and of having known the raucous good humour of the Saturday night crowds and the background of the quiet river, flowing 'unnoticed and apparently unconcerned'. The Lyric Movement for viola and small orchestra was written during his last illness. It has a warmth and sensuous beauty that he had denied himself for many years. Holst had completed only one movement, the Scherzo, of the symphony he was writing at the time of his death. The few bars of sketches for the slow movement (now in the British Library) suggest that, as in the Lyric Movement, he was nearer than ever before to his own ideal of 'tender austerity'.

Two contrasting characteristics are recognizable in much of Holst's music. One is scherzando: its recurring rhythmic patterns can sound brittle and edgily precise, or robust and ironically deliberate. The other is contemplative, and its slow, quietly balanced phrases can seem timelessly remote. Such moods were not familiar to listeners in the early 1920s; they felt more secure when one of his sweeping modal tunes moved reassuringly above the steps of a descending bass (a characteristic of his music that was in danger of becoming a mannerism). Holst's contemporaries found the skilful counterpoint of his later works too 'cerebral', and they were disconcerted by the austerity of his bitonal harmony, and also by the economy of his writing. During the first quarter of the 20th century most English composers still needed a 'bridge passage' to lead from one idea to another, and they still prepared the way for a final cadence. Holst went straight from one idea to the next, and having said what he wanted to say, he stopped. It is this economy in Holst's writing that has influenced later English composers. His own pupils knew what they owed him; Rubbra has said 'with what enthusiasm did we pare down our music to the very bone!'. The English composers who were just beginning to write at the time of Holst's death could learn from him by listening to his works. Tippett has been influenced by the vitality of his counterpoint, and Britten acknowledged his lasting debt to Holst's directness of thought.

WORKS

Edition: *Collected Facsimile Edition of Autograph Manuscripts of the Published Works*, ed. I. Holst, i–iv (London, 1974–83) [CFE]; numbering in I. Holst: *A Thematic Catalogue of Gustav Holst's Music* (1974) is indicated by H

Numbers in right-hand margins denote references in the text.

STAGE

op.		ref.
	Lansdown Castle (operetta, 2, A. C. Cunningham), 1892, Cheltenham, 7 Feb 1893, unpubd; H. Appx I, 21	161
—	The Revoke (opera, 1, F. Hart), 1895, unpubd, H7	
1	The Idea (children's operetta, Hart), c1898, H21	
11	The Youth's Choice (opera, 1, Holst), 1902, unpubd, H60	
23	Sita (opera, 3, Holst, from the Ramayana), 1900–06, unpubd, H89	155
25	Sāvitri (chamber opera, 1, Holst, from the Mahābharata), 1908; cond. H. Grunebaum, London, 5 Dec 1916, H96, CFEi	157, 161–2
27a	The Vision of Dame Christian, masque, 1909, unpubd, H101	
—	The Sneezing Charm (incidental music, C. Bax), 1918, unpubd, H143	
—	7 Choruses from Alcestis (Euripides, trans. Murray), 1920, H146	
—	The Lure, ballet, 1921; recorded 1981, LSO, cond. D. Atherton, H149	
39	The Perfect Fool (opera, 1, Holst), 1918–22; cond. E. Goossens, London, Covent Garden, 14 May 1923, H150	162
42	At the Boar's Head (opera, 1, after Shakespeare: Henry IV), 1924; cond. M. Sargent, Manchester, 3 April 1925, H156	162
45/1	The Golden Goose (choral ballet, J. Joseph), 1926; cond. Holst, Hammersmith, 24 May 1926, H163	161
45/2	The Morning of the Year (choral ballet, S. Wilson), 1926–7; BBC National Orch, cond. Holst, London, Royal Albert Hall, 17 March 1927. H164	161
—	The Coming of Christ (incidental music, Masefield), 1927; cond. Holst, Canterbury, 28 May 1928, H170	161
50	The Wandering Scholar (chamber opera, 1, C. Bax), 1929–30; cond. J. E. Wallace, Liverpool, 31 Jan 1934, H176, CFEi	162

CHORAL WITH ORCHESTRA OR ENSEMBLE

op.		ref.
5	Clear and Cool (C. Kingsley), chorus, orch, 1897, unpubd, H30	
17	King Estmere (anon.), chorus, orch, 1903; cond. E. Mason, London, Queen's Hall, 4 April 1908. H70	
26	Choral Hymns from the Rig Veda (trans. Holst): 1st group: Battle Hymn, To the Unknown God, Funeral Hymn, chorus, orch, 1908–10; Newcastle, 6 Dec 1911, H97 2nd group: To Varuna, To Agni, Funeral Chant, female chorus, orch, 1909; cond. Mason, Queen's Hall, 22 March 1911, H98 3rd group: Hymn to the Dawn, Hymn to the Waters, Hymn to Vena, Hymn of the Travellers, female chorus, harp, orch, 1910; Blackburn, 16 March 1911, H99 4th group: Hymn to Agni; Hymn to Soma, Hymn to Manas, Hymn to Indra, male chorus, str, brass, perc, 1912, cond. Mason, Queen's Hall, 18 March 1914, H100	157
—	O England my Country (G. K. Menzies), chorus 1v, orch, 1909; H103	
—	Christmas Day (trad.), chorus, orch, 1910, H109	157
30	The Cloud Messenger (Kalidasa, trans. Holst), chorus, orch, 1909–10; cond. Holst, Queen's Hall, 4 March 1913, H111	
31/1	Hecuba's Lament (Euripides, trans. Murray), A, female chorus, orch, 1911; H115	
—	2 Psalms: Psalm 86 (J. Bryan), Psalm 148 (F. R. Gray), T, chorus, str, org, 1912, H117	156
31/2	Hymn to Dionysus (Euripides, trans. Murray), female chorus, orch, 1913; cond. Holst, Queen's Hall, 10 March 1914, H116	
—	A Dirge for Two Veterans (Whitman), male chorus, brass, perc, 1914, H121	160
—	3 Carols: I saw three ships (trad.), Christmas Song (trans. J. Joseph), Masters in this Hall (W. Morris), chorus 1v, orch, 1916–7, H133	
36a	Three Festival Choruses: Let all mortal flesh (liturgical, trans. G. Moultrie), Turn back O Man (C. Bax), A Festival Chime (C. Bax), chorus, orch, 1916; cond. Holst, Thaxted Church, 27 May 1917, H134	161

No.	Work	pp.
37	The Hymn of Jesus (Apocryphal Acts of St John, trans. Holst), 2 chorus, female semichorus, orch, 1917; cond. Holst, Queen's Hall, 25 March 1920, H140	118, 149, 158, 159-60
38	Ode to Death (Whitman), chorus, orch, 1919; cond. E. Coates, Leeds, 6 Oct 1922, H144	160
—	Short Festival Te Deum, chorus, orch, 1919, H145	161
—	I vow to thee, my country (C. Spring Rice), chorus 1v, orch, c1921 [arr. from The Planets, no.4], H148	
41	First Choral Symphony (Keats), S, chorus, orch, 1923-4; cond. Coates, Leeds, 7 Oct 1925, H155, CFEiv	150-51, 160
44	7 Partsongs (Bridges): Say who is this?, O Love, I complain, Angel Spirits of Sleep, When we first met, Sorrow and Joy, Love on my heart from Heaven fell, Assemble all ye maidens, S, female chorus, str, 1925-6, H162	161
51	A Choral Fantasia (Bridges), S, chorus, org, str, brass, perc, 1930; cond. Holst, Gloucester, 8 Sept 1931, H177	160
53	6 Choruses (medieval Latin, trans. Waddell): Intercession, Good Friday, Drinking Song, A Love Song, How mighty are the Sabbaths, orch, Before Sleep, male chorus, str/org/pf, 1931-2, H186	161

OTHER CHORAL

(unaccompanied unless otherwise stated)

No.	Work	pp.
—	Light Leaves Whisper (Hart), chorus, c1896, H20	
—	Clouds o'er the Summer Sky (Hart), female chorus 2vv, pf, c1898, H40	
9a	5 Partsongs: Love is Enough (W. Morris), To Sylvia (F. Thompson), Autumn Song (W. Morris), Come away, Death (Shakespeare), A Love Song (W. Morris), chorus, 1897-1900, no.4 unpubd, H48	
9b	Ave Maria, 8-part female chorus, 1900; London, 23 May 1901, H49	155
—	I love thee (T. Hood), chorus, n.d., H57	
12	5 Partsongs: Dream Tryst (F. Thompson), Ye Little Birds (T. Heywood), Her eyes the glow-worm lend thee (R. Herrick), Now is the month of Maying (anon.), Come to me (C. Rossetti), chorus, 1902-3, nos.3, 5 unpubd, H61	
—	Thou didst delight my eyes (Bridges), chorus, before 1904, H58	
20a	In Youth is Pleasure (R. Wever), chorus, n.d., H76	160
—	Songs from The Princess (Tennyson): Sweet and low, The splendour falls, Tears, idle tears, O swallow, swallow, Now sleeps the crimson petal, female chorus 3-8vv, 1905, H80	
20b	4 Old English Carols (anon.): A babe is born, Now let us sing, Jesu, thou the Virgin-born, The Saviour of the World, chorus or female chorus, pf, 1907, H82	156
—	2 Carols (anon.): A Welcome Song, chorus, ob, vc, before 1908, Terly Terlow, chorus, ob, vc, 1916, H91	
—	Pastoral (anon.), female chorus, c1908, H92	
44	4 Partsongs (J. G. Whittier): Song of the Ship-builders, Song of the Shoemakers, Song of the Fishermen, Song of the Drovers, female chorus, pf, 1910, H110	
—	2 Eastern Pictures (Kalidasa, trans. Holst): Spring, Summer, female chorus, harp, 1911, H112	
—	The swallow leaves her nest (T. L. Beddoes), female chorus, before 1913, H119	
—	The Homecoming (Hardy), male chorus, 1913, H120	
—	Nunc dimittis (liturgical), chorus 8vv, 1915; Westminster Cathedral, 4 April 1915, H127	
34/1	This have I done for my true love (trad.), chorus, 1916; cond. Holst, Thaxted Church, 19 May 1918, H128	161
34/2	Lullay my liking (anon.), S, chorus, 1916, H129	161
34/3	Of one that is so fair (anon.), S, A, T, B, chorus, c1916, H130	161
34/4	Bring us in good ale (anon.), chorus, 1916, H131	
36b	6 Choral Folk Songs (trad.): I sowed the seeds of love, There was a tree, Matthew, Mark, Luke and John, The Song of the Blacksmith, I love my love, Swansea Town, arr. chorus/male chorus (excluding no.2), 1916, H136	
—	Diverus and Lazarus (trad.), arr. chorus, c1917, H137	
—	2 Partsongs (Whittier): The Corn Song, Song of the Lumbermen, female chorus 2vv, pf, 1917, H138	
—	A Dream of Christmas (anon.), female chorus 2vv, str/pf, 1917, H139	
43/1	The Evening-watch (H. Vaughan), chorus 8vv, 1924; cond. Holst, Gloucester, 10 Sept 1925, H159	160

43/2 Sing me the men (D. M. Dolben), chorus 9vv, 1925, H160 — 156

— 2 anthems (Bridges): Man born to toil, Eternal Father, chorus, org, bells ad lib, S in no.2, 1927, H168, H169 — 156

— Wassail Song (trad.), arr. chorus, c1928–30, H182

— 12 Welsh Folk Songs (trad., trans. S. Wilson): Lisa Lan, Green Grass, The Dove, Awake, awake, The Nightingale and Linnet, The Mother-in-law, The First Love, O 'twas on a Monday morning, My sweetheart's like Venus, White Summer Rose, The Lively Pair, The Lover's Complaint, arr. chorus, 1930–31, H183 — 157

— 8 Canons (medieval Latin, trans. Waddell), equal vv: If you love songs, 3vv, Lovely Venus, 3vv, The Fields of Sorrow, 3vv, David's Lament for Jonathan, 3vv, O Strong of Heart, 9vv, Truth of all Truth, 6vv, Evening on the Moselle, 2vv, pf, If 'twere the Time of Lilies, 2vv, pf, 1932, H187 — 161

ORCHESTRAL AND BAND
(including works with solo voice)

— A Winter Idyll, 1897, unpubd; BBC, 1983, H31

6 Örnulf's Drapa (Ibsen, trans. W. Archer), Bar, orch, 1898, unpubd, H34

7 Walt Whitman, ov., 1899, unpubd; London, 23 July 1982, H42 — 155

8 Symphony 'The Cotswolds', F, 1899–1900, unpubd, except for 2nd movt as Elegy In Memoriam William Morris; Bournemouth, 24 April 1902, H47

10 Suite de ballet, Eb, 1899, rev. 1912; cond. Holst, London, 20 May 1904, H43 — 155

13 Indra, sym. poem, 1903, unpubd, H66

18 The Mystic Trumpeter (Whitman), S, orch, 1904, rev. 1912; cond. Holst, Queen's Hall, 29 June 1905, H71 — 155

19/1 A Song of the Night, vn, orch, 1905; London, 20 Sept 1984, H74

19/2 Invocation, vc, orch, 1911; cond. L. Ronald, Queen's Hall, 2 May 1911, H75

21/1 Songs of the West, 1906–7, unpubd, H86 — 156

21/2 A Somerset Rhapsody, 1906–7; cond. Mason, Queen's Hall, 6 April 1910, H87

22 Two Songs without Words: Country Song, Marching Song, chamber orch, 1906; cond. Holst, London, RCM, 19 July 1906; Marching Song arr. military band, 1930; H88 — 156

28/1 Suite no.1, Eb, military band, 1909, H105 — 156

28/2 Suite no.2, F, military band, 1911; Royal Albert Hall, 30 June 1922, H106 — 156

29/1 Beni Mora, oriental suite, 1909–10; cond. Holst, Queen's Hall, 1 May 1912, H107 — 157

— Phantastes, suite, F, 1911, unpubd, withdrawn, H108

— Incidental Music to a London Pageant, military band, unison chorus, 1911; Crystal Palace, 1911, H114

29/2 St Paul's Suite, str, 1912–13, H118, CFEii — 160

32 The Planets: Mars, Venus, Mercury, Jupiter, Saturn, Uranus, Neptune (with female chorus 8vv), 1914–16; New Queen's Hall Orch, cond. Boult, Queen's Hall, 29 Sept 1918 (private perf.); LSO, cond. Coates, Queen's Hall, 15 Nov 1920 (public perf.); H125, CFEiii — 148, 149, 155, 157, 159, 163

33 Japanese Suite, 1915; ? Coliseum, 1916, H126

— The Perfect Fool (ballet music from op.39), 1918; cond. Coates, Queen's Hall, 1 Dec 1921, H150

40/1 A Fugal Overture, 1922; as ov. to The Perfect Fool; cond. Goossens, Covent Garden, 14 May 1923, H151 — 118, 162

40/2 A Fugal Concerto, fl, ob, str, 1923; University of Michigan, 17 May 1923 (private perf.); cond. Holst, Queen's Hall, 11 Oct 1923 (public perf.); H152, CFEii — 162–3

— The Golden Goose, suite [from op.45/1], arr. I. Holst, 1970, H163

— Dances from The Morning of the Year [from op.45/2], arr. I. Holst and C. Matthews, 1981, H164

47 Egdon Heath, Homage to Hardy, 1927; New York SO, cond. W. Damrosch, New York, Mecca Auditorium, 12 Feb 1928; CBSO, cond. Holst, Cheltenham, 13 Feb 1928; H172 — 163–4

— A Moorside Suite, brass band, 1928; Crystal Palace, 29 Sept 1928, H173; 2nd movt 'Nocturne' arr. str orch, ?1928 — 156

— The Dream-City, S, orch, arr. C. Matthews from 12 Songs: London, 1984, H174

49 Double Concerto, 2 vn, 1929; A. Fachiri, J. d'Aranyi, cond. O. Fried, Queen's Hall, 3 April 1930, H175, CFEii — 164

52 Hammersmith: Prelude, Scherzo, military band, 1930; 'Washington, 17 April 1932; 2nd version, orch, 1931; BBC SO, cond. Boult, Queen's Hall, 25 Nov 1931, H178 — 164

— Jazz-band Piece, 1932; ed. I. Holst as Capriccio, 1967; London, Queen Elizabeth Hall, 10 Jan 1968, H185

Brook Green Suite, str, 1933; cond. Holst, London, St Paul's Girls' School, March 1934, H190, CFEii | 160

Lyric Movement, va, chamber orch, 1933; L. Tertis, BBC SO, cond. Boult, London, BBC studio, 18 March 1934, H191, CFEii | 164

Scherzo, 1933–4; BBC SO, cond. Boult, Queen's Hall, 6 Feb 1935, H192 | 164

CHAMBER AND INSTRUMENTAL

String Trio, g, 1894; Aldeburgh, 1984, H Appx I, 34

2 Fantasiestücke, ob, str qt, 1896, rev. 1910, unpubd, H8

3 Quintet, a, pf, ob, cl, hn, bn, 1896, unpubd, H11

14 Wind Quintet, A♭, 1903; Nash Ensemble, London, Wigmore Hall, 15 Sept 1982, H67

7 Scottish Airs, arr. str, pf, 1907, H93

Phantasy (British trad.), str qt, 1916, unpubd, withdrawn; arr. I. Holst as Fantasia on Hampshire Folksongs, str orch, 1970, H135

Toccata, pf, 1924, H153

Terzetto, fl, ob, va, 1925; London, 2 March 1926, H158

46/1 Chrissemas Day in the morning, pf, 1926, H165

46/2 2 Folk Song Fragments: O I hae seen the roses blaw, The Shoemaker, pf, 1927, H166 | 163

Nocturne, pf, 1930, H179

Jig, pf, 1932, H179

SONGS

(for voice and piano unless otherwise stated)

4 Songs: Slumber-song (Kingsley), Margrete's Cradle-song (Ibsen, trans. Archer), Soft and gently (Heine), unpubd, Awake, my heart (Bridges), 1896–8, H14

15 6 Songs, Bar, pf: Invocation to the Dawn (Rig Veda, trans. Holst), Fain would I change that note (anon.), The Sergeant's Song (Hardy), In a wood (Hardy), Between us now (Hardy), I will not let thee go (Bridges), 1902–3, nos.2, 4, 5, 6 unpubd, H68

16 6 Songs, S, pf: Calm is the morn (Tennyson), My true love hath my heart (P. Sidney), Weep you no more (anon.), Lovely kind and kindly loving (N. Breton), Cradle Song (Blake), Peace (A. Hyatt), 1903–4, nos.1, 2, 5, 6 unpubd, H69

24 Hymns from the Rig Veda (trans. Holst): Ushas [Dawn], Varuna I [Sky], Maruts [Stormclouds], Indra (God of Storm and Battle), Varuna II [The Waters], Song of the Frogs, Vac [Speech], Creation, Faith, 1907–8, H90 | 156–7

— The heart worships (A. Buckton), 1907, H95

35 4 Songs (anon, 15th century), S/T, vn: Jesu sweet, now will I sing, My soul has nought but fire and ice, I sing of a maiden, My Leman is so true, 1916–17; Thaxted Church, 27 May 1917, H132 | 156

48 12 Songs (H. Wolfe): Persephone, Things lovelier, Now in these fairylands, A Little Music, The Thought, The Floral Bandit, Envoi, The Dream-city, Journey's End, In the Street of Lost Time, Rhyme, Betelgeuse, 1929; Paris, 9 Nov 1929, H174 | 157

EDITIONS

H. Purcell: *The Gordian Knot Untied, The Virtuous Wife, The Married Beau*, suites, str orch, ww ad lib

J. S. Bach: *Fugue à la gigue*, orch/military band

Several sets of 17th- and 18th-century canons and glees

Principal publishers: Boosey & Hawkes, Faber, Novello, Oxford University Press, Stainer & Bell

BIBLIOGRAPHY

E. Evans: 'Modern British Composers: 6. Gustav Holst', *MT*, lx (1919), 524, 588, 657

R. Vaughan Williams: 'Gustav Holst', *ML*, i (1920), 181, 305; repr. in *National Music and other Essays* (London, 1963)

K. Eggar: 'How they make music at Morley College', *Music Student*, xiii (1921), 359

C. Bax: *Inland Far* (London, 1925)

F. Gray: *And gladly wolde he lerne and gladly teche* (London, 1931)

A. Bliss: 'Gustav Holst: a Lonely Figure in Music', *Radio Times*, xliii (15 June 1934), no.559, p. 819

A. Boult: 'Gustav Holst: the Man and his Work', *Radio Times*, xliii (15 June 1934), no.559, p.819

E. Evans: 'Gustav Holst', *MT*, lxxv (1934), 593

A. Foster: 'Gustav Holst – an Appreciation', *MMR*, lxiv (1934), no.758, p.126

G. Jacob: 'Holst the Composer', *R.C.M. Magazine*, xxx (1934), 81; repr. in lxxx/2 (1984), 85

R. Capell: 'Death comes to Satyavan', *Radio Times*, xlix (18 Oct 1935), no.629, p.15

C. Bax: *Ideas and People* (London, 1936) [chap. 6 on Holst]

I. Holst: *Gustav Holst: a Biography* (London, 1938, 2/1969)

W. Mellers: 'Holst and the English Language', *MR*, ii (1941), 228; repr. in *Studies in Contemporary Music* (London, 1947)

E. Rubbra: *Gustav Holst* (Monaco, 1947)

R. Vaughan Williams: 'Holst', *DNB*

I. Holst: *The Music of Gustav Holst* (London, 1951, rev. 3/1985, incl. *Holst's Music Reconsidered*)

R. Cantrick: '*Hammersmith* and the two Worlds of Gustav Holst', *ML*, xxxvii (1956), 211

M. Tippett: 'Holst – Figure of our Time', *The Listener*, lx (13 Nov 1958), 800

U. Vaughan Willams and I. Holst, eds.: *Heirs and Rebels* (London, 1959/R1974) [incl. correspondence between Holst and R. Vaughan Williams, and writings]

J. Warrack: 'A New Look at Gustav Holst', *MT*, civ (1963), 100

U. Vaughan Williams: *R.V.W. – a Biography of Ralph Vaughan Williams* (London, 1964)

A. Boult: 'Interpreting *The Planets*', *MT*, cxi (1970), 263

——: *My Own Trumpet* (London, 1973)

——: 'Gustav Holst', *R.C.M. Magazine*, lxx (1974), 52

I. Holst: *Holst* (London, 1974, 2/1981)

——: 'Holst and the Royal College of Music', *R.C.M. Magazine*, lxx (1974), 49

Bibliography

——: *A Thematic Catalogue of Gustav Holst's Music* (London, 1974)

S. Lloyd and E. Rubbra, eds: *Gustav Holst: Collected Essays* (London, 1974)

H. Ottaway: 'Holst as an Opera Composer', *MT*, cxv (1974), 473

M. Short, ed.: *Gustav Holst (1874–1934): a Centenary Documentation* (London, 1974)

——: *Gustav Holst: Letters to W. G. Whittaker* (Glasgow, 1974)

J. Warrack: 'Holst and the Linear Principle', *MT*, cxv (1974), 732

F. Wilkinson: 'Gustav Holst as a Friend', *R.C.M. Magazine*, lxx (1974), 54

I. Holst and C. Matthews, eds.: *Gustav Holst: Collected Facsimile Edition of Autograph Manuscripts of the Published Works* (London, 1974–83)

D. R. Boyer: 'Holst's *The Hymn of Jesus*: an Investigation into Mysticism in Music', *MR*, xxxvi (1975), 272

I. Holst (compiled): *A Scrapbook for the Holst Birthplace Museum* (Cheltenham, 1978)

J. N. Moore, ed.: *Music and Friends: Seven Decades of Letters to Adrian Boult* (London, 1979)

P. Pirie: *The English Musical Renaissance* (London, 1979)

I. Holst: 'Holst's *At the Boar's Head*', *MT*, cxxiii (1982), 321

M. Kennedy: 'The English Musical Renaissance, 1880–1920', *Gramophone*, lx (1982), 211

I. Holst: 'Holst in the 1980s', *MT*, cxxv (1984), 266

S. Lloyd: *H. Balfour Gardiner* (Cambridge, 1984)

C. Matthews: 'Some Unknown Holst', *MT*, cxxv (1984), 269

WILLIAM WALTON

Hugh Ottaway

CHAPTER ONE

Life

William Turner Walton was born in Oldham on 29
March 1902. He was the second of four children born
to Charles Walton, an Oldham choirmaster and singing teacher, and his wife Louisa (née Turner), who
was also a singer. As a boy he took piano and
violin lessons, without any marked success, and he
sang in his father's choir at St John's church,
Werneth. There is no evidence that he had a particular interest in music, but he had a good voice and
was a natural singer. Accordingly, his father decided
that he should compete for a place as a chorister at
Christ Church Cathedral, Oxford, which he did, successfully. In retrospect, this looks like a far-sighted foster-
ing of talent, but in fact it was a bid to procure a better
general education than that provided by the local
elementary school.

Walton entered the Oxford choir school in 1912, at
the age of ten. Almost at once he began to develop
musically, and by the time he was 12 he had started to
compose. Included in his juvenilia was a good deal of
unaccompanied choral music, some of it elaborate, a
number of solo songs and some piano and organ music.
The dean of Christ Church, Thomas Strong, took an interest in the boy, in due course persuaded his father to
let him become an undergraduate, and arranged for him
to do so at the early age of 16. However, when Walton

left Oxford at the end of 1920, it was without a degree; he had passed the second BMus examination in June of that year, but had repeatedly failed Responsions, which he needed for an obligatory BA course.

For about the next ten years, on and off, he lived in Chelsea or abroad as the 'adopted, or elected, brother' of Osbert and Sacheverell Sitwell, whom he had met at Oxford. Although viewed with alarm in Oldham, this was an excellent arrangement, giving Walton the freedom to compose and greatly broadening his cultural experience. *Façade*, *Portsmouth Point*, the Sinfonia concertante and Viola Concerto were written during those years. The Viola Concerto (1928–9) stands at the beginning of Walton's maturity – indeed, some regard it as his finest achievement; but Walton did not begin to get an income from his music for another five years, when, thanks to the enthusiasm of the director Paul Czinner, he started composing for films. In addition to the Sitwells, a number of friends and admirers – notably Mrs Samuel Courtauld, who left him a small legacy, and Lady Wimborne – helped him through this difficult period. And so there is no tale of teaching or music copying, although for a time he did try 'arranging for jazz band'. Among his musical friends in the 1920s were the composers Berners, Van Dieren, Lambert and Warlock, his publisher Hubert Foss (of Oxford University Press, which publishes virtually all his works apart from the Piano Quartet and a couple of early songs) and the pianist Angus Morrison, each of whom was a formative influence.

Apart from involving himself with the Composers' Guild and the Performing Right Society, Walton generally limited his public life to composing and conducting his music. In both these activities he was largely self-taught. He was always a 'reluctant' rather than a 'compulsive' composer, and some of his finest works gave him a great deal of trouble. In *Belshazzar's Feast*, for instance, he was held up for seven months on the word 'gold', and in the First Symphony both the slow movement and the finale brought long delays. His output was relatively small, but an impressively large part of it is of major importance.

At 46 Walton met and married Susana Gil, an Argentinian many years younger than himself. They made their home on Ischia, an event which for Walton was the climax of a long affection for Italy, going back to his first visit with the Sitwells in the 1920s. His tendency to 'Mediterraneanize' his music, already evident in the Violin Concerto (1938–9), was strengthened. Most of his later works, from *Troilus and Cressida* onwards, were written in response to commissions. As well as composing he toured abroad conducting or attending performances of his own music – notably, in Australia and New Zealand (1964) and the USSR (1971) – and often visited Britain, particularly for concerts and recordings.

During more than 50 years as a composer, Walton experienced in turn notoriety, fashionableness and popular acceptance. This progression brought with it many honours, including seven doctorates, the first two being from the universities of Durham (1937) and Oxford (1942), the Gold Medal of the Royal Philharmonic Society (1947), a knighthood (1951), the Order of Merit (1967) and the Benjamin Franklin Medal (1972). In 1978 he was elected an honorary member of the American Academy and Institute of Arts and Letters, and in 1982 received an Ivor Novello Award. He died in Ischia on 8 March 1983.

CHAPTER TWO

Works

Of Walton's juvenilia, interpreting this fairly broadly, at least eight items have survived: a song, a waltz for piano in the Library at Christ Church, Oxford, an organ piece in the British Library, a choral work, and four published works: *A Litany* ('Drop, drop slow tears') for soprano, alto, tenor and bass, *The Winds* and *Tritons*, both solo songs, and the Piano Quartet. This last, revised in 1921, won a Carnegie Award. Although derivative, it shows growing signs of Walton's lyricism, and there are also some rhythmic and harmonic characteristics; it was revised again in 1976. The first works of the crucial, exploratory, Sitwellian period – a String Quartet and *Façade* – immediately followed.

When played at the first festival of the ISCM (Salzburg, 1923), the String Quartet was acclaimed by Berg, but Walton soon withdrew it (the parts still exist): 'full of undigested Bartók and Schoenberg' was his verdict later. The fate of *Façade* could not have been more different. Originally conceived by the Sitwells as an 'entertainment' for their drawing-room (see Sitwell), this has become Walton's most popular work. The idea may have owed something to *Pierrot lunaire*, but the influences revealed in Walton's contribution – instrumental 'backings' for the declamation of some experimental poems by Edith Sitwell – are predominantly Parisian, with Ravel in evidence as well as the postwar school. Although by no means representative of Walton's output, the sensitive stylishness of *Façade* (in its second version, 1923), with its sharply contrasting moods of spirited parody and languorous melancholy, is a clear pointer to the mature composer, in a way that the String Quartet, from all accounts, was not.

Between *Façade* and his next important composition, the overture *Portsmouth Point*, Walton spent more than a year (1923–4) immersed in jazz, 'writing and scoring fox-trots for the Savoy Orpheus Band and working at a monumentally planned concerto for two pianofortes, jazz band and orchestra' (Lambert). This remains legendary; no trace of the foxtrots has been found, and the 'concerto' (*Fantasia concertante*) was withdrawn, and possibly destroyed, when about to be performed. Clearly, something of the syncopation in *Portsmouth Point* and in the works that followed derives from this experience. Equally clearly, Walton was still finding his way, reacting sharply first against a Schoenbergian intellectualism and then against its antidote. *Portsmouth Point* again suggests Parisian influences – Stravinsky or Honegger – but is strongly characterized and established an incisive, scherzando style that is decidedly personal.

At this stage the young composer was keen to gain the interest of Dyagilev, to whom an intended ballet was played on two pianos by Angus Morrison and Walton himself, but the commission he hoped for did not follow. At Lambert's suggestion the music was remodelled as a work for piano and orchestra, the Sinfonia concertante. With its blend of neo-classical and neo-romantic elements, this is the expression of an arresting but not yet unified personality.

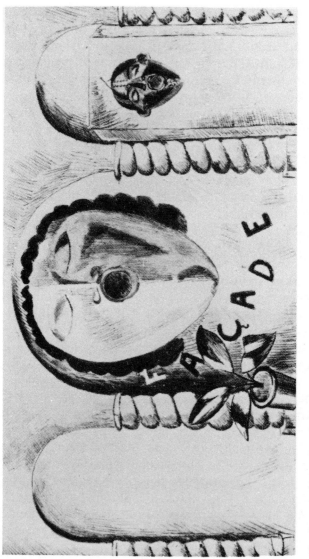

17. Screen design by Frank Dobson for the first public performance of Walton's 'Façade' (London, 12 June 1923)

In his mid-20s, and widely regarded as an *enfant terrible*, Walton was achieving a position quite different from that of any other English composer. He was often thought of as an English extension of Les Six, but the continental figure he had most in common with was probably Prokofiev. It seems likely that Prokofiev's Violin Concerto no.1 served as a model for his own Viola Concerto, a masterpiece written for Tertis but first played by Hindemith. At once deeply poetic and of real formal stature, this commanded a response far beyond the 'modern music' circles of the day, and it gave Walton the confidence to challenge English musical conservatism in its innermost stronghold, the choral festival. This he did with *Belshazzar's Feast*, which, although first given at the Leeds Festival (1931), was commissioned by the BBC, where Edward Clark was a valuable ally.

It was generally recognized that *Belshazzar's Feast* was the biggest landmark in English choral music since *The Dream of Gerontius*. The fresh and vivid musical imagery, the flair for dramatic effect and realistic expression of violent collective emotions are among the qualities that struck home directly and have continued to do so. Some, however, resisted its frankly pagan tone, or its musical modernity, or both: the Three Choirs Festival did not give a performance until 1957. 'Modernity', not 'modernism': like the Viola Concerto, *Belshazzar's Feast* is notable for its underlying sense of tradition, no less than for its individuality. This may well explain why the choral writing, at first thought immensely demanding, is now comfortably within the range of most large choral societies.

The first performance of *Belshazzar's Feast* was conducted by Sargent, who in the course of the next ten years became Walton's foremost interpreter, a role that was later Szell's and then Previn's. But in the mid-1930s, the conductor most often associated with Walton's music was Harty, who gave both first performances of the Symphony no.1 (the first three movements in December 1934, and the complete work in November 1935). Indeed, Harty became involved as soon as the symphony was projected and, with Foss, did what he could to encourage the composer to wrestle with his problems. For the work proved peculiarly recalcitrant and was not completed until two and a half years after the time set initially, if unrealistically, for its performance. Briefly, the chronology is as follows: early in 1932 a false start was made with an Allegro theme, later to become the flute theme at the beginning of the Andante; in spring 1933 the first two movements were completed in short score; after a gap of several months the discarded Allegro revealed itself as the germ of the Andante; while writing the Andante, Walton sketched the opening and close of the finale; in spring 1934, probably, the full score of the first three movements was completed; and in summer 1935 the finale was completed after a long delay, the fugue subject having been written only at the beginning of July.

Mason's comment that 'the impulse is no longer the *desire* to express for others, but the *necessity* to express for himself' may help to explain Walton's problems. The symphony stands firmly in the conflict-and-triumph tradition of Beethoven's Fifth, and a sense of personal commitment is strongly communicated. Whatever reservations there may be about the finale, for example that it 'provides a physical rather than an intellectual answer to

the questioning and agitated mood of the opening'
(Lambert), this work remains one of the most important
symphonies of its time. To some extent Walton adopted
the techniques of Sibelius, notably the building-up of
tension over a succession of pedal points. This is particularly marked in the first movement, but only as an
influence that has been thoroughly absorbed and
individualized. In the fugue subject at the centre of the
finale, Walton's affinity with Hindemith is declared, and
in the radiant rhetoric with which the finale begins and
ends – a vein already met with in *Belshazzar's Feast*
(see the invocation to the God of Gold and the final
alleluias) – there is a feeling for pageantry that opens up
comparisons with Elgar.

In the coronation march *Crown Imperial* (1937),
Elgar is more directly invoked, in a way that was later
confirmed by parts of the film scores for *Henry V* and
Richard III. But the next major work was the Violin
Concerto, commissioned by Heifetz and completed just
ten years after the Viola Concerto. The concertos share
a similar basic plan (a centrally placed scherzo flanked
by predominantly lyrical movements), but in the Violin
Concerto the lyricism is more sensuously indulgent and
the enjoyment of technical virtuosity a more important
part of the conception. Although shaped and controlled
with a craftsman's detachment, this is a work with
Romantic antecedents; it is also the most notable violin
concerto by an English composer since Elgar's and one
of the supreme examples of Walton's feeling for orchestral colour.

It was with the two concertos, *Belshazzar's Feast* and
the First Symphony that Walton established his position
as a major composer, at first in Britain and the USA,

and from the 1940s onwards more widely. During the war years his only concert work was the overture *Scapino*, written for the 50th anniversary of the Chicago SO. This is highly polished 'entertainment' music, a successor to *Portsmouth Point*, only smoother and rhythmically less complex. Apart from two ballet scores, *The Wise Virgins*, an arrangement of music by Bach, and *The Quest*, an original score written in five weeks, Walton's main concern in those years was music for films, including a number of 'patriotic' films, such as *The Next of Kin* and *The First of the Few*, to which his labour was officially directed.

The Next of Kin (1941) was probably Walton's sixth film score. His first was *Escape me Never* (1934), and by the time he came to work on the first of Laurence Olivier's three Shakespeare films (*Henry V*, 1943–4) he was not only highly proficient but one of the most distinquished composers for the medium. 'Doing films', he remarked, 'gave me a lot more fluency'; it also showed him his ability to seize on a mood or situation immediately and vividly, and it extended the range of his expressive resources. The same qualities are evident in the music for *Christopher Columbus*, a BBC radio programme written by MacNeice for the 450th anniversary of Columbus's first voyage to America; this highly characteristic score led directly to the collaboration with Olivier on *Henry V*, *Hamlet* and *Richard III*, which together mark the climax, but not quite the end, of this aspect of his work. As late as 1969 Walton wrote a big score for *The Battle of Britain*, but only a part of it was used.

The immediate postwar years were a critical time for Walton's reputation. His music had reached a wide audience, but he had written no major work since 1939. His admirers looked for a composition that in imaginative power and emotional commitment would be a true successor to the First Symphony. Others, misled by his former radicalism, felt that he was a modernist who had 'gone wrong'; as early as the Violin Concerto there had been deprecating talk of a 'creative relaxation' and a 'lowering of tension'. There is much confusion here. Despite the efforts of the Sitwells and Van Dieren to persuade him otherwise in the 1920s, Walton was never really an intellectual modernist. He had always been an artist of the intuitive sort 'with a strong feeling for lyricism' (his own words), a liking for rhythmic excitement and a flair for precise workmanship. As his sympathies broadened, so the more traditional facets of his work became more evident. He then turned to chamber music, perhaps in reaction to his excessive concentration on film music, and in a string quartet and a sonata for violin and piano redefined his imaginative world with great sensitivity.

The String Quartet in A minor (1945–7) is beautifully written for the medium, in a way that underlines the precise, almost Ravelian aspect of Walton's art. It also has an air of composed withdrawal, despite the rhythmic vitality of the scherzo and the finale; the slow movement particularly has an inwardness that speaks of a deeply personal motivation. In 1971–2, at the suggestion of Neville Marriner, Walton adapted the quartet for string orchestra, renaming it Sonata. Apart from one or two tiny modifications, three of the four movements are straight transcriptions; but in the first movement there are cuts, compressions, changes of key, rewritings and many instances of retexturing, which amount to a reappraisal and tautening of the whole expression (see Ottaway, 1974). The Sonata for violin and piano (1949) is a wholly lyrical composition in two movements, an intended scherzo having been extracted and published separately as one of Two Pieces for violin and piano. This was written for Menuhin and Kentner, who made 'many valuable suggestions' and gave the first performance. Too much emphasis has been given to the presence of a little 12-note idea in the piano as a 'coda' to the theme of the second movement ('Variazioni', cf the theme of the finale of the Second Symphony), for in this work the composer's tonal allegiances are particularly strong. Although the piano is an instrument that Walton never mastered (but always used), its role in the Violin Sonata is both resourceful and effective; there is also a fine piano accompaniment in the original version of *A Song for the Lord Mayor's Table*.

During the next four or five years (1950–54), Walton was much preoccupied with his first opera, *Troilus and Cressida* (libretto by Christopher Hassall), from which he turned aside only to write the *Coronation Te Deum* and a second coronation march, *Orb and Sceptre*. The view of Cressida derives from Chaucer, not Shakespeare, and becomes a projection of one of the central themes of Romanticism: that of the lonely individual in a hostile and perplexing world. The principal characters are straightforwardly presented, the emotions are clear and strong, and the musico-dramatic treatment relates pre-eminently to the Italian tradition. When produced at Covent Garden in 1954, and subsequently at La Scala and elsewhere, *Troilus and Cressida* was said by some to be 'hopelessly out of date, both musically and psychologically', but it was generally agreed that, in terms of theatrical effectiveness, Walton's achievement could hardly be faulted. Whether the Romantic 'grand manner' was valid for an artist in the mid-1950s depends on what he did with it. There is evidence, internal and otherwise, that Walton was deeply involved in his opera: the *Troilus* sound is distinctive and is echoed many times in later works. Musically, where there are weaknesses, as in some of the writing for Troilus (for instance, 'Child of the wine-dark wave' in Act 1), it is not because the manner is Romantic, but because, at those particular moments, the composer's response seems conventionally appropriate rather than keenly felt. In general, the level of invention is high, communicating a wide range of emotion and a strong sense of atmosphere. The characterization of Pandarus suggests a debt to Britten; otherwise the style is an amalgam of most Waltonian elements, and the finish is both sumptuous and precise. In 1975–6 Walton made some cuts and also modified the part of Cressida, lowering the pitch in certain places to suit the voice of Janet Baker (Covent Garden, 1976).

The other opera, *The Bear* (after Chekhov), completed 13 years later, is a very different proposition. Described as an 'extravaganza in one act', this comic work satirizes Romantic attitudes, engages in some brilliant musical parody, and in spirit comes closer to *Façade* than almost anything from the intervening years. Thus *The Bear* complements *Troilus*, to which it also makes a good deal of (perhaps) knowing allusion, and emphasizes the craftsman–entertainer, by no means the least of Walton's roles.

In the years after *Troilus*, Walton was generally content to write commissioned works. In some cases, however, the creative idea came first and the commission followed. There was little fundamental development; the refinement of gesture, colour and texture was clearly a primary concern. In 1961 he even revised the scoring of the Viola Concerto, reducing the size of the orchestra and adding an important harp part (a comparison of the two versions makes a revealing study). Such refinement is immediately evident in the Cello Concerto, written for Pyatigorsky in 1956. This stands in much the same relation to the more sumptuous aspects of *Troilus* as does the String Quartet in A minor to the film music that preceded it: 'the harmony is a shade less sweet and the mood more serene and "objective" with less of his old nostalgic bitter-sweet melancholy' (Mason).

In the Partita for orchestra, written for the 40th anniversary of the Cleveland Orchestra, and the Second Symphony, commissioned by the Royal Liverpool Philharmonic Society, 'objectivity' tends to express itself as a steely glitter, a brilliant but sometimes brash exploitation of orchestral virtuosity. However, in each of these three-movement works there is a slow movement of tenderness and warmth, the one in the symphony recalling some of the most poignant moments in *Troilus*. A comparison of the Second Symphony with the First suggests a markedly different balance of creative forces. The First is a work of passion in which the intense emotional drive has conditioned the musical style. But in the outer movements of the Second a passionate style is an end in itself: the style is the passion, and the musical achievement is in no small measure a triumph of Walton's professionalism.

It has sometimes been asked how far this latterday

18. William Walton

brilliance and detachment indicates that the old entertainer was determined to show that he could still do
his tricks. Certainly Walton was irritated by the recurring charge of 'relaxation', to which much in the Partita
and the Second Symphony might be construed as a
more or less deliberate reply. Perhaps the most extreme
example of this concern with a hard-edged orchestral
stylishness is the *Capriccio burlesco*, a short, high-
spirited piece written in 1968 to mark the 125th season
of the New York PO.

The craftsman's skill is again evident in the two works
in variation form – Variations on a Theme by Hindemith (1962–3) and Improvisations on an Impromptu
of Benjamin Britten (1969) – but here there is also an
undoubted concern with the deeper potentiality of the
musical material; indeed, the Hindemith Variations,
commissioned by the Royal Philharmonic Society for
its 150th concert, must be reckoned one of Walton's
most satisfying achievements. The 'theme' is nothing
less than a passage of about 35 bars from the beginning
of the slow movement of Hindemith's Cello Concerto,
and the work also contains references to a characteristic
phrase from the opera *Mathis der Maler*. In the background is some 40 years' responsiveness to Hindemith's
music, and in the foreground many a revealing insight
into what that responsiveness meant for Walton's own
music. In a letter of appreciation, Hindemith particularly commended 'the honest solidity of workmanship ... something that seems almost completely lost
nowadays'. Walton's use of the term 'improvisation' (see
also the finale of the Cello Concerto) denotes something
freer than variation, and in the work based on the theme
of the slow movement ('Impromptu') from Britten's

Piano Concerto op.13, the tendency is for different aspects of the theme to be seized on in turn as a basis for invention. Commissioned by Dr Ralph Dorfman for the San Francisco SO, this is in scale and emotional range the smaller of the two works, but it has a distinctive presence and the closeness of its musical thought is impressive.

Walton's development can thus be outlined largely in terms of the orchestral and instrumental works, the two operas and *Belshazzar's Feast*, but there are other works requiring mention. Neither *In Honour of the City of London* (1937) nor the *Gloria* written in 1961 'to celebrate the 125th anniversary of the Huddersfield Choral Society and the 30th year of Sir Malcolm Sargent as its conductor' has enjoyed much success with British choral societies. Both pieces are effectively written, mostly in Walton's radiant, rhetorical manner, but their impact hardly compares with that of *Belshazzar's Feast*. One of Walton's problems was his tendency always to do his best work the first time he used a form or medium. There are, however, several admirable pieces for smaller choral forces, some with organ or orchestra, others unaccompanied. Among the former are the *Missa brevis* (1966) commissioned by the Friends of Coventry Cathedral, the *Jubilate Deo* (1972) written for the English Bach Festival, a *Magnificat* and *Nunc dimittis* for the 900th anniversary of Chichester Cathedral (1975) and a setting of George Herbert's *Antiphon* for the 150th anniversary of St Paul's Church, Rochester, New York (1977). While such compositions did not engage the whole of Walton's powers, they certainly offered scope for his fastidious ear, and in a medium that he came to understand when still a boy.

191

The unaccompanied pieces include three carols, a wedding anthem, a setting of words by Masefield, *Where does the uttered music go?*, for the unveiling of the memorial window to Sir Henry Wood in St Sepulchre's, Holborn, in 1946, and the motet *Cantico del sole* written for the 21st Cork International Choral and Folk Dance Festival, 1974.

Walton's feeling for unaccompanied voices was so natural and idiomatic that his failure to write more for this medium is regrettable. Still more regrettable is his very intermittent attention to the solo song. The Three Songs to words by Edith Sitwell, which originally formed part of a set of five for voice and orchestra (*Bucolic Comedies*, 1924, withdrawn), and the two song cycles, *Anon. in Love* for tenor and guitar (1960) and *A Song for the Lord Mayor's Table* for soprano and piano (1962), contain many fine settings in which Walton's wit and sensibility are happily blended. Both cycles were later arranged for voice and orchestra.

Although some problems concerning the early works still remain, Walton's music is now well documented. For the most detailed and reliable information, see Craggs, 1977; for analysis of works, see Howes.

Numbers in right-hand margins denote references in the text.

OPERAS AND BALLETS

The First Shoot (ballet, 1), 1935; cond. F. Collinson, London, Adelphi, 4 Feb 1936

The Wise Virgins (ballet, 1) [arr. of Bach], 1940; cond. C. Lambert, London, Sadler's Wells, 24 April 1940 — 184

The Quest (ballet, 1), 1943; cond. Lambert and J. Clifford, London, New Theatre, 6 April 1943 — 184

Troilus and Cressida (opera, 3, C. Hassall), 1950–54, rev. 1975–6; cond. M. Sargent, London, Covent Garden, 13 Dec 1954; cond. L. Foster, Covent Garden, 12 Nov 1976 — 177, 186–7, 188, 191

The Bear (extravaganza, 1, P. Dehn, after Chekhov), 1965–7; cond. J. Lockhart, Aldeburgh, Jubilee Hall, 3 June 1967 — 182, 191

ORCHESTRAL

Pedagogic Overture 'Dr Syntax', 1921, withdrawn — 179

Fantasia concertante, 2 pf, jazz band, orch, ?1924, withdrawn

Portsmouth Point, ov., 1925; Tonhalle Orch., cond. V. Andrae, Zurich, Tonhalle, 22 June 1926 — 176, 179, 184

Siesta, small orch, 1926; Aeolian Chamber Orch., cond. W. Walton, London, Aeolian Hall, 24 Nov 1926

Façade, suite no.1, 1926; Lyceum Theatre Orch., cond. Walton, London, Lyceum, 3 Dec 1926

Sinfonia concertante, orch, pf obbl., 1926–7, rev. 1943; Y. Bowen, RPO, cond. E. Ansermet, London, Queen's Hall, 5 Jan 1928 — 176, 179

Viola Concerto, 1928–9, rev. 1961; P. Hindemith, Henry Wood SO, cond. Walton, Queen's Hall, 3 Oct 1929 — 176, 181, 183, 188

Symphony no.1, bb, 1932–5; LSO, cond. H. Harty, Queen's Hall, 3 Dec 1934 [movts 1–3]; BBC SO, cond. Harty, Queen's Hall, 6 Nov 1935 [complete] — 177, 182–3, 164, 188

Crown Imperial, coronation march, 1937; Coronation Orch., cond. A. Boult, Westminster Abbey, 12 May 1937 — 183

Façade, suite no.2, 1938; New York Philharmonic SO, cond. J. Barbirolli, New York, Carnegie Hall, 30 March 1938

Violin Concerto, 1938–9, rev. 1943; J. Heifetz, Cleveland Orch, cond. A. Rodzinski, Cleveland, Severance Hall, 7 Dec 1939 — 177, 183, 184

Music for Children, 1940; LPO, cond. B. Cameron, Queen's Hall, 16 Feb 1941 — 184

Scapino, comedy ov., 1940; Chicago SO, cond. F. Stock, Chicago, Orchestra Hall, 3 April 1941

The Wise Virgins, suite, 1940

Spitfire Prelude and Fugue [from film score The First of the Few], 1942; Liverpool PO, cond. Walton, Liverpool, Philharmonic Hall, 2 Jan 1943

Two Pieces, str [from film score Henry V], 1944

Orb and Sceptre, coronation march, 1953; Coronation Orch., cond. Boult, Westminster Abbey, 2 June 1953 — 186

Johannesburg Festival Overture, 1956; South African Broadcasting Corporation, cond. M. Sargent, Johannesburg, City Hall, 25 Sept 1956

Cello Concerto, 1956; G. Piatigorsky, Boston SO, cond. C. Munch, Boston, Symphony Hall, 25 Jan 1957 — 188

Partita, 1957; Cleveland Orch, cond. G. Szell, Severance Hall, 30 Jan 1958 — 188, 190

Symphony no.2, 1959–60; Royal Liverpool PO, cond. J. Pritchard, Edinburgh, Usher Hall, 2 Sept 1960 — 186, 188, 190

Granada Prelude, call signs and end music [for Granada Television], 1962

Variations on a Theme by Hindemith, 1962–3; RPO, cond. Walton, London, Royal Festival Hall, 8 March 1963 — 190

Capriccio burlesco, 1968; New York PO, cond. A. Kostelanetz, New York, Philharmonic Hall, 7 Dec 1968 — 190

The Battle of Britain, suite [from film score], arr. Carl Davis, 1985; Bournemouth SO, cond. Davis, Bristol, Colston Hall, 10 May 1985 — 184

Improvisations on an Impromptu of Benjamin Britten, 1969; San Francisco SO, cond. J. Krips, San Francisco, War Memorial Opera House, 14 Jan 1970 — 190

Sonata, str [arr. of Str Qt, a], 1971–2; Academy of St Martin-in-the-Fields, cond. N. Marriner, Perth, W. Australia, Octagon Theatre, 2 March 1972 — 185–6

Varii capricci [free transcr. of 5 Bagatelles for gui], 1976; LSO, cond. A. Previn, Royal Festival Hall, 4 May 1976

Prelude [from Granada Television music], 1977; Young Musicians' SO, cond. J. Blair, London, St John's, Smith Square, 25 June 1977

Prologo e Fantasia, 1981; National SO of Washington, DC, cond. M. Rostropovich, Royal Festival Hall, 20 Feb 1982

BRASS BAND AND BRASS ENSEMBLE

March for concert band [from Granada Television music], 1966 — 191

The First Shoot [arr. from ballet], brass band; Black Dyke Mills Band, Grimethorpe Colliery Band, cond. E. Howarth, London, Royal Albert Hall, 7 Sept 1981

A Queen's Fanfare, 1959

Anniversary Fanfare, 1973

Fanfare for the National, 1976

Roaring Fanfare, 1976 — 191

Salute for the 100th birthday of Robert Mayer, 1979

Birthday Fanfare, 1982

CHORAL

(with orchestra)

The Forsaken Merman (Arnold), S, T, SATB, orch, 1916, unperf. — 191

Belshazzar's Feast (O. Sitwell, after Bible), Bar, SATB, orch, 1929–31; D. Noble, Leeds Festival Chorus, LSO, cond. Sargent, Leeds Town Hall, 8 Oct 1931 — 36, 177, 181–2, 183, 191

In Honour of the City of London (Dunbar), SATB, orch, 1937; Leeds Festival Chorus, LPO, cond. Sargent, Leeds Town Hall, 6 Oct 1937 — 191

Coronation Te Deum, SATB, orch, org, 1952–3; Coronation Choir and Orch, Kneller Hall Trumpeters, O. Peasgood, cond. W. McKie, Westminster Abbey, 2 June 1953 — 186

Gloria, A, T, B, SATB, orch, 1961; M. Thomas, R. Lewis, J. Cameron, Huddersfield Choral Society, Royal Liverpool PO, cond. Sargent, Huddersfield Town Hall, 24 Nov 1961 — 191

(with organ)

The Twelve (W. H. Auden), SATB, org, 1965; Christ Church Cathedral Choir, R. Bottone, cond. S. Watson, Oxford, Christ Church Cathedral, 16 May 1965 — 191

Missa brevis, SSAATTBB, org/orch, 1966, Choir of Coventry Cathedral, cond. D. Lepine, Coventry, 10 April 1966 — 191

Jubilate Deo, SSAATTBB, org, 1972; Christ Church Cathedral Choir, S. Darlington, cond. S. Preston, Christ Church Cathedral, 22 April 1972 — 191

Magnificat and Nunc dimittis, SATB, org, 1975; Chichester Cathedral Choir, I. Fox, cond. J. Birch, Chichester Cathedral, 14 June 1975 — 191

Antiphon, SATB, org, 1977; St Paul's Church Choir, D. Craighead, cond. D. Fetler, Rochester, NY, St Paul's Church, 20 Nov 1977 — 191

(unaccompanied)

A Litany (P. Fletcher), SATB, 1916 — 175, 191, 192

Make we joy in this fest (trad. carol), SATB, 1931 — 178

Set me as a seal upon thine heart (Song of Solomon), SATB, 1938; St Mary Abbots Church Choir, choirmaster F. G. Shuttleworth, London, St Mary Abbots, 22 Nov 1938

Where does the uttered music go? (J. Masefield), SATB, 1946; BBC Chorus, Theatre Revue Chorus, cond. L. Woodgate, London, St Sepulchre's, Holborn, 26 April 1946 — 192

What cheer (trad.), SATB, 1961

All this time (early Eng.), SATB, 1970

Cantico del sole (St Francis), SATB, 1974; BBC Northern Singers, cond. S. Wilkinson, Cork, University College, 25 April 1974 — 192

King Herod and the Cock (trad.), SATB, 1977; King's College Choir, cond. P. Ledger, Cambridge, King's College Chapel, 24 Dec 1977

SOLO VOCAL

Tell me where is fancy bred (Shakespeare), S, T, 3 vn, pf, 1916 — 175, 178

The Winds (Swinburne), 1v, pf, 1918; O. de Foras, G. Bryan, London, Aeolian Hall, 30 Oct 1929 — 178

Tritons (Drummond), 1v, pf, 1920; de Foras, Bryan, Aeolian Hall, 30 Oct 1929 — 178

Façade (E. Sitwell), reciter, fl + pic, cl + b cl, sax, tpt, perc, vc, 1921–2, final rev. 1942; E. Sitwell, R. Murchie, P. Draper, F. Moss, H. Barr, C. Bender, A. Gauntlett, cond. Walton, 2 Carlyle Square, Chelsea, 24 Jan 1922 (private perf.), Aeolian Hall, 12 June 1923 (public perf.); C. Lambert, J. Francis, R. Temple Savage, F. Johnson, R. Walton, J. Blades, S. Trau, cond. W. Walton, Aeolian Hall, 29 May 1942 — 176, 178, 187

Façade 2 [8 pieces perf. with 1921–2 versions but not pubd in 1942], 1979; P. Pears, R. Adeney, T. King, S. Trier, C. Steele-Perkins, J. Blades, C. Tunnell, cond. S. Bedford, Snape Maltings, 19 June 1979 — 176, 178

Bucolic Comedies (E. Sitwell), 5 songs, 1v, orch, 1924, withdrawn, 3 rev. as 3 Songs, 1v, pf, 1932; D. Stevens, H. Foss, London, Wigmore Hall, 10 Oct 1932 — 192

Under the Greenwood Tree (Shakespeare) [from film score As you like it], 1v, pf, 1936

Anon. in Love (anon.), 6 songs, T, gui/orch, 1960; Pears, J. Bream, Ipswich, Shrubland Park Hall, 21 June 1960 — 192

A Song for the Lord Mayor's Table (various), 6 songs, S, pf/orch, 1962; E. Schwarzkopf, G. Moore, London, Goldsmiths' Hall, 18 July 1962 — 186, 192

CHAMBER AND INSTRUMENTAL

Choral Prelude on 'Wheatley,' org, 1916 — 175, 178

Waltz, c, pf, 1916

Piano Quartet, 1918–19, rev. 1921 and 1976; P. Tas, J. Lockyer, J. Gaballa, G. Bryan, Aeolian Hall, 30 Oct 1929 — 176, 178

String Quartet, 1919–22; McCullagh Qt, London, RCM, 5 July 1923; withdrawn — 178, 179

Toccata, vn, pf, ?1923; K. Goldsmith, A. Morrison, London, Queen's Square, 12 May 1925; withdrawn

Duets for Children, pf, 1940

String Quartet, a, 1945–7; Blech Qt, London, BBC, 4 May 1947 — 185, 188

Sonata, vn, pf, 1949; Y. Menuhin, L. Kentner, Zurich, Tonhalle, 30 Sept 1949 — 185, 186

Two Pieces, vn, pf, 1949–50 — 186

Five Bagatelles, gui, 1972; J. Bream, Bath Assembly Rooms, 27 May 1972

Passacaglia, vc, 1982; M. Rostropovich, London, Royal Festival Hall, 16 March 1982

INCIDENTAL MUSIC
(for the theatre)

The Son of Heaven (Strachey), London, Scala, 12 July 1925

The Boy David (Barrie), Edinburgh, King's, 21 Nov 1936

Macbeth (Shakespeare), Manchester, Opera House, 16 Jan 1942 — 192

(for the cinema)

Escape me never, 1934 — 184, 188

As you like it, 1936 — 184

Dreaming Lips, 1937

A Stolen Life, 1939

Major Barbara, 1941 — 184

The Next of Kin, 1941 — 184

The First of the Few, 1942

The Foreman went to France, 1942

Went the day well?, 1942

Henry V, 1943–4 — 183, 184

Hamlet, 1947–8 — 184

Richard III, 1955 — 183, 184

The Battle of Britain, 1969 [score used only in part; see 'Orchestral'] — 184

Three Sisters, 1970

(for radio)

Christopher Columbus (MacNeice), A, T, B, 2 speakers, SA speaking chorus, TB speaking chorus, gui, orch; BBC Chorus, BBC SO, cond. Boult, 12 Oct 1942 — 184

(for television)

March for A Hist.   e English Speaking Peoples, ABC television, 1959

Series title music for BBC TV Shakespeare Series, BBC television, 1978

Principal publisher: Oxford University Press

BIBLIOGRAPHY

C. Lambert: 'Some Recent Works by William Walton', *The Dominant*, i (1928), 16

B. de Zoete: 'William Walton', *MMR*, lix (1929), 321, 356

H. J. Foss: 'William Walton', *The Chesterian*, xi (1930), 175

A. Hutchings: 'The Symphony and William Walton', *MT*, lxxviii (1937), 211

A. Frank: 'The Music of William Walton', *The Chesterian*, xx (1939), 153

H. J. Foss: 'William Walton', *MQ*, xxvi (1940), 456

F. Merrick: 'Walton's Concerto for Violin and Orchestra', *MR*, ii (1941), 309

E. Evans: 'William Walton', *MT*, lxxxv (1944), 329, 364

C. Mason: 'William Walton', *British Music of our Time*, ed. A. L. Bacharach (Harmondsworth, 1946), 137

K. Avery: 'William Walton', *ML*, xxviii (1947), 1

O. Sitwell: *Laughter in the Next Room* (London, 1949)

H. Murrill: 'Walton's Violin Sonata', *ML*, xxxi (1950), 208

D. Mitchell: 'Some Observations on William Walton', *The Chesterian*, xxvi (1952), 35, 67

F. Reizenstein: 'Walton's "Troilus and Cressida" ', *Tempo*, no.34 (1954–5), 16

H. Rutland: 'Walton's New Cello Concerto', *MT*, xcviii (1957), 69

P. Evans: 'Sir William Walton's Manner and Mannerism', *The Listener*, lxii (1959), 297

M. Schafer: *British Composers in Interview* (London, 1963), 73ff

F. Howes: *The Music of William Walton* (London, 1965, rev. 2/1974)

J. Warrack: 'Sir William Walton talks to John Warrack', *The Listener*, lxxx (1968), 176

F. Aprahamian: 'Walton Retrospective', *Music and Musicians*, xx/11 (1971–2), 22

H. Ottaway: 'Walton's First Symphony', *MT*, cxiii (1972), 254

——: *William Walton* (Sevenoaks, 1972, rev. 2/1977)

C. Palmer: 'Walton's Film Music', *MT*, cxiii (1972), 249

F. Routh: *Contemporary British Music: the 25 Years from 1945 to 1970* (London, 1972), 25ff

E. Rubbra: 'William Walton's Seventieth Birthday', *The Listener*, lxxxvii (1972), 394

H. Ottaway: 'Walton's First and its Composition', *MT*, cxiv (1973), 998

S. R. Craggs: *Sir William Walton, O.M.: a Catalogue, Annotated Bibliography and Discography of his Musical Works* (diss., Library Association, 1973)

H. Ottaway: 'Walton Adapted', *MT*, cxv (1974), 582

Bibliography

J. Churchill: 'The Church Music of Sir William Walton', *Music: The AGO and RCCO Magazine*, xi (1977), 40

S. R. Craggs: *William Walton: a Thematic Catalogue* (London, 1977) [incl. essay by M. Kennedy]

H. Ottaway: 'Walton at 75', *Hallé Magazine* (1977), 2, 32

S. R. Craggs: *William Turner Walton: his Life and Music* (diss., U. of Strathclyde, 1978)

A. Orga: 'Sir William Walton: Some Thoughts', *Composer*, no.68 (1979–80), 11

P. Driver: 'Façade Revisited', *Tempo*, no.133–4 (1980), 3

A. Poulton: *The Recorded Works of Sir William Walton* (Kidderminister, 1980)

W. K. Fulton: *Selected Choral Works of William Walton* (diss., Texas Technical U., 1981)

B. Northcott: 'In Search of Walton', *MT*, cxxiii (1982), 179

C. Moorehead: 'Beyond the Façade ... the reluctant Grand Old Man', *The Times* (29 March 1982), 5

F. Whitsey: 'Plants for a Music Maker', *Country Life* (1 April 1982), 890

G. Widdicombe: 'Behind Walton's Façade', *Observer Magazine* (7 Feb 1982), 28

——: 'Grand Old Man of British Music', *Observer* (28 March 1982), 32

E. Greenfield: 'Sir William Walton (1902–1983), *Gramophone*, lx (1982–3), 1244

H. Cole: 'Walton in Retrospect', *Country Life* (31 March 1983), 766

G. Widdicombe: 'The Quiet Musician of Ischia', *Observer* (13 March 1983), 7

S. R. Craggs: 'Façade and the Music of Sir William Walton', *Library Chronicle of the University of Texas at Austin*, no.25–6 (1984), 101

N. Tierney: *William Walton: his Life and Music* (London, 1984)

MICHAEL TIPPETT

Ian Kemp

CHAPTER ONE

Life

Michael Kemp Tippett was born in London on 2 January 1905. His father, who was of Cornish descent, spent most of his life as a kind of entrepreneur; his mother came from a Kentish family and was closely associated with the suffragette movement. Shortly after Tippett was born the family moved from Middlesex to Wetherden, a small village in Suffolk, where he spent his childhood. By this time his father had retired and invested his money in a hotel at Cannes, and the two sons became fluent French speakers when they were very young. Tippett's early education was undertaken by his mother and a governess. When he was nine he was sent to preparatory school, and at 13 he won a scholarship to Fettes College, Edinburgh. He intensely disliked Fettes and was withdrawn in 1920, transferring to Stamford Grammar School in Lincolnshire, where he found conditions more congenial.

Tippett had no musical training during his childhood, apart from piano lessons, and when, after leaving Stamford Grammar School, he expressed his intention of becoming a composer, neither he nor his parents had much knowledge of what this implied. At first it was decided that he should train as a professional pianist, and he stayed on in Stamford so that he could continue studying with Frances Tinkler (who had also taught Malcolm Sargent). Six months later his parents discovered by chance that if their son wanted to become a composer the better course would be to send him to the Royal College of Music in London. Tippett began there a few weeks after the beginning of the summer term in 1923.

Tippett's first study was composition, with Charles Wood. When Wood died, in 1926, Tippett transferred to C. H. Kitson, whose methods he found unproductive. His second study was the piano, with Aubin Raymar, and he also studied conducting with Sargent and Boult. After leaving the RCM in 1928 he decided to settle in Oxted, Surrey, renting a flat at Hazelwood School, the local preparatory school, where in 1929 he was asked to teach French. Part-time schoolteaching, the first of various occupations undertaken to earn enough money to live on and to give some freedom to compose, continued until 1932. He remained in Oxted until 1951, having built a cottage there in 1938. In 1951 he moved to Tidebrook Manor, near Wadhurst in Sussex, in 1960 to Parkside, in Corsham, Wiltshire and in 1970 to a house near Calne, Wiltshire, where he now lives.

In 1924, when still a student, Tippett had agreed to conduct a small choral group in Oxted, in the first instance so that he could extend his knowledge of English madrigals. Later he persuaded the local dramatic society, the Oxted and Limpsfield Players, to collaborate with his choir and venture into opera. He was able to explore the choral and operatic repertory more or less as he wished, and in the process he not only gained further experience of practical music-making but also acquired first-hand knowledge of the English operatic tradition, with performances of Vaughan Williams's *The Shepherds of the Delectable Mountains*, his own realization of the 18th-century ballad opera *The Village*

Opera and Stanford's *The Travelling Companion*. In April 1930 he gave a concert of his own music, which revealed to him that his technique was still immature. Remembering a single tutorial given at the RCM by R. O. Morris, he persuaded Morris to accept him as a pupil, and from September 1930 until July 1932 he studied fugue and 'free composition' with him.

Shortly afterwards Tippett was asked to take charge of music at an annual work-camp in the East Cleveland district of north Yorkshire, where unemployment was particularly severe. The success in 1933 of *The Beggar's Opera* at Boosbeck, a small mining village, encouraged him to write a ballad opera of his own, *Robin Hood*, for the following year. The importance of the work-camps to him was, however, more political than musical. An early dislike of middle-class values had encouraged left-wing views, even in his schooldays. The miserable conditions at Boosbeck led him to a more radical commitment; eventually in the mid-1930s, when the realities of communism and fascism came more into the open, he became Trotskyite in sympathy, espousing an explicitly pacifist rather than political viewpoint. Efforts to provide activities for the unemployed in London were centred on Morley College at that time, and in 1932 Tippett was asked to conduct what became the South London Orchestra (Morley College Professional Orchestra), formed to enable unemployed musicians to continue playing. Having given up schoolteaching, he also found a job as conductor of two choirs run by the Royal Arsenal Co-operative Society. the only such society directly affiliated to the Labour Party. The South London Orchestra gave concerts in various parts of London and continued to flourish long after other 'classes' for the

19. Michael Tippett

unemployed at Morley had stopped. It disbanded in October 1940, when Morley College was almost destroyed in an air raid. At the same time its director of music, Arnold Foster, was evacuated from London. Tippett was asked to succeed him.

In November 1940 Tippett joined the pacifist organization, the Peace Pledge Union, and when his call-up papers arrived he registered as a conscientious objector. His case was not heard until February 1942, when he was directed to non-combatant military duties. He appealed, and in May that year was directed to full-time work in air-raid precautions, the fire service or on the land. He refused to comply, believing that he could best serve the country as a musician. In June 1943 he was brought before Oxted Police Court and sentenced to three months' imprisonment. At Wormwood Scrubs he qualified for one-third remission and was released on 21 August.

During the intervening years Tippett had already made Morley College an important centre of musical activities in London. By the end of the war the choir had grown from eight to 70 voices, and his concert series, emphasizing early music (especially Purcell, Dowland and Monteverdi) and new music, with little or nothing from the 19th century, had become far the most enterprising in Britain. Concerts continued on a larger scale after the war and reached a climax in 1951, when a series of three was given in the newly opened Royal Festival Hall. The same year Tippett resigned from Morley College, having discovered that he could earn a reasonable income from the BBC as a broadcaster (he eventually edited selected talks and published them as *Moving into Aquarius*) and that he could therefore devote more time to composition.

Tippett continued to broadcast, on radio and television, and to conduct, both with professional orchestras in Britain and abroad (notably the USA) and with amateurs (notably with the Leicestershire Schools Symphony Orchestra, with which he began an association in 1965). From 1969 to 1974 he was a director of the Bath Festival, greatly extending its range and restoring its financial stability. In 1959 he was made a CBE, in 1966 he was knighted, in 1979 he was made a Companion of Honour, and in 1983 he received the Order of Merit. He has received several honorary degrees and various other tokens of public regard.

CHAPTER TWO

Works

I Earlier works

Tippett began studying music relatively late in life, at the age of 18. In someone less single-minded this might have been a disadvantage, but he was mature enough to realize that his first priority would be to develop a technique, and he was patient enough to accept that this would take a long time. He followed a self-imposed regimen with remarkable persistence. His early works reveal some of the characteristics of his subsequent output, notably his concern for contrapuntal textures, for extended melodic line and for classical structures; but as a whole they represent an apprenticeship rather than a search for a style. By 1934 he had written in all the principal genres and, notably in passages from *Robin Hood* and the Symphony in B♭, had provided evidence of a natural breadth of phrase and of a potentially novel rhythmic style. His attempts to transcend the twin influences of Sibelius and a folksong style, dominant in English music of the 1930s, were not fulfilled however until he was 30, when he wrote the earliest of his acknowledged works, the String Quartet no.1 (1934–5). Even this did not entirely satisfy him and eight years later he replaced the original first and second movements with a single new one. Apart from the occasional performance in unpretentious surroundings, his first work to be put before a wider public was the Piano Sonata no.1 (then called 'Fantasy Sonata') of 1936–8, issued as a gramophone recording in 1941. He did not gain recognition as a composer of stature, however, until the first performance of his oratorio *A Child of our Time* in 1944.

Tippett was thus slow to develop and even slower to be noticed. Yet these early years also speak of a conviction that if his music had any quality it would find its place, and that he would, in time, achieve an individual style. This moment of recognition came specifically in the finale of the String Quartet no.1, whose manuscript bears the inscription 'Damn braces. Bless relaxes' (from the 'Proverbs of Hell' in Blake's *Marriage of Heaven and Hell*). The original version of this work still contains a number of unassimilated influences (especially in its second movement, a rather academic allegro of Sibelian formal character) and as a whole is uncomfortably disparate in style. But in its first and slow movements Tippett discovered a melodic–harmonic language of genuine originality, and in the finale a rhythmic language that was to prove more significant. This movement is a fugue, like many others in his output. Its long principal theme contains the first appearance of his typically lilting yet asymmetric patterning of long and short beats; the combination of counter-melodies makes the movement branch out into a rhythmic polyphony, later to form the essence of his style. At a time when the radicalism of music was reckoned in harmonic terms above all, the relatively diatonic nature of the quartet's harmony tended to obscure its real individuality, which was in the area of rhythmic counterpoint and the fresh and lucid textures it produced.

Subsequent works developed this aspect of his style,

and it quickly became his most immediately recognizable fingerprint. The opening subject of the Concerto for Double String Orchestra of 1938–9 (ex.1) and the beginning of the scherzo in the String Quartet no.2 of 1941–2 (ex.2) illustrate the salient points (the examples are notated in the real rather than published rhythms, which are a compromise in the interests of ensemble).

Ex.1

The ingredients of the style are not in themselves new. Syncopation and beats of unequal length derive from Tippett's interest in English Renaissance music and to some extent from Stravinsky; the anticipatory rhythm (with the crescendo) in the first bar of ex.1 derives from jazz. What is new is the particular synthesis, and the momentum resulting from the cut and thrust of polyphonic rhythms (see ex.1). In general Tippett has abandoned conventional reiterated accompanimental patterns; and his rhythmic accents do not divide (aurally, at any rate) into small multiples of a unit of pulse, as in Stravinsky or Messiaen. Instead they fall into extended and flowing beats of irregular length. Each bar of ex.2 constitutes one such beat. This imparts a dancing, bounding, almost airborne quality to the music.

Ex.2

The 'harmony' of ex.1 is a composite modality, resulting from the Mixolydian lines and a consequent unity of sound. Harmony in Tippett's early music is often created in this way – as the presentation of a tonality, which will then be placed as an important structural ingredient. While functional harmonic progression is not discarded, more characteristic is the use of harmony as a 'colouring', to achieve some expressive

209

or dramatic purpose. In ex.3, part of the first episode in
the fugal slow movement of the Quartet no.2, the purpose of the harmonies is not to effect a modulation to
the middle entries (this is in fact made two bars later in a
progression involving two chords only); rather it
provides some brief and consoling escape after the rigid
ordering of entries in the exposition. The vertical
elements issue out of the part-writing, an effect reminiscent of Purcell at his more anguished. The climactic
chord of C major in the third bar is thus in no way a
structural use of the tonality of C. It offers a momentary

Ex.3

glimpse of the associations suggested by that particular
way of laying out the chord – of, for example, the rapt
spirituality of the slow movement of Beethoven's op.132
Quartet. Tippett's sensitivity to tonal colour of this sort
is also used on a bolder scale. The Double Concerto is
in A, yet it ends with a new cantabile melody in C. This

could be related to the idea of progressive tonality, or even to the residue of a Sibelian apotheosis. But the chief aural effect is to highlight the broad exultant sound of the tonality of C major, used to create a liberating gesture required by the tension of the work. The Piano Concerto of 1953–5 also concludes in C major, and for similar reasons.

Up to the Symphony no.1 of 1944–5 Tippett's harmony was triadic in origin, but with that work harmony based on 4ths entered his idiom. The obvious model for this was Hindemith. Tippett succeeded, however, in investing 4ths with a highly individual and often very sensuous character, partly through a Debussy-like concentration on the sound *per se* and partly through a subtle transitional technique (involving the alteration of one note). The finest examples are to be found in *The Midsummer Marriage* and the Piano Concerto.

Two other aspects of Tippett's style at this time require comment: his use of traditional structural processes, and of widely different musical idioms in the same work. Up to the Symphony no.2 of 1956–7, he was continually fascinated by classical forms, especially sonata and fugue. This was in part the result of his admiration for Beethoven, in part perhaps a feeling that the most complex of musical forms were the ones to strive after, and in part an indication of his sympathy with the broadly neo-classical temper of music in the 1930s and 1940s. But there were crucial differences between his neo-classicism and that of, say, Stravinsky or Hindemith. Whereas Stravinsky used classical forms to highlight the objectivity of his music and Hindemith to demonstrate their relevance to a contemporary climate, Tippett was far more subjective, using them to express his personal belief that music symbolized a dramatic flow in the psyche and that dynamic musical forms representing both duality and singleness were paramount. Sonata and fugue thus represented archetypal vehicles for containing and articulating such feelings. Few 20th-century composers have grappled with them so persistently. Although Tippett's early maturity certainly dates from the Quartet no.1, subsequent works up to the Quartet no.3 can also be seen as exercises on a grand scale, in which the composer examined his ability to manipulate these forms and, in particular, to place them in a complete work so that the emotional and dramatic weight of the sonata allegro, for example, is tested in different contexts. Thus the sonata allegro of the (original) Quartet no.1 comes second (in fact, the form of this movement derives from the gradual extension of a number of separate motifs after the manner of Sibelius rather than Beethoven, but the function remains the same); in the Piano Sonata no.1 it is third; in the Double Concerto, first; in the Quartet no.2, last; and in the Symphony no.1, again first. Thus every possible placing for this type of movement has been tried out and with it a solution of the consequent problem of dramatic balance over the work as a whole. All three quartets similarly address themselves to the use of fugue, notably the third, three of whose five movements are fugues and in which there is no sonata allegro at all. *A Child of our Time* is dense with fugal textures and the Symphony no.1 concludes with a double fugue that triumphantly sets the seal on Tippett's skill as a contrapuntist.

These forms also enabled Tippett to reconcile the demands of taut musical argument with his naturally expansive lyricism. The opening sonata movement of the Double Concerto, for example, is built up entirely from material in the first statement (ex.1), material which underlies the whole work. In *A Child of our Time* the process was of a different kind. Here Tippett presented himself with the problem of integrating the language of negro spirituals with his own style, and in order to achieve some unity of language he reduced the spirituals to their simplest common denominator, a minor triad with added 7th, and based his own music on constituents of this matrix.

The use of negro spirituals in a work of highly sophisticated European sensibility, or, expressed in another way, Tippett's characteristic mixing of genres, is one of his most individual traits. The oratorio is the most celebrated instance in his early work, but it is not the only one. The Sonata no.1 includes folksong and jazz alongside classical procedures, and the Double Concerto also includes folksong. It would be idle to pretend that the effect of these partnerships is always wholly integrated. But it would be missing the point to say that they were merely the result of an eclectic mind or of an immature technique. In Tippett's case they reflect a considered philosophy of music's nature and function. This was given open expression in *A Child of our Time*, the text of which he wrote himself. In November 1938 Herschel Grynsban, a 17-year-old Polish Jew sheltering in Paris, assassinated a minor Nazi diplomat in order to lodge a desperate protest at the Nazi persecution of his parents. The boy was imprisoned and disappeared. The Nazis retaliated with the most savage pogrom experienced up to that time. With the outbreak of war ten months later the brutality

20. *Scene from Act 3 of Tippett's opera 'The Knot Garden', first performed at Covent Garden on 2 December 1970, with Jill Gomez as Flora, Thomas Hemsley as Mangus, Raimund Herincx as Faber, Thomas Carey as Mel and Robert Tear as Dov (design by Timothy O'Brien)*

acquired official sanction. It was typical of Tippett that his emotional response to the fate of Grynsban and European Jews should be so intense, and that he should attempt to confront so enormous an issue as man's inhumanity to man; and it was natural that to him music should provide the most immediate symbol of the subconscious roots of this contemporary and eternal tragedy. What was unusual was his proposition that man must recognize the 'light' and the 'shadow' in his own personality (set out in the penultimate section of the oratorio) and that a constructive acceptance of both good and evil was the only alternative to a divided world. War was thus a civil war, fratricide and even suicide. This was perhaps too theoretical for general understanding at that time, although Tippett's ability to express both the dark instincts associated with war and the assurance of compassion and peace in terms neither jingoistic nor facile certainly was powerful enough to win him recognition as a composer. For him, however, the belief set out in the oratorio was of fundamental importance. The opera *The Midsummer Marriage* was a dramatization of its meaning and later (1965) he wrote: 'It is the only truth I shall ever say'.

If it is accepted that a balanced personality has come to terms with all its components, whether honourable or otherwise, 'intellectual' or 'emotional', it follows that exclusive pursuit of one, in the interests of purity, therapy or whatever else, is dangerous. It also follows that incompatibility between styles is an illusion. When using negro spirituals in the oratorio Tippett was not merely lighting on a brilliantly imaginative contemporary substitute for the Lutheran chorale in his formal scheme (the work is based on a combination of the

215

traditions enshrined in *Messiah* and Bach's Passions), he was also demonstrating the universal relevance of a supposedly foreign style and culture. The emotional release contained in, for example, 'Nobody knows' does not depend on mystic identification with the and does not depend on a mystic identification with the plight of oppressed blacks, even though blacks alone experienced the misery that gave rise to the music and invented that particular musical archetype (from another amalgam, it may be said, of African and European cultures). Neither was Tippett content merely to juxtapose a developed Western language with 'authentic' spirituals in a sort of surrealistic collage. Integration of language is also part of the philosophy. Ex.4 gives the opening of 'Nobody knows'. Tippett's setting is

Ex.4

direct enough to be almost a quotation, and with its quasi-canonic part-writing and irregular accentuation it is still consistent with his own style. Ex.5 gives the opening of the alto solo 'The soul of man', a number that shows obvious thematic derivations from the spiritual, both motivically and rhythmically, and that is at the same time entirely personal, not least in its subtle yet natural diction.

Ex.5

By 1946, when Tippett began to work on *The Midsummer Marriage*, his first full-length opera, he had developed an original and flexible instrumental and vocal language (the dancing coloratura of the cantata *Boyhood's End* of 1943 is particularly relevant in this respect). This did not make composition any easier,

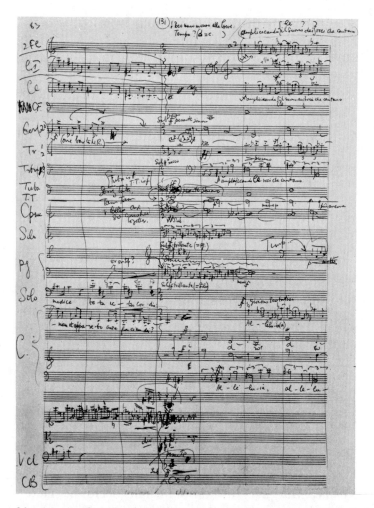

21. Autograph MS of the beginning of St Augustine's 'Vision' from part 2 of Tippett's 'The Vision of St Augustine', composed 1963–5

however, and the opera took about seven years to write, interrupted only by the composition of the Suite in D (largely a reworking of pre-existing material) and the song cycle *The Heart's Assurance* (a major work and one of his most impassioned). The opera was harshly undervalued after its first performances in 1955, partly because its 'images of abounding, generous, exuberant beauty' (from Tippett's essay 'A Composer and his Public' in *Moving into Aquarius*) – created precisely because they were lacking in contemporary music – were considered an anachronism in the ascetic and unresponsive musical climate of the time, and partly because Tippett's own text seemed obscure and pretentious, the narrative element being too tenuous for sympathetic understanding of the protagonists' activities. Yet later performances revealed that the obscurities had been exaggerated, and that the music was of a sustained and exuberant lyricism unequalled in English music.

All the same the work is highly complex and little help is provided by reporting that it is simply the story of lovers eloping, quarrelling and, after a period of mysterious experiences, being reconciled. The difficulty lies in the mysterious experiences, for here Tippett took his characters into regions of the subconscious quite different from the reasonably logical supernatural worlds of fairy tale and myth. This leads to scenes that appear inconsequential and unmotivated, and characters that appear to lack substance and differentiation as human beings. Yet Tippett's main thesis, that difficulties in marriage or, on a wider scale, difficulties in all forms of personal and social contact arise from people's ignorance of themselves, is not only reasonable but particularly suitable for treatment through the medium most powerfully able to project metaphors of subconscious activity. The

music itself illuminates understanding, and a little knowledge of the theories of Jung clarifies matters further.
The opera is, on one level, an exploration of the meaning
of Jung's 'light' and 'shadow', of the exhortation 'dare
the grave passage' in *A Child of our Time*. It also
dramatizes the battle of the sexes and, in particular, the
battle of the generations, the representative of the older
generation being defeated by the younger. As a whole it
is an affirmation of youth and vitality.

Structurally the opera is traditional, with few
procedures that cannot be traced back to Verdi or
Wagner. What singles it out in this respect is the use of
ballet as an integral part of the action (rather than
dramatic colouring or formal contrast), its skilful transitions between the real and the supernatural and its
almost tangible sense of place. That place is the English
countryside, nowhere more vividly evoked than in the
Ritual Dances of Act 2, which succeed in converting
the rather pallid pastoralism of earlier English composers into something far more precisely focussed and
alive with movement. The essence of the opera however
remains in its singing and its wide variety of style, from
the capricious and lyric to the heroic and monumental.

Far from exhausting Tippett's creative imagination,
the proliferation of musical gesture in this large work
opened out further areas for exploration. The rapt,
almost ecstatic calm of such a passage as that in ex.6,
from Jenifer's aria 'Sweet was the peace' in Act 1,
turned out to be a particularly fruitful area of musical
experience. The characteristically pure yet densely elab-
orated lines became even more profusely decorated in
subsequent works, notably the Fantasia concertante of
1953 and the Piano Concerto of 1953–5.

221

With the Symphony no.2 a noticeable change of style set in. Although its lines are frequently as elaborate as those of its predecessors and its structures remain severely classical, the work is more taut and alert; here Tippett began to explore the possibilities of a non-diatonic harmony based on the superposition of related tonalities, most clearly evident in the last chord of the work, which combines the tonalities of C, G and A. Although this interest in the vertical does not inhibit the natural flow of the music, it certainly accounts for shorter and more compact sub-sections, suggesting an aesthetic in which argument is replaced by statement.

II Later works

The implications of this were fully realized in *King Priam* (1958–61), which contrasts so markedly with *The Midsummer Marriage* that, if the evidence of the Symphony no.2 were not there to suggest otherwise, it might have been regarded as a drastic attempt to renew creativity by disregarding past achievement. Almost everything about it is the opposite of the earlier work: instead of an original libretto the work has a text based on Homer (though still written by the composer); instead of giving a message of encouragement it concentrates on the difficulties of marriage, on the impossibility of avoiding the dead hand of fate, and on war; instead of being swept into the drama, the audience is kept at its distance; the singing style is declamatory rather than lyrical; the orchestra is split up into small autonomous ensembles and emphasizes wind and brass rather than strings; the harmony is acid rather than euphonious. Most of all, the sense of surging momentum is discarded in favour of a succession of sharply differentiated structural units. Why Tippett's style changed in this way is a matter for speculation. The important matters concern the new idiom itself. Structurally the work follows an alternating pattern of scene and sung interlude, the scenes presenting rather than developing situations, and the interludes reinforcing this objectivity by discussing the implications of the series of fateful choices made in the scenes. Tonality is not abandoned, but mostly acts as a means of confirming the colour of a scene or episode, whose character is established more by its instrumentation and tempo. Melodic material is succinct and non-developmental, built up in a succession of self-contained groups. Cohesion is achieved through the manipulation of a basic thematic cell, of a semitone plus one other interval – another semitone, a minor 3rd, a perfect or augmented 4th. These features are illustrated in ex.7, part of the monologue in Act 1 scene ii, in which Priam discovers that Paris, the son whom he had ordered to be killed, is alive and will join his family in Troy.

All subsequent works owe something to *King Priam*. The opera emphasized the futility of attempting to create a present paradise. Translated into terms applicable to instrumental music this meant that Tippett began to doubt the validity of using evolutionary structures that reached out towards a conclusion. The Concerto for Orchestra (1962–3), while elaborating the mixed-ensemble format of the opera, deploys numerous and distinct gestures in a kind of circular formal scheme, the three movements ending inconclusively. This work celebrates the richness of the present rather than points towards a future. Much the same could be said of the Piano Sonata no.2 (1962), though its structure is more concentrated and though, as in the Concerto, its 'de-

Later works

velopment' sections reveal that the Beethovenian in-
heritance is not buried.

The work most concerned with the present, and that
on a mystic scale, is *The Vision of St Augustine* (1963–
5), arguably Tippett's most remarkable work. Here the
paradox of the post-*Priam* works becomes acute, for
whereas individual sections remain essentially static,
their disposition creates a tension whose release, once
achieved, inevitably recalls an aesthetic associated with
Beethoven. There results a kind of dynamic calm, which,
at the climactic point of *St Augustine*, a metaphor of the
vision of eternity experienced by Augustine and described in his *Confessions*, succeeds in making articulate
a sense of everlasting present, of timelessness. As a
preparation for this moment in the work Tippett sub-
verted the baritone's central narrative by continually
introducing enormous choral parentheses, representing
the density of thought and feeling embracing the simple
account of the circumstances leading up to the vision. In
order to achieve the desired effect of wide areas of
feeling surging out of the single vocal line, Tippett asked
for the chorus to be rearranged into two divisions only,
of male and female voices; this enabled him to write
such a passage as ex.8, whose top line, for example, is
divided between contraltos and sopranos as is conveni-
ent.

In its use of choral note-clusters, ecstatic vocal
ornamentation and extremely complex textures, *St
Augustine* is symptomatic of the acceleration in
Tippett's stylistic development in later years. The major
works following it have intensified this process and
testify to his refusal to retreat into a private world of
reminiscence, and his determination to wrestle with

Ex.8

major issues in a contemporary fashion. At the same time these works continue to draw from traditional genres, further demonstrating his belief that such genres in their essence embody fundamental musical gestures and that their use should not be confused with a vain attempt to restore defunct manners. Thus *St Augustine* is in the tradition of *The Dream of Gerontius* or *Sea Drift*; *The Knot Garden* (1966–9), *Songs for Dov* (1969–70) and the Symphony no.3 (1970–72) similarly reassert the vitality of opera, song cycle and symphony.

The Knot Garden demonstrates that if the trappings are discarded, opera remains as powerful and immediate an art form as ever. What Tippett discarded are the explanations of why his situations exist, leaving him free to concentrate on the emotional substance of clashes of personality and their outcome. His unusually candid if stylized presentation of raw human relationships and of the need to make a success of the seemingly incompatible ones has produced a score of lapidary compression, notable for its metallic sonorities, its use of a 12-note theme (though not serial technique) to represent fractured relationships and its revival of blues and boogie-woogie in a manner analagous to his use of spirituals in *A Child of our Time*.

Boogie-woogie reappears as a linking refrain in the semi-autobiographical *Songs for Dov*, as do small quotations from Beethoven, Wagner, Musorgsky and himself in a kind of collage that postulates an integration of cultures, periods and life styles. The Symphony no.3 continues to explore the seemingly inexhaustible flow of invention stimulated by the 'light' and the 'shadow'. The abstract musical argument of the first part is answered by the overtly human involvement of the second, where blues again express a basic human predicament and where Beethoven's vision of universal brotherhood (quotations from the finale of his Ninth Symphony) is held to account.

The range of reference is even wider in Tippett's

fourth opera, *The Ice Break* (1973–6), where a blues style again stands for human warmth but where many more diverse strands of high and popular culture are alluded to in his anxiety to transfigure clashes of age, race and social system. The short scenes of *The Knot Garden* are separated by transitional passages, called 'dissolve' (deriving from television techniques); in *The Ice Break* however there are no transitions at all. The resulting counterpoint between an intimate, family drama involving the principal characters and unpredictable, eruptive scenes involving the chorus is the most original feature of the opera, and it also contributes to that ironic attitude towards the human condition which typifies Tippett's music from *The Knot Garden* to *The Ice Break*.

In his Symphony no.4 (1976–7) Tippett inaugurated what can be interpreted as a 'late' period in his output, a series of works concerned with the idea of comprehensiveness, or with summarizing his artistic position. The classicizing tendencies of his earlier works and the more expressionistic tendencies of his subsequent ones are not lost sight of, but they are subsumed within a synthesis which, despite its challenging, passionate (and no longer ironic) agnosticism, speaks of a new creative assurance. The first three of these works – the symphony, the String Quartet no.4 (1977–8) and the Triple Concerto (1978–9) – demonstrate this in the broad sweep of their designs, their continuous cyclic structures and in a new harmonic sumptuousness. In the *Mask of Time* (1980–82), a huge and avowedly summatory work, completed when Tippett was nearly 78, absorbing references to several of his works from *King Priam* onwards and embracing features of his style

Numbers in right-hand margins denote references in the text.

STAGE

The Village Opera (ballad opera, 3) [realization with added music of orig. version by C. Johnson, 1729], vv, 9 insts, 1927–8, unpubd — 202–3

Don Juan (incidental music, Flecker), 1930, lost

Robin Hood (folksong opera, 2, Tippett, D. Ayerst, R. Pennyman), vv, 5 insts, 1934, collab. Ayerst, Pennyman, unpubd — 203, 206

Robert of Sicily (play for children, C. Fry, after Browning), children's choruses, 5 insts, 1938, unpubd

Seven at One Stroke (play for children, Fry), children's choruses, 6 insts, 1939, unpubd

The Midsummer Marriage (opera, 3, Tippett), 1946–52; cond. J. Pritchard, London, Covent Garden, 27 Jan 1955 — 211, 215, 217, 219–21, 222

King Priam (opera. 3, Tippett), 1958–61; cond. Pritchard, Coventry, Belgrade, 29 May 1962 — 222–5, 226, 229

The Tempest (incidental music, Shakespeare), London, Old Vic, 29 May 1962

The Knot Garden (opera, 3, Tippett), 1966–9; cond. C. Davis, Covent Garden, 2 Dec 1970 — 214, 228, 229

The Ice Break (opera, 3, Tippett), 1973–6; cond. Davis, Covent Garden, 7 July 1977 — 229

CHORAL

The Undying Fire (H. G. Wells), Bar, chorus, orch, c1927, unpubd

Psalm in C ('The Gateway') (Fry), chorus, orch, 1930, unpubd

Miners (J. Wogan), chorus, pf, c1935, unpubd

A Song of Liberty (Blake), chorus, orch, 1937, unpubd

A Child of our Time (Tippett), oratorio, S, A, T, B, chorus, orch, 1939–41; J. Cross, M. McArthur, P. Pears, R. Lloyd, London Region Civil Defence Choir, Morley College Choir, LPO, cond. W. Goehr, London, Adelphi Theatre, 19 March 1944 — 207, 212, 213, 215–17, 221, 228

Two Madrigals, SATB, 1942: The Source (E. Thomas), The Windhover (Hopkins); Morley College Choir, cond. W. Bergmann, London, Morley College, 17 July 1943

Plebs angelica, motet, SSAATTBB, 1943–4; Fleet Street Choir, cond. T. B. Lawrence, Canterbury Cathedral, 16 Sept 1944

The Weeping Babe (E. Sitwell), motet, S, SATB, 1944; BBC Singers, cond. L. Woodgate, BBC, 24 Dec 1944

Dance, Clarion Air (Fry), madrigal, SSATB, 1952; Golden Age Singers, Cambridge University Madrigal Society, cond. B. Ord, London, Royal Festival Hall, 1 June 1953

Bonny at Morn (arr. of Northumbrian folksong), unison, 3 rec, 1956

Four Songs from the British Isles, SATB, 1956: Early One Morning, Poortith Cauld, Lilliburlero, Gwenllian; London Bach Group, cond. J. Minchinton, Abbaye de Royaumont, 6 July 1958

Crown of the Year (Fry), cantata, SSA, 2 rec/2 fl, ob, cl, cornet/tpt, perc, handbells, pf, str qt, 1958; Badminton School Choir, cond. Tippett, Badminton School, 25 July 1958

5 spirituals (arr. from A Child of Our Time), chorus, 1958

Wadhurst (Unto the Hills) (J. Campbell), hymn tune, 1958

Lullaby (Yeats), 6 solo vv/A, SSTTB, 1959; Deller Consort, London, Victoria and Albert Museum, 31 Jan 1960

Music (Shelley), unison, str, pf ad lib, 1960; East Sussex and West Kent Choral Festival Combined Choirs, cond. T. Harvey, Tunbridge Wells, Assembly Hall, 26 April 1960

Magnificat and Nunc dimitis, SATB, org, 1961; St John's College Chapel Choir, cond. G. Guest, Cambridge, 13 March 1962

The Vision of St Augustine (St Augustine, Bible), Bar, chorus, orch, 1963–5; D. Fischer-Dieskau, BBC Chorus, BBC SO, cond. Tippett, Royal Festival Hall, 19 Jan 1966 — *218, 226–8*

The Shires Suite (various), chorus, orch, 1965–70; Schola Cantorum of Oxford, Leicestershire Schools SO, cond. Tippett, Cheltenham, Town Hall, 8 July 1970 (1st complete perf.)

The Mask of Time (Tippett and others), S, A, T, B, chorus, orch, 1980–82; F. Robinson, Y. Minton, R. Tear, J. Cheek, Tanglewood Festival Chorus, Boston SO, cond. C. Davis, Boston, Symphony Hall, 5 April 1984 — 229

ORCHESTRAL

Concerto, D, chamber orch, 1928–30, lost

Symphonic Movement, c1930–31, unpubd

Symphony, B♭, 1933, rev. 1934, unpubd — 206

Concerto, double str, 1938–9; South London Orch, cond. Tippett, Morley College, 21 April 1940 — 208–9, 210–11, 212, 213

Fantasia on a Theme of Handel, pf, orch, 1939–41; P. Sellick, LSO, cond. Goehr, London, Wigmore Hall, 7 March 1942

Symphony no.1, 1944–5; Liverpool PO, cond. M. Sargent, Liverpool, Philharmonic Hall, 10 Nov 1945 — 211, 212

Little Music, str, 1946; Jacques Orch, cond. R. Jacques, Wigmore Hall, 9 Nov 1946

Ritual Dances from The Midsummer Marriage, chorus ad lib, orch; Basel Kammerorchester, cond. P. Sacher, Basel, Musiksaal, 13 Feb 1953

Suite, D (Suite for the Birthday of Prince Charles), 1948; BBC SO, cond. A. Boult, BBC, 15 Nov 1948 — 219

Fantasia concertante on a Theme of Corelli, str, 1953; BBC SO, cond. Tippett, Edinburgh, Usher Hall, 29 Aug 1953 — 221

Divertimento on Sellinger's Round, chamber orch, 1953–4; Collegium Musicum Zurich, cond. Sacher, Zurich, Tonhalle, 5 Nov 1954

Piano Concerto, 1953–5; L. Kentner, CBSO, cond. R. Schwarz, Birmingham, Town Hall, 30 Oct 1956 — 211, 221

Symphony no.2, 1956–7; BBC SO, cond. Boult, Royal Festival Hall, 5 Feb 1958 — 211, 222

Praeludium, brass, bells, perc, 1962; BBC SO, cond. A. Dorati, Royal Festival Hall, 14 Nov 1962 — 223

Concerto for Orchestra, 1962–3; LSO, cond. Davis, Usher Hall, 28 Aug 1963

Braint (final variation in Severn Bridge Variations, collab. Arnold, Hoddinott, Maw, Jones, Williams), 1966; BBC Training Orch, cond. Boult, Swansea, Brangwyn Hall, 11 Jan 1967

Symphony no.3, S, orch, 1970–72; H. Harper, LSO, cond. Davis, Royal Festival Hall, 22 June 1972 — 228

Symphony no.4, 1976–7; Chicago SO, cond. G. Solti, Chicago, Orchestra Hall, 6 Oct 1977 — 229

Conc., vn, va, vc, 1978–9; G. Pauk, N. Imai, R. Kirshbaum, LSO, cond. Davis, London, Royal Albert Hall, 22 Aug 1980 — 229

BRASS BAND AND BRASS ENSEMBLE

Fanfare no.1, 4 hn, 3 tpt, 3 trbn, 1943; Band of the Northamptonshire Regiment, cond. C. Marriott, Northampton, St Matthew's Church, 21 Sept 1943

Fanfare no.2, 4 tpt, 1953

Fanfare no.3, 3 tpt, 1953; RAF St Mawgan trumpeters, St Ives Church Tower, 6 June 1953

Wolf Trap Fanfare, 3 tpt, 2 trbn, tuba, 1980; members of National SO of Washington, cond. H. Wolff, Virginia, 29 June 1980

Festal Brass with Blues, brass band, 1983; Fairey Engineering Band, cond. H. Williams, Hong Kong, 6 Feb 1984

SOLO VOCAL

3 songs (C. Mew), 1v, pf, 1929: Sea Love, Afternoon Tea, Arracombe Fair, lost

Boyhood's End (W. H. Hudson), cantata, T, pf, 1943; P. Pears, B. Britten, Morley College, 5 June 1943 — 217

The Heart's Assurance (S. Keyes, A. Lewis), song cycle, S/T, pf, 1950–51; Pears, Britten, Wigmore Hall, 7 May 1951 — 219

Words for Music Perhaps (Yeats), speaker(s). b cl, tpt, perc, pf, vn, vc, 1960; B. Duffell. S. Manahan, A. McCelland, cond. Tippett, BBC, 8 June 1960

Songs for Achilles (Tippett), T, gui, 1961; Pears, J. Bream, Aldeburgh, Great Glemham House, 7 July 1961

Songs for Ariel (Shakespeare) [from incidental music to The Tempest], 1v, pf/hpd, 1962, arr. 1v, fl/pic, cl, hn, perc, hpd, 1964; G. Burgess, V. Pleasants, London, Fenton House, 21 Sept 1962

Songs for Dov (Tippett), T, small orch, 1969–70; G. English, London Sinfonietta, cond. Tippett, Cardiff, University College, 12 Oct 1970 — 228

CHAMBER AND INSTRUMENTAL

Bolsters: The House that Jack Built, Cheerly Men, Yang-Tsi-Kiang, Three Jovial Huntsmen [arr. from unperf. ballet], pf trio, c1926–7, unpubd

Sonata, c, pf, c1928, unpubd

String Quartet, F, 1928, rev. 1930, unpubd

String Quartet, f, 1929, unpubd

Variations for Dudley [Parvin], pf, 1929, unpubd

10 Variations on a Swiss Folksong as Harmonized by Beethoven [WoO64], pf, 1929, unpubd

Variations: Jockey to the Fair, pf, 1930, unpubd

Sonata, e, vn, pf, c1930, frags.

String Trio, B♭, 1932, unpubd; orchd 1932, frags.

String Quartet no.1, 1934–5, rev. 1943; Brosa Qt, London, Mercury — 206, 207, 212

Theatre, 5 Dec 1935; Zorian Qt, Wigmore Hall, 26 Feb 1944 (rev. version)

Piano Sonata no.1, 1936–8, rev. 1942; P. Sellick, London, Queen Mary Hall, 11 Nov 1938 — 207, 212, 213

String Quartet no.2, 1941–2; Zorian Qt, Wigmore Hall, 27 March 1943 — 208, 209–10, 212

String Quartet no.3, 1945–6; Zorian Qt, Wigmore Hall, 19 Oct 1946 — 212

Preludio al Vespro di Monteverdi, org, 1946; Geraint Jones, Westminster, Central Hall, 5 July 1946

Four Inventions, 2 rec, 1954; F. Dinn, W. Bergmann, London, Froebel Institute, 1 Aug 1954

Sonata, 4 hn, 1955; Dennis Brain Wind Ensemble, Wigmore Hall, 20 Dec 1955

Piano Sonata no.2, 1962; M. Kitchin, Edinburgh, Freemason's Hall, 3 Sept 1962 — 223

In Memoriam Magistri, fl, cl, str qt, 1971; London Sinfonietta, cond. E. Howarth, London, St John's, Smith Square, 17 June 1972

Piano Sonata no.3, 1972–3; P. Crossley, Bath, Assembly Rooms, 26 May 1973

String Quartet no.4, 1977–8; Lindsay Qt, Bath, Assembly Rooms, 20 May 1979 — 229

The Blue Guitar, gui, 1982–3; J. Bream, Pasadena, Ambassador Auditorium, 9 Nov 1983

Piano Sonata no.4, 1983–4; Crossley, Los Angeles, Japan–America Theatre, 14 Jan 1985 — 205, 219

See also 'Brass band and brass ensemble'

Principal publisher: Schott

WRITINGS

'A Child of our Time', *The Listener*, xxxviii (1945), 66

'Purcell and the English Language', *Eight Concerts of Henry Purcell's Music*, ed. W. Shaw (London, 1951), 46

Moving into Aquarius (London, 1958, 2/1974)

'Holst: Figure of our Time', *The Listener*, lx (1958), 800

'Our Sense of Continuity in English Drama and Music', *Henry Purcell: Essays on his Music*, ed. I. Holst (London, 1959), 42

'Conclusion', *A History of Song*, ed. D. Stevens (London, 1960)

'At Work on King Priam', *The Score*, no.28 (1961), 58

'The Gulf in our Music', *The Observer* (14 May 1961), 21

'Thoughts on Art and Anarchy', *The Listener*, lxv (1961), 383; repr. in M. Bowen (1980)

'Towards the Condition of Music', *The Humanist Frame*, ed. J. Huxley (London, 1961), 211; repr. in Bowen (1980)

'King Priam: some Questions Answered', *Opera*, xiii (1962), 297

'A Child of our Time', *The Composer's Point of View*, ed. R. S. Hines (Norman, Oklahoma, 1963), 111; repr. in Bowen (1980)

'The Composer Speaks', *Audio and Record Review*, ii/6 (1962–3), 27 [conversation between I. Kemp, M. Rayment and Tippett]

'Michael Tippett', *British Composers in Interview*, ed. M. Schafer (London, 1963), 92

'Music on Television', *The Listener*, lxxi (1964), 629

'An Englishman Looks at Opera', *Opera News*, xxix (2 Jan 1965), 7

'Music and Poetry', *Recorded Sound*, no.17 (1965), 287

'Music for our Time', *The Sunday Telegraph* (3 Jan 1965)

'Schoenberg's Letters', *Composer* (1965), no.15, p.2; repr. in Bowen (1980)

'Schoenberg's Moses and Aaron', *The Listener*, lxxiv (1965), 164; repr. in Bowen (1980)

'The BBC's Duty to Society', *The Listener*, lxxiv (1965), 302

'Waiting for the Public Ear', *The Guardian* (6 April 1968)

'The Festival and Society', *MT*, cx (1969), 589

'The Noise in the Pool at Noon', *The Listener*, lxxxii (1969), 804 [on Ives]; repr. in Bowen (1980)

Untitled essay on the Concerto for Orchestra, *The Orchestral Composer's Point of View*, ed. R. S. Hines (Norman, Oklahoma, 1970), 203

'My Kind of Music', *The Observer* (17 Oct 1973)

'A Personal View of Music in England', *Festschrift für einen Verleger: Ludwig Strecker zum 90. Geburtstag*, ed. C. Dahlhaus (Mainz, 1973), 61

'Michael Tippett Talking about the PPU', *The Pacifist*, xiii/3 (1974), 11 [conversation between M. Soloman and Tippett]

'Michael Tippett', *Hi-Fi News and Record Review* (1975), Jan, 115

'Michael Tippett on Ice', *The Observer* (3 July 1977)

'Back to Methuselah and The Ice Break', *Shaw Review*, xxi (1978), 100

E. William Doty Lectures in Fine Arts, 2nd ser. 1976 (Austin, Texas, 1979)

Review of Shostakovich's *Testimony*, *Quarto*, no.3 (1980), 7

ed. M. Bowen: *Music of the Angels* (London, 1980) [collected articles and interviews]

'The Mask of Time: Work in Progress', *Comparative Criticism: a Yearbook*, iv, ed. E. S. Shaffer (Cambridge, 1982), 19

BIBLIOGRAPHY

J. Amis: 'New Choral Work by Michael Tippett', *MT*, lxxxv (1944), 41

C. Mason: 'Michael Tippett', *MT*, lxxxvii (1946), 137

S. Goddard: 'Michael Tippett and the Symphony', *The Listener*, xliii (1950), 84

J. Amis: 'A Child of our Time', *The Listener*, xliv (1951), 436

A. E. F. Dickinson: 'Round about The Midsummer Marriage', *ML*, xxxvii (1956), 50

C. Mason: 'Michael Tippett's Piano Concerto', *The Score*, no.16 (1956), 63

W. Mellers: 'Michael Tippett and the String Quartet', *The Listener*, lxvi (1961), 405

I. Kemp, ed.: *Michael Tippett: a Symposium on his 60th Birthday* (London, 1965) [incl. R. Donington: 'Words and Music', 87; P. Evans: 'The Vocal Works', 135; W. Mann: 'The Operas: an Allegory and an Epic', 114; C. Mason: 'The Piano Works', 194; W. Mellers: 'Four Orchestral Works' (Conc. for double str orch, Sym. no.1, Sym. no.2, Conc. for Orch), 162; A. Milner: 'Style', 211; A. Ridout: 'The String Quartets', 180]

E. Rubbra: 'The Vision of Saint Augustine', *The Listener*, lxxvi (1966), 74

T. Souster: 'Michael Tippett's Vision', *MT*, cvii (1966), 20

J. Warrack: 'The Knot Garden', *MT*, cxi (1970), 1092

B. Northcott: 'Tippett Today', *Music and Musicians*, xix/3 (1970–71), 34

T. Sutcliffe: 'Tippett and the Knot Garden', *Music and Musicians*, xix/4 (1970–71), 52 [interview]

A. E. F. Dickinson: 'The Garden Labyrinth', *MR*, xxv (1971), 176

B. Northcott: 'Tippett's Third Symphony', *Music and Musicians*, xx/10 (1971–2), 30 [interview]

F. Routh: 'Michael Tippett', *Contemporary British Music* (London, 1972), 282

D. Cairns: 'The Midsummer Marriage', *Responses* (London, 1973), 33

M. A. Sheppach: *The Operas of Michael Tippett in the Light of Twentieth-century Opera Aesthetics* (diss., U. of Rochester, NY, 1975)

J. Agar: *An Approach to the Operas of Michael Tippett* (diss., U. of East Anglia, 1976)

D. Fingleton: 'The Ice Break', *Music and Musicians*, xxv/11 (1976–7), 28

J. Clapham: 'Tippett's Concerto for Double String Orchestra', *Welsh Music*, v/6 (1977), 47

Bibliography

'The Composer as Librettist', *Times Literary Supplement* (8 July 1977), 834 [conversation between Tippett and P. Carnegy]

R. E. Jones: *The Operas of Michael Tippett* (diss., U. of Wales, Cardiff), 1977

Michael Tippett: a Man of our Time (London, 1977) [exhibition catalogue]

G. N. Odam: *Michael Tippett's Knot Garden: an Exploration of its Musical, Literary and Psychological Construction* (diss., Southampton U., 1977)

J. Warrack: 'The Ice Break', *MT*, cxviii (1977), 553

P. Andrews: 'Sir Michael Tippett – a Bibliography', *Brio*, xv/2 (1978), 33; repr. with addenda (Bedford, 1980)

M. Hurd: *Tippett* (London, 1978)

R. E. Rodda: *The Symphonies of Sir Michael Tippett* (diss., Case Western Reserve U., 1979)

E. Walter White: *Tippett and his Operas* (London, 1979)

A. Woolgar: 'A Tippett Discography', *Records and Recordings*, xxiii/5 (1979–80), 26

E. Hughes and T. Day: 'Discographies of British Composers, 4: Sir Michael Tippett', *Recorded Sound*, no.78 (1980), 73

L. Kovnatskaya: 'Maykl Tippet', *SovM* (1980), no.11, p.123

D. Matthews: *Michael Tippett* (London, 1980)

'Tippett at 75', *Composer*, no.70 (1980), 1–37 [essays by S. Aechternacht, S. Clarke, P. Crossley, P. Garvie, P. Gellhorn and F. Routh]

M. Bowen: *Michael Tippett* (London, 1982)

B. V. Vaughn: *The Hope of Reconciliation: a Stylistic Characteristic . . . Culminating in The Ice Break* (diss., Ohio State U., 1982)

F. Sternfeld and D. Harvey: 'A Musical Magpie: words and music in Michael Tippett's operas', *Parnassus: Poetry in review*, x/2 (1982), 188

A. Whittall: *The Music of Britten and Tippett: Studies in Themes and Techniques* (Cambridge, 1982)

P. Driver: 'The Mask of Time', *Tempo*, no.149 (1984), 39

I. Kemp: *Tippett: the Composer and his Music* (London, 1984)

A. Whittall: 'The Transcendental Guest', *Times Literary Supplement* (28 Dec 1984), 1493

M. Bowen: 'Travels with my Art', *The Guardian* (2 Jan 1985)

A. Clements: 'Tippett at 80', *Opera*, xxxvi/1 (1985), 16

P. Dennison: 'Reminiscence and Recomposition in Tippett', *MT*, cxxvi (1985), 11

P. Driver: 'Tippett at 80: a Personal Tribute', *MT*, cxxvi (1985), 11

N. John, ed.: *Operas of Michael Tippett* (London, 1985)

G. Lewis: 'Tippett: the Breath of Life – an Approach to Formal Structure', *MT*, cxxvi (1985), 18

G. Lewis, ed.: *Michael Tippett O.M.: a Celebration* (Tunbridge Wells, 1985) [incl. M. Bowen: ' "Dare, Divining, Sound" ', 215; A. Broadbent and G. Lewis: 'Tippett on Record', 235; S. Clarke: 'Birth and Renewal', 47; P. Dennison: 'Tippett and the New Romanticism', 175; R. E. Jones: 'Ritual, Myth and Drama', 59; R. F. Jones; 'Tippett's Atonal Syntax', 119; G. Lewis: ' "Spring come to you at the farthest/In the very end of harvest." ', 199; D. Matthews: ' "Mirror upon mirror mirrored" ', 35; W. Mellers: 'Song and Dance Man', 23; N. Morris: ' "Simply the thing I am shall make me live" ', A. Whittall: 'Tippett and the Modernist Mainstream', 109]

D. Matthews and A. Payne: 'Sir Michael Tippett: a Birthday Offering', *Music and Musicians* (1985), Jan, 7

M. Wren: 'A Piece for our Time: Theological Reflections on Sir Michael Tippett's "The Mask of Time" ', *Theology*, lxxxviii (1985), 209

BENJAMIN BRITTEN

Peter Evans

CHAPTER ONE

Life

Edward Benjamin Britten was born in Lowestoft on 22 November 1913. His mother was an amateur singer and his early musical experience was on a homely level. But at the Norwich Festival of 1924, the boy, who had been composing prolifically but without guidance from the age of five, attracted the interest of Frank Bridge, and became his pupil. Bridge was at this time abandoning the elegant but rather faded idiom of his early work in favour of an experimental style that was then exceptional in England for showing acquaintance with the music of Bartók and of Schoenberg's school. A highly professional craftsman, he required Britten's precocious invention to be supported on extensive technical foundations. The keenly developed ear, rather than theoretical preconceptions, was to be the final arbiter, but the widest exploration of other composers' music could aid the development. Britten was helped both to acquire a superb compositional technique and to look beyond the limited horizons of the selfconsciously nationalist manner that then enjoyed favour in much institutional teaching.

In 1930, however, Britten entered the Royal College of Music, where he developed impressive pianistic skills under Harold Samuel and Arthur Benjamin. After Bridge's enlightened and concentrated training, composition study with Ireland seemed less than ideally stimulating, and the difficulty of securing performances for his music added a further disappointment. His official op.1, the Sinfonietta (1932), shows how he continued to look abroad for stimulus. After hearing *Wozzeck* in 1934, he visited Vienna, but plans for studying with Berg foundered on opposition at home. The Sinfonietta had been performed at a Macnaghten–Lemare concert a year earlier; other chamber music and choral pieces were given in that series and the Phantasy for oboe quartet at the Florence ISCM Festival of 1934. In 1935 Britten found a new outlet for his talents in providing music for a series of documentary films made by the General Post Office. By satisfying the highly particularized yet diverse demands of this medium from very slender and often unconventional resources, he cultivated the expressive immediacy and technical aptitude that were to distinguish his operatic work.

W. H. Auden was a fellow member of the film unit, and the collaboration proved congenial enough to be maintained outside their studio work. It gave rise to social and political commentaries, sometimes bitterly ironic, like the song cycle with orchestra *Our Hunting Fathers* (1936) and the choral *Ballad of Heroes* (1939), music of a brilliance British critics found almost suspect. Auden's emigration to the USA helped to bring to a focus in Britten a discontent that seems to have been compounded of political despair, artistic exasperation and the sense of social estrangement which homosexuality still exacted: he left England for North America in 1939. With him was the tenor Peter Pears, whose individual artistry was to inspire many of the composer's greatest operatic roles and song cycles. The set of Michelangelo Sonnets (1940) was the first of these; together with the Rimbaud cycle *Les illumina-tions* (1939) it completed Britten's emancipation from native inhibitions in setting texts. But instrumental scores were still predominant at this stage, and the two concertos (of 1938 and 1939), the *Sinfonia da requiem* (1940) and the First Quartet (1941) show increasing structural subtlety. A first operatic essay, however, *Paul Bunyan* (1941), to an Auden libretto, was withdrawn (it was revived in 1976); before its epoch-making succes-sor was conceived, Britten had returned to England.

Only after having uprooted himself had he come to recognize his own heritage. A chance reading of an article by E. M. Forster on the Suffolk poet Crabbe crystallized Britten's resolve to leave for home; even on the voyage he began to refine and diversify his command of English verse-setting in *A Ceremony of Carols* (1942). The highly characteristic *Serenade* (1943) marked a new stylistic poise, and at this time, discovering the commanding stature of Purcell (see *Rejoice in the Lamb*, 1943), he began to develop a comparably meticulous declamation. During these war years Britten, a conscientious objec-tor, was engaged, often with Pears, in giving concerts to audiences of all kinds. Pears also took part in the productions of the Sadler's Wells Opera Company: its director, Joan Cross, arranged that the opera on which Britten had been working since the beginning of 1944, *Peter Grimes*, should be performed to mark the reopen-ing of the Sadler's Wells Theatre on 7 June 1945. Its emphatic success stamped Britten as the most gifted music dramatist England had produced since Purcell, and its eager acceptance by foreign houses showed the judgment to be more than parochial.

The years following *Grimes* were amazingly prolific,

241

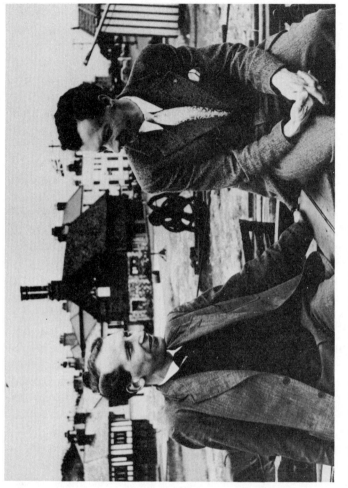

22. *Benjamin Britten (right) with Eric Crozier in front of the Moot Hall, Aldeburgh, 1949*

such works as the Donne Sonnets, the Second Quartet, the orchestral *Young Person's Guide to the Orchestra* (Variations and Fugue on a Theme of Purcell), the cantata *St Nicolas* and the *Spring Symphony* all appearing as interludes in a succession of opera scores. Yet a country with a history of the most fitful support of opera (and with only two established opera houses) was scarcely ready for a full-scale native repertory. So Britten turned to the medium of chamber opera, using an orchestra of solo instruments and few enough singers to be deployed on modest provincial stages. *The Rape of Lucretia* (1946) and *Albert Herring* (1947) successfully put these resources to contrasted ends, and in 1947 the special company formed to present the works became the English Opera Group. A year later the new group helped to launch, under Britten's direction and in the small Suffolk town where he had recently settled, the first Aldeburgh Festival. Despite his occasional acceptance of commissions from elsewhere, the production of music to be included in the festival's programmes was the composer's principal activity for the rest of his life, while most of his finest work as a pianist and conductor was done there. Britten's preference for writing with highly specific, and often domestically familiar, performing conditions in mind is equally clear in his compositions for amateurs, especially children (*Noye's Fludde* of 1957 is his masterpiece in this field), the works he wrote for his friends to play at Aldeburgh, and the three 'parables' written during the 1960s for performance in Orford Church during the festivals.

However, large-scale opera was not neglected, even though it could find no place at Aldeburgh. For the Festival of Britain in 1951, Britten was commissioned to write *Billy Budd*, produced at Covent Garden in December that year; in June 1953 his next opera was also launched there, *Gloriana*, a study of Queen Elizabeth I presented as a tribute to Elizabeth II at the time of her coronation. Another important commission was for the chamber opera *The Turn of the Screw* (1954), given at the Venice Biennale; this was the first score in which Britten adapted some features of 12-note practice to his own ends. A recital tour by Britten and Pears which took them to the Far East in 1955 proved influential: Balinese music affected the sonorities of the full-length ballet *The Prince of the Pagodas*, presented at Covent Garden on 1 January 1957, while the Japanese noh play *Sumidagawa* and its musical conventions determined the nature of the first parable, *Curlew River*, in 1964, a crucial turn in the composer's stylistic development. Before that drastic paring down of his textures there was a magnificently rich operatic score in *A Midsummer Night's Dream*, for the 1960 Aldeburgh Festival. In the same year Britten executed a commission for the University of Basle with the genial *Cantata academica*, while at the end of 1961 he completed a work that seemed to offer a comprehensive review of many aspects of his style, the *War Requiem*, given in May 1962 to celebrate the consecration of the new Coventry Cathedral. The *Requiem* had a great impact on its early audiences, and marked a second peak (*Grimes* and its aftermath being the first) in Britten's esteem with the general public.

In 1961 an artistic partnership with Rostropovich began that proved very fruitful, the Cello Sonata of that year being followed by the Cello Symphony (1963) and three solo cello suites. Britten visited Russia in 1963, the year of his 50th birthday (an event signalled in England by many celebratory performances, and a volume of essays on and around the composer). On a return visit to the USSR in 1965, he and Pears stayed in a Composers' House in Armenia, where the cycle *The Poet's Echo* on Pushkin poems was written for Rostropovich's wife, Vishnevskaya. Also in that year Britten was commissioned by the United Nations to write an anthem, *Voices for Today*, which was given its first performances simultaneously in London, Paris and New York.

The scope of the Aldeburgh Festival was much enlarged by the opening in 1967 of a concert hall, the Maltings at Snape. Though this could also house bigger opera productions, its first result was to bring into greater prominence Britten's powers as a conductor of the orchestral repertory. Indeed, his next opera, *Owen Wingrave* (1970), was written for no stage but in response to a BBC commission for a television opera, first transmitted in 1971; it was subsequently staged at Covent Garden in May 1973. One month later, the composer's only opera for the enlarged Aldeburgh Festival resources, *Death in Venice*, was produced. Though a serious illness prevented Britten from conducting, the work gave to Pears perhaps the most demanding role assigned him in some 35 years of their musical partnership.

In the three years after *Death in Venice*, Britten was too ill to produce work on the largest scale, yet he was able to complete a fifth canticle and a cycle of Burns songs (both for Pears and both with harp accompaniment, for Osian Ellis), some choral pieces and an orchestral suite on folktunes. The dominating works of this final period are a solo cantata with orchestra, *Phaedra*, written for Janet Baker, and a third string quartet. No less significant for a conspectus of his life's work was the release in 1976, for performance by the English Music Theatre Company (successor to the English Opera Group), of his 1941 operetta, *Paul Bunyan*.

Britten received numerous honours from British and foreign learned societies and universities; his speech on receiving the Aspen Award in 1964 is an important statement of his artistic beliefs. He became a Companion of Honour in 1952 and a member of the Order of Merit in 1965. He was made a life peer (the first musician to be so honoured) in 1976; he died at Aldeburgh in the same year, on 4 December.

CHAPTER TWO

Instrumental music

Until Britten returned to England in 1942, instrumental writing was predominant in his output: 18 out of his first 25 sizable scores are chamber and orchestral works. The majority of these depend on that juxtaposition of 'characteristic' kinds of music proper to the suite and the variation set, but across this decade can also be seen the refinement of an individual view of sonata structure. Whatever capacity Britten demonstrated for drawing the most various thematic characters from a restricted store of motivic shapes, his most ambitious structures depend on the behaviour, not merely the demeanour, of their themes. The principal early scores seem to prepare therefore for a development from which the composer was subsequently deflected, only isolated works returning to the problems of 'absolute' structure they investigate.

The op.1 Sinfonietta of 1932 owes its chamber-orchestral disposition (and much more) to Schoenberg's First Chamber Symphony, but the typical sonority is less opaque. The persistent motivic use of a major 7th, which often draws the music into conflicting tonal orbits, creates a tension that is unexpected in the context of a rather modal melodic vocabulary. In the first movement the peak is deferred through a middle section that avoids both tonal and thematic crisis until the restatement, which presents both subjects simultaneously; even then a decisive outcome is postponed until their reappearance at the end of the tarantella finale. Cyclic structures of the kind encouraged by the Cobbett chamber music competitions were essayed in the Phantasy Quintet for strings (1932) and the Phantasy for oboe and strings (1932). The oboe quartet is quasi-programmatic, notably in its emergence from and return to silence through a cryptic march; Frank Bridge's *Oration* may have influenced this scheme, though the pastoral lyricism of Britten's central section stems from less adventurous English models. The uncertainty of tone was to recur for some years yet, though the solitary early piano work, *Holiday Diary*, is notable for the establishment, in 'Sailing', of a wholly personal sonorous formula, of mild diatonic dissonance. By contrast, the Violin Suite op.6, written in Vienna, attempts some wilfully 'modern' sophistications, but is at its most acute in the blatant parody of its Waltz.

Britten took parody techniques much further in the string-orchestral Variations on a Theme of Frank Bridge op.10 (1937), ranging from the lampooning 'Aria italiana' through the Gallic insouciance of the 'Romance' to the pungent wit of the harmonic displacements in the 'Wiener Walzer'. This brilliant performance reflects a young man's delight in his craft, but there were also signs that more than a pasticheur was in the making: the cogent dramaticism of Britten's introduction to Bridge's theme and its final reharmonization in a rich but taut D major are both prophetic, while the power of the somewhat Mahlerian Funeral March is disconcerting only because as yet it lacks an appropriate context. The appearance of a mordant waltz and a smartly vulgar march in the Piano Concerto op.13 (1938) suggests that Britten was continuing to borrow received manners, yet the opening Toccata explores the contrast between percussive piano figurations and sustained orchestral sonorities in a big sonata essay. In the Violin Concerto op.15 (1939) Britten produced a highly original structure in which only the lyrical first subject returns, at last in an indisputably tonic D major, the exposition having been more a revolt against F than a definition. Variations that are no longer genre pieces are amassed into an impressively bulky passacaglia finale, sounding at its turn to D major a note of bold simplicity that foreshadows the *Grimes* style.

Two more important works in D form the peak of Britten's early instrumental period: the *Sinfonia da requiem* op.20 (1940) and the First Quartet op.25 (1941). The programmatic movement titles of the symphony are not interpreted in inertly apt music: 'Lacrymosa' treads steadily forward to an explosive confrontation of its contrasted elements rather than a recapitulatory consolidation, and the 'Dies irae' scherzo (the finest of several dances of death in early Britten) projects its thematic fragments dynamically across broad spans before they are splintered apart again in graphic enactment of chaos. With the slow finale, 'Requiem aeternam', Britten's debts to Stravinsky and Mahler (still distinct strains in, say, *Our Hunting Fathers*) are fused into a peculiarly luminous sound; the D major and B♭ major strata which co-exist here filter into brightness the constituents of the first two movements' brooding D minor. The four-movement design of the string quartet suggests deference to Classical example, but the detailed working is not derivative: for example, the movements' key relationship, D–F–B♭–D, also operates within the first and last movements. The alternation of slow and fast sections provides a more fundamental source of dramatic contrast in the first movement than the sonata pattern of the allegros. Both this and the ardent slow movement offer original expressive schemes in idiomatic quartet terms.

The success of *Peter Grimes* and of his own kind of chamber opera set Britten on a new course, from which instrumental scores became an occasional distraction. The Second Quartet (1945), in tribute to Purcell, culminates in an even bigger ground-bass finale than the Violin Concerto's, a Chacony that is a tour de force, both of variation techniques and of oblique relationships to the C which is the quartet's centre. The first movement extends the practice of simultaneous restatement to material that was presented in three successive stages (the second two of these having stemmed from the first); the various time-levels at which modulation operates contribute to the structural subtlety. A Purcell theme prompted a less sophisticated piece in the following year, the orchestral *Young Person's Guide* (composed for a film, 1946); this has exceeded its didactic function to become a popular concert piece.

Two smaller instrumental works, the sombre *Lachrymae* variations for viola and piano and the *Metamorphoses after Ovid* for solo oboe appeared in 1950–51, but there followed ten years with no instrumental score from Britten. It was the artistry of the Soviet cellist Rostropovich that reawakened Britten's interest and, beginning with the Cello Sonata op.65 (1961), he wrote five works for that artist. With movement titles like 'Elegia' and 'Marcia' the Sonata might appear another 'characteristic' work, but its principal movements, though small in scale, make their points against the background of sonata practice. A remarkable economy of material (much of it derives simply from the juxtaposition of tone and semitone) unobtrusively tightens a work of great delicacy; though it is sometimes bizarre, it is far less assertively brilliant than were many of the earlier instrumental works. Still further from the conventional virtuoso's music is the concerto Britten wrote for Rostropovich in 1963, the kind of partnership involved being made clear in the title, 'Symphony for Cello and Orchestra'. Its opening movement is Britten's most spacious sonata plan, and to allow a full exchange of material between the participants there is an unabridged restatement, leaving to a rich coda the typical contrapuntal conflation of themes. As in the sonata, much is made from cells as minute as the semitone step (e.g. in the second subject), yet the paragraphs grow convincingly. The spectral scherzo is almost all derived from a three-note cell (again, tone plus semitone), and the profound adagio and variation set share thematic features that make of them one impressive final block in Britten's most commanding instrumental work. As well as the three suites for solo cello, inventive responses to Rostropovich's skills and a temptingly restrictive medium, there are other tributes to distinguished players, like the Harp Suite and the *Nocturnal* (after Dowland) for guitar, a set of quasi-programmatic variations still more poetic than *Lachrymae*.

In the last years of his life Britten released for publication a string quartet of 1931 that antedates the op.1 Sinfonietta but shares many of its features, notably in weaving a texture of Schoenbergian motivic density from material which still echoes the modal rhapsody of

251

CHAPTER THREE

Solo vocal music

Numbering well over 100 settings, Britten's contributions to the literature of song dominate his native scene; and few of his contemporaries elsewhere offer formidable rivalry. In remaining faithful to the 19th-century medium of solo voice and piano, he recognized the simple practicality that singers still perform far more often in recitals than with the specialized ensembles of so much modern music; indeed, the majority of his songs were written to enlarge the repertory of his own superlative recital partnership with Pears. Yet his practice of conceiving his songs as cycles (ranging typically between five and nine settings) that, although not concerned with narrative sequence, do not effectively split up, his tendency to write with a quite particular vocal timbre as his ideal, and his assumption that his interpreter will bring pronounced literary sensibilities to bear have all restricted the frequency with which this repertory is to be heard.

The range of verse he set from English sources alone is remarkably wide, while cycles from Rimbaud, Michelangelo, Hölderlin and Pushkin, all set in the original languages, could suggest a selfconscious virtuosity. In fact, the German and Russian texts were chosen as tributes to the songs' dedicatees, but the early cycles, both written during Britten's American period, seem to have been part of a necessary process of emancipation. By mastering these unfamiliar worlds of feeling, he acquired the confidence to re-approach his native territory without the defensive irony of the pasticheur. Before he left England, the dominating influence of Auden had set the tone of Britten's social commentary, from lacerating irony to calculated banality, while musical models as various as Mahler, Berg and Stravinsky could be accommodated only by treating the choice of style as commentary in itself. Thus the 'symphonic cycle' *Our Hunting Fathers* op.8 (1936) uses Stravinsky as a route to the hard brilliance of 'Rats away' while the final sequence, including a Funeral March, inevitably evokes Mahler. But Messalina's grief, drawn with a compassion that is Britten's own, allows one to forget models. This score, Britten's first for full orchestra, remains extraordinarily incisive, and the ultimate unity of Auden's rather prickly anthology, on man's relations with the animal world, is countered musically by an embracing tonal plan and by motivic recurrences, notably of a 'canker' shape (including major 3rd darkening to minor) characteristic of later Britten. The Auden cycle with piano *On this Island* op.11 (1937) abandons such unification for a sequence of neatly realized songs, and the pastiche ranges from glittering Baroque ornament to the clipped rhythms and complacent vacuity of sophisticated 1930s dance music (exploited more consistently in the *Cabaret Songs*, to Auden texts, of 1937–9). But when irony is least in evidence, as in the 'Nocturne', Britten is content to rely on the simplest of means to fashion his most satisfying expressive shapes.

The pervasive Lydian inflections of *Les illuminations* op.18 (1939) may owe something to Fauré, but their extensions towards the major scale with flattened 7th and sharpened 4th, and thence towards tritonally opposed centres (B♭ and E) as structural poles (commonly marked by fanfares), are notable moves into quintessential Britten territory. A new subtlety of mood is more apparent in modest songs like 'Antique' and 'Départ' than in the heavily neo-classical 'Royauté' or the spectral Mahlerian march of 'Parade' (adapted from an earlier quartet movement). After this cycle with string orchestra, unified by a motto theme, the Michelangelo Sonnets op.22 (1940) again revert to self-contained structures. In the Rimbaud songs, the orchestra's opulent harmonic textures were the musical essence, the voice enunciating often in an inflected monotone. But the clean bright piano textures of the Michelangelo settings, though unified by pithy motifs and admitting illuminating comments, remain subservient to the great arcs, spanning complete songs, of the voice. In learning thus from Italian models, Britten finally broke free from English inhibitions of 'good taste' and prepared the way to the ample melodic shapes of his early operatic style. The simplification of texture throws greater weight than ever on the placing of modulatory twists: a song like 'Sonnet XXX' sidesteps banality with breathtaking assurance.

These contrasted achievements behind him, Britten sampled his new-found Englishness in choral contexts and then was ready to celebrate it by devising a comprehensive anthology of English poems, the *Serenade* op.31 for tenor, horn and strings (1943). Despite the framing horn solo and some effective cross-references, this cycle is unified by its succession of nocturnal moods rather than by common motifs. Its imagery, reliant on resources as simple as juxtaposed triads and semitonal deflections, and its frequently nostalgic tone seem legacies from a Romantic world of sound, yet the harmonic structures are newly imagined (the Keats sonnet), the tonal shifts elusive (Blake's *Elegy*), while Baroque devices like ground and fugue find an entirely original expressive synthesis (*Lyke-wake Dirge*). The dexterity with which Jonson's *Hymn to Diana* is transformed into a scherzo-like ritornello aria reflects a superb technical equipment and a mercurial imaginative response to the suggestiveness of words. In the Donne Sonnets op.35 (1945) Britten faced the challenge of Purcell in setting texts of truly Baroque elaboration in a manner that recalls the *Harmonia sacra* both in fevered spirituality and vocal declamation. Rhythmic vitality in the melody is offset by persistent *Affekt* figurations in the piano, and a tension results that is not released by apparent restatements (see 'O my black soule'). The gentle fluidity Britten had learnt in *Les illuminations* is still admitted, but as relief from apocalyptic vision rendered in fantastic detail. The final song achieves a powerful climax by pitting against a five-bar ground bass a mounting stream of metric and tonal contradictions. After this emotionally demanding cycle, *A Charm of Lullabies* op.41 (1947) can appear unduly relaxed, offering few of the previous anthology's flights of imagination.

Six years later the Hardy cycle *Winter Words* op.52 afforded a remarkable contrast to the Donne settings: the pruning of textural detail, partly a response to Hardy's homely verse, also indicated a new direction in Britten's work. His choice of poems ensures that the restrained tone is not a monotonous one, and a mood like that created by the first song's tonal obliquities is subtly compounded. In strophic pieces like *Midnight on the Great Western*, obviously illustrative figures are assimilated structurally, while the jostling images of *The Choirmaster's Burial* fuse into that rarity, a successful ballad. But the simplicity of the last song is the most daring: this cry for a primeval nescience matches the poet's spare phraseology yet forms the climax of an inevitable musical growth. Spareness of another kind is to be heard in the poignant miniatures Britten made of Waley's translation in Songs from the Chinese op.58 (1957). The accompanying guitar's evanescence (especially in glissandos) provides an apt symbol for moods of autumnal disillusionment, of vanished sweetness, that pervade the poems and Britten's settings. In *The Old Lute* harmonic progression is replaced by a single complex in which any or all notes of the mode can appear together; such embalmed music was to be explored later in the church parables. The individual sonority of the Chinese Songs is won from slender means, but in the *Hölderlin-Fragmente* op.61 (1958) Britten's self-denial is more fundamental, all sonorous charm being renounced at times. In place of the early cycles' exuberant imagery, apparently 'abstract' motifs are worked out. But the piano's 12 different root triads in *Sokrates und Alcibiades* against the singer's graceful line symbolize, as certainly as in *Billy Budd*, a beauty that must awaken love; and the trance-like crossing of lines in the final song perfectly combines fidelity to the poem with musical logic.

The Hölderlin cycle is unlikely ever to become popular, for its texts invite thought as much as sensation; it was withheld from publication until 1963. Shortly before its composition Britten addressed in a

23. *Benjamin Britten and Peter Pears in 1967*

cycle with orchestra the wider audience that had welcomed the *Serenade*. The *Nocturne* op.60 (1958) is another anthology of poems on night, sleep and dreams, but the use of a new obbligato instrument in each setting encourages more fantastic illustrative detail. The cycle is bound into a continuous structure by a ritornello for the string orchestra, as of a sleeper's deep breathing; the individual songs thus intrude like a chain of dreams. That many of the verses Britten set are extracted from larger contexts (and thus lack finality) aids this impression, while enigmatic and obsessive texts conjure up a less neatly picturesque nocturnal world than that of the *Serenade*. Simple strophic forms are replaced by a free arioso style, and the tonal situations are far more fluid. The Shakespeare sonnet which ends the cycle turns to a consistent symbolism the semitonal relations that control so much of the *Nocturne*: music which offers C minor and/or Db major simultaneously seems to hover on the border between waking and dreaming.

Britten's first three cycles were written for the soprano Sophie Wyss, and all but one of the next eight for Pears. So the Songs and Proverbs of William Blake op.74 (1965), a creative response to the unique baritone timbre of Fischer-Dieskau, are distinctive in both tessitura and vocal style. Pears's nervous energy, as discernible in the controlled ecstasy of his cantabile as in the precision of his melismata, was best suited to aspiration (which need not imply optimism); Fischer-Dieskau, no less 'intellectual' a singer than Pears, seems better adapted to expressions of world-weariness, even of fatalism, tempered by philosophic resignation. Pears chose the verses for the Blake cycle, the proverbs (which Britten based on a 12-note aphorism) forming transi-

tions, musical and textural, between seven songs that
touch on a remarkable range of Blake's themes. *A
Poison Tree*, a dramatically developing song of a kind
rare in Britten, reaches its terrible climax through a
burgeoning of contrapuntal texture. *Ah Sunflower*, ex-
pressing passionate longings against the dragging under-
tow of a weighty piano bass line, is also difficult to
parallel. But, as in other Britten cycles, it is the final
song that distils the essence of the poet's message: its
symbol of eternity is fused with the burden of human
misery in an ostinato (the last segment of the proverbs'
row) that closes the cycle in profound, yet resigned,
sadness. Britten's use of loose alignment in the proverbs
was an early adaptation from his 'parable' techniques.
The Pushkin cycle *The Poet's Echo* op.76 (1965), written for Vishnevskaya, makes more extensive use of these
innovations, most memorably in the multiple echoes
superimposed in the first song; appropriately these
sounds reverberate faintly in the later songs too, notably
The Nightingale and the Rose, a piece of fragile beauty,
and *Lines Written during a Sleepless Night*, a troubled
fantasy around the ostinato of ticking time. With the
cycle of 'lyrics, rhymes and riddles' by the Scottish poet
William Soutar, named after the ninth song *Who are
these Children?* op.84 (1969), Britten accepted free
alignment as one more procedure among very many;
indeed, the cycle seems almost a retrospective exhibition
of his song techniques. The pieces in Scots dialect are
miniatures deftly wrought from simple materials, but the
four English songs show Britten at his most committed,
for Soutar's denunciation of man the murderer, and his
impassioned concern for children in a world ordered by
their guilty elders, recall preoccupations of the com-

poser. He returned to Scots verse in *A Birthday Hansel*
op.92 (1975), settings of Burns for voice and harp, and
was far more open to suggestion from native musical
idioms than in the Soutar cycle. Pentatonicism, drones
and so on are fused into typical ambivalent tonal contexts without suffering the distortions of parody.

Britten's last vocal work was also his only true solo
cantata, *Phaedra* op.93 (1975), written for Janet Baker
and scored for strings and percussion, with harpsichord
and cello for the recitatives. This continuo group does
not very convincingly assume responsibility for making
psychological points, but the rest of this dramatic scena,
an intense miniature in Britten's operatic manner, is
strengthened by detailed tonal and motivic symbolism.
With its reminders of *Lucretia*, it also points up how
sparing the composer became of that early lyrical ef-
fusion in these ascetic last scores.

To five extended vocal pieces Britten gave the title
'canticle'. All treat religious subjects though their
diverse texts, from miracle play to Sitwell and Eliot, are
without liturgical associations. The first (1947) sets
Francis Quarles's rapturous meditation around 'My
beloved is mine and I am his' as a miniature cantata for
tenor and piano, tonally unified, and with textures alternating between homophony and nervously lithe counterpoint. Graphic imagery is never disruptive, and quiet
ecstasy never challenges order. In *Abraham and Isaac*
(1952) an alto is added, facilitating the representation of
father (tenor), son (alto) and the voice of God (both
voices in speech rhythm at close intervals). A dramatic
scene of many short sections is built from a few musical
shapes. With a sonata-like logic as well as patent symbolism, the two chief themes, of God and of man, which,

before the central action, were originally divided by the greatest gulf (E♭–A) finally are at one in the E♭ tonic. Contemporary with *Billy Budd*, this piece reflects the opera's compassion for both sacrificial victim and anguished celebrant, but final deliverance is painted with a radiance that looks forward to *Noyes Fludde*. So artless a tone is nowhere to be heard in the third canticle, *Still Falls the Rain* (1954), a schematic alternation between declamatory tenor recitatives (unified by the refrain of the title words), and a set of variations for horn and piano. The instrumental theme consists solely of whole-tone steps and falling 4ths, but the variations alternately contract and widen these intervals; each variation is echoed as a piano commentary on the following recitative. These two planes merge in the final variation, where voice and horn in serenely diatonic mirror movement signal the 'Dawn' that follows the terrible night (a commentary on the wartime raids couched in the imagery of a Passion scene). This also provides the resolution of a key dichotomy that has affected the whole canticle, a piece that takes its place with the opera that immediately preceded its composition, *The Turn of the Screw*, among Britten's supreme imaginative feats in the adaptation of abstract procedures to specifically expressive ends. In 1971 Britten turned again to his 'canticle' type of setting, to accommodate Eliot's *Journey of the Magi* (for countertenor, tenor and baritone). This narrative piece is less terse than the Sitwell setting, yet Britten's primary material is now still more restricted: two intervallic cells that interact to create the harmonic events of almost every bar. Melodically they are supplemented by the plainsong *Magi videntes stellam*: appearing when the Magi arrive at the place appointed, it is recalled imperfectly as they rationalize a disturbing experience. After the chilled passion of this familiar Eliot, the tone of his early *The Death of Saint Narcissus* seems lacerating. In setting this poem as his last canticle (1974), Britten reflected a preoccupation with death that haunts much of his late music, yet his art remained free from disruptive over-emphasis. Simply by amplifying the poem's correspondences, a controlled structure has been created, supported by a characteristic tonal argument: intermingled C major and C♯ minor are finally resolved into their common pitch, E. This fifth canticle is for tenor with harp, prompting Britten to newly imagined accompaniment figurations; but his power is clearest in a voice part which captures contrasted expressive nuances yet spans the piece as one subtly organized line.

CHAPTER FOUR

Choral works

The choral variations *A Boy was Born* (1933) are settings of chiefly 15th-century Christmas texts, but
Britten was at pains to avoid limply decorous modality and ad hoc textural illumination, which are the
stock English responses to such texts. The initial
four notes (i.e. those to the title words) form a motif
from which the whole cycle is built; though the structural and textural procedures are more common in 'absolute' instrumental composition, the poems' varying
moods are given an incisive edge. *Ballad of Heroes*
(1939), a political piece for a very general public, is less
intensively written, but retains interest for some prophetic touches. With another Auden text, *Hymn to St
Cecilia* (1942), Britten struck his most characteristic
vein of choral sonority. Instrumental effects are still
cultivated (the mercurial scherzo tinkles like a magic
glockenspiel), but broad triadic writing brings a new
repose. Yet the Lydian sweetness of 'O dear white children' is underlined by a tension inevitably discharged at
'O weep, child'. Long-term planning, as much as the
recurrences of the memorable opening invocation,
draws three sections of the poem into a remarkably
unified emotional span. *A Ceremony of Carols*, written
at the same time, reverts more obviously to the English
tradition sidestepped by *A Boy was Born*, but the use of
single vocal lines and their canonic multiplication and of

an elaborate tonal plan gives this cycle strength as well as manifold felicitous colourings. The radiant tone and simple harmonic resources are maintained in the cantata *Rejoice in the Lamb* (1943). The range of Christopher Smart's eccentric imagery produces a musical diversity that a blatantly Purcellian 'Hallelujah' refrain strives to unify like a verse anthem; less obviously, motivic principles forge subtle connections between the most unlike contexts.

Britten's first large-scale choral and orchestral work, written in 1949, clearly owed little to native oratorio traditions: it converted the English choir, large and a little ponderous, into an apparently virtuoso body. But criticism remained ponderous, much of it wasted on the title, *Spring Symphony*. Brimming over with the prodigal invention of the post-*Grimes* period, this work shows little concern for economical developmental processes hallowed by Classical precedent, but the arrangement of its poetic anthology in four groups roughly corresponds to the shape of a Classical succession of movements. The juxtaposition of three slow settings or three scherzo settings, however, impelled the composer to aim for pointed contrasts within his groups: constantly new permutations of solo voices, choral textures and chamber orchestra scorings contribute to the kaleidoscopic enchantment of this work. As befits the subject, bright airy moods predominate, though the shadows of the slow section blacken startlingly at the climax of the Auden setting. The finale is an extended May Day pageant, shaped as a ternary design weighty (and tonally stable) enough to draw the whole work together in a blaze of optimism. An echo of this ebullience may be heard in the *Cantata academica*, written ten years later. The worthy Latin text, in praise of the University of Basle (which commissioned the work for its quincentenary), sounds a note of academic dignity, but Britten, thinking perhaps of students as much as of studies, set it with a light touch. In fact, the cantata is replete with selfconsciously 'learned' devices including super-ordering of its movements' tonal fixed points (pedals but not necessarily tonics) by a series that is heard melodically in the central movement; this also includes a flippantly erudite fugue.

In the *War Requiem* (1961) Britten for the first time employed the choral and orchestral medium to treat the topics that most exercised him. Instead of another opera presenting a parable of innocence and wickedness, he overtly denounced the bestiality of war in interleaving the Requiem text with war poems of a victim, Wilfred Owen. The latter are reserved for the tenor and baritone soloists and illuminated by the intricate detail of a chamber orchestral accompaniment, whereas the Latin text veers between liturgical impassivity (boys' voices with organ) and mankind's mingled mourning, supplication and guilty apprehension (chorus with broad orchestral textures, sublimated at times by soprano soloist). The planes are spatially separated and the work's dramatic impact depends chiefly on stark confrontations rather than symphonic working-out. But persistent tritonal relations (most schematic in the mirrored scalic movement of the Agnus Dei) provide an audible unifying factor as well as a fund of symbols.

The *Requiem*'s fusion of diverse traits from earlier Britten suggested a determination to give his utmost in preaching an urgent text. It was perhaps over-performed initially, blunting the sense of outrage, but its power to impress should effortlessly outlive the contempt that was a common critical second thought. Like an appendix to the *Requiem*, the *Cantata misericordium* (1963) also culminates in a soft, bright music of sleep. But violence is less the central issue here than man's need to counter it with compassion; the parable of the Good Samaritan is simply told – in Latin, chiefly to give the cantata, written for the centenary of the Red Cross, easy international currency. Modest instrumental resources contribute an individual colouring while the major 3rd relationship (F♯ and D) that predominates substitutes ambivalence for the oppositions in the *Requiem*. The many short sections are drawn together by a ritornello for string quartet, ensuring that one constantly reflects on the moral even while glimpsing successive stages of the action. In its delicate structural and tonal balance this is one of Britten's most beautifully realized works. Another 'international' work, the anthem *Voices for Today* (1965), suffers from too many and varied texts: though they all share one vision, of a peaceful future, cumulative musical momentum is sacrificed until the final section, setting excerpts from Virgil's fourth eclogue. Ten years later, the eight medieval lyrics, *Sacred and Profane* (1974–5), for five voices, show a darkened horizon: though a remarkable range of moods is encompassed with little recourse to the mock-archaic, the work is most memorable for its death-obsessed settings.

Although Britten was sometimes called on to produce church music, he showed no sustained interest; thus a *Te Deum* of 1934 received its *Jubilate* only in 1961. The 1944 *Festival Te Deum* and the wedding anthem *Amo ergo sum* (1949) are patently occasional pieces, the former a rare example of polymetric writing and the

CHAPTER FIVE

Music for children and amateurs

Britten's refusal to adopt the loftiest view of the composer's mission made him ready to provide music that can please amateur performers, however young, while stretching their powers. His remarkable ability in such music was to treat fundamentally simple yet freshly imagined ideas with an ingenuity that prevents their descent to a banal or cloying level. *Friday Afternoons* op.7 (1933–5) offered children a delightful escape from the clichés of school songbooks, while *The Ballad of Little Musgrave and Lady Barnard* (1943) cleverly tapped the modest vocal resources of a prisoner-of-war camp. But *St Nicolas* (1948) harnessed amateur forces to professional, without embarrassing either. Apart from the dominating tenor role of Nicolas, this cantata is sung by amateur choral groups and accompanied by strings – of which only a solo quartet needs to be professional – piano duettists, organist and percussionists, led by one professional. Very distinctive sonorous contrasts result from this disposition, and they are put to dramatic ends, as when the simple choral writing of the opening invocation gives way to impassioned eloquence at the reply of the saint's spirit. Even the naivety of episodes like the 'Pickled Boys' finds a congruous place in a scheme that refused to respect traditional stylistic proprieties.

In *The Little Sweep* (1949) children are given operatic roles, while the audience acts as opera chorus. The work, originally preceded by a play in which children and adults plan their production together, demonstrates the mechanics of opera and its ability to tell a story with an emotional intensity that, invested only in words, could appear an embarrassment. Like much other Britten this is a parable about cruelty and compassion. If its moral is inscribed somewhat in black and white (adults are all caricatures), the poignant figure of Rowan, caught between the worlds of those who have and those who have not, is subtly realized in music. Expressive effects are typically created by playing off unchanging elements against tellingly varied ones: Sam's refrain 'How shall I laugh and play?' and the many ostinato movements encourage the listener to respond to crucial modifications.

A still more ambitious entertainment for performance by children is *Noye's Fludde* (1957): the few adult soloists and ten professional players are heavily outnumbered by children's voices and instruments (including bugles, recorders, handbells and teacups). Inspired by the naive stylized language of the miracle play, Britten struck here a vein of childlike music that communicates very powerfully; in fact it depends on compositional skills of a high order. The three hymns which act as buttresses in the total structure are drawn into elaborate relationships with other material, but also colour much that is apparently quite independent of them. Thus, although superficially no more than a series of delightful tableaux, the work remains perennially satisfying (and not only to young audiences) because it is magnificently integrated. Psalm cl, set by Britten in 1962, takes the 'ad lib' principle further than any other

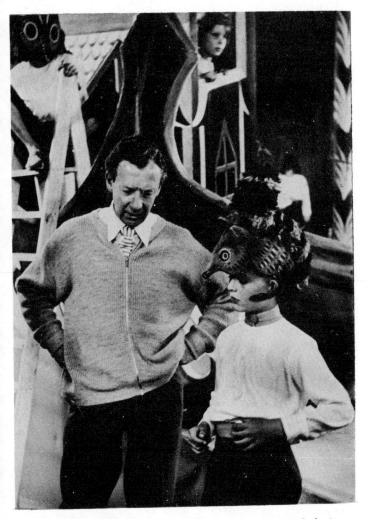

24. *Benjamin Britten in conversation with a Squirrel during a rehearsal of 'Noye's Fludde' in 1958*

of his scores for amateurs, but still contrives to make some delicate points.

Two works for rather special children are the *Gemini Variations* (1965) and *The Golden Vanity* (1966). The variations, on a Kodály theme, were written for two talented Hungarian brothers, and ingeniously provide for them as flautist and violinist but also as solo or duo pianists. The 'vaudeville' on the traditional ballad was also written for quasi-professional continental performers, the Vienna Boys' Choir, and it too is deftly made, though it lacks something of the warmth with which Britten responded to English amateurish enthusiasm. An unexpected transfer to this context of a continental 'ballad' was the *Children's Crusade* (1968), a setting of Brecht, made for the Wandsworth School Boys' Choir (with their own percussionists, two pianists and an organist) to perform in St Paul's Cathedral on the jubilee of the Save the Children Fund. Brecht's calculatedly flat presentation of a harrowing narrative is matched by Britten's consistently syllabic word-setting, his avoidance of 'set piece' elegances and of any elegiac commentary on the children's fate. Musical pattern-making is left to the instruments, two of the principal structures applying Britten's characteristic modifications of 12-note principle. A curiously laconic piece, it disturbingly reveals the child's world as a microcosm of our own. The *Welcome Ode* op.95 (1976) is noteworthy in that Britten's last completed work proved to be a piece, unpretentious and as optimistic as the *Spring Symphony* finale, for young people's chorus and orchestra.

CHAPTER SIX

Dramatic works

At the revival in England in 1976 (35 years after its first performance in New York) of Britten's first opera, *Paul Bunyan*, the eventual unveiling of what had been a tantalizingly inaccessible work revealed no obvious reasons for its suppression. Inevitably its succession of mainly strophic pieces, with continuity dependent on a spoken title role and a ballad-singer narrator, gives no opportunity for the musically integrated act structures of Britten's mature operas, and the range of evident models, many of them from American popular music, can appear disconcerting. But the musical invention is not only effervescent but often subtle and moving. If the modish tone of, say, the Telegraph-boy's song recalls that of the final song in *On this Island*, in the blues quartet a popular style has been made poignant, while at a few moments like Inkslinger's soliloquy a character is illuminated in startling relief. In the prologue, the haunting choral refrain is similarly prophetic of Britten's later penetrating simplicity, while the wide range of orchestral colourings of the whole operetta confirm how well prepared he was for the synthesis of his talents called for by *Peter Grimes*.

It is too early to predict whether *Bunyan* will become a repertory piece; perhaps an over-refinement of detail is all that stands between it and the truly popular success accorded to the best in musical comedy. With *Peter*

25. Peter Grimes (Peter Pears) and Ellen Orford (Joan Cross) in a scene from the first performance of the opera (London, 1945)

Grimes (1945) over-familiarity is the more likely handicap to critical evaluation: a work that was audacious in its assumption that an English operatic tradition could exist can now appear unadventurous by comparison with the composer's later achievements, not to speak of other more radical operatic styles. Britten had been deliberately cultivating a lucid manner, shunning complexities though not subtleties, in the compositions following his return to England; *Peter Grimes* provided an impressive test of its range. Flexible modality, with a penchant for Lydian and Phrygian inflections, prevents the staleness a scalic melodic norm might induce, and tonal ambivalence (of many kinds in addition to the fundamental tritonal relationship A–E♭) reveals dramatic potentialities within a primarily triadic vocabulary. Though the initial impression may be of too many minor figures, each given its deft character-sketch, these fall into place as details illuminating a composite character, the crowd, that is a menacing force in the opera: with the sturdy choral textures of *Peter Grimes*, an English speciality was effectively transplanted to the stage at last. The two main characters, Peter in particular, are rounded out musically by set arias that exploit sweeping cantabile phrases with few 'tasteful' inhibitions, but also afford innumerable acute psychological insights. The 'number' principle does not exclude wide-ranging motivic usages: the repercussions of Grimes's 'and God have mercy upon me' (a characteristic Lydian shape) can be sensed in every subsequent development. Recitative, though sometimes too evidently a connecting mechanism, maintains momentum while giving a fine cutting edge to the language. The orchestra, still used in an essentially traditional manner,

275

contributes luminous accompanimental detail; its interludes are vivid mood-pictures, tightly enough organized to make good concert pieces, but their tensions are truly of the drama (most notably in the storm and the brooding Passacaglia). The final interlude reveals as certainly as that of *Wozzeck* how deeply bound up the composer was in the fate of his flawed hero.

For, while *Peter Grimes*, with its pub, dance-hall and church scenes, can be prized for its graphic depictions of an enclosed English community, these are attendant upon more fundamental themes: innocence a prey to violence, the outsider a prey to society. Since the composer's death, the view has gained currency that his predilection for operatic characters who assume the burden of what society has chosen to regard as their guilt reflects an equivocal response to his own homosexuality. The relationship appears most direct in the cases of Grimes, Vere and Aschenbach, but parables of a similar kind may be discerned in *Owen Wingrave* and *The Rape of Lucretia*. In no other Britten work is a message so didactically presented as in *Lucretia* (1946), the first of the chamber operas. The Male and Female Chorus who observe the action, pointing out motives and morals, finally attempt an interpretation of the antique tragedy in terms of Christian morality. Though it has been much criticized, musically the sublime resolution of this final section is the goal towards which the whole opera has been directed, as is confirmed by the elaborate but highly consistent tonal scheme, turning about the C major of Lucretia's purity and its recovery in the epilogue's state of blessedness. No less pervasive is the use of motifs, those of Lucretia and Tarquinius undergoing innumerable transformations as a clue both to suppressed meanings and to a still wider symbolism, of the female and male forces. Woman's passive role is underlined by the various reflective ensembles, sensuously beautiful in sound, in which the women occupy themselves in household tasks. The invasion of this world by the ruthless vigour of Tarquinius is vividly prefigured in his ride to Rome. *Lucretia* shows a greater flexibility than *Peter Grimes* in effecting transitions between the driest (piano-accompanied) recitative and the most lavish cantabile. Set pieces are even more prevalent, but the voice often moves quite freely in relation to a coherent musical design maintained in the orchestra. Britten's chamber orchestra (quintets of strings and wind, harp, percussion) is deficient in warmly blurred tutti, strong in 'characteristic' solo dispositions. So set pieces tend to treat colourings with an almost Baroque consistency, as in the purple mourning of the english horn in Lucretia's last aria.

The symmetry of casting in *Lucretia* was appropriate to so conscious an enactment of tragedy. Turning one year later to domestic comedy in *Albert Herring*, Britten sought to depict a heterogeneous assembly of English character-types by means verging on caricature. He drew on a wide range of stock musical idioms – Victorian anthem, Empire-builders' march, drawing-room ballad and so on – but by adroit techniques of distortion, primarily harmonic, was able to convey, not the falsity of a sentiment so much as its disproportion to the situation. Even the inane flatulence of Lady Billows's clichés can give way to a sustained emotional fervour represented by Britten in terms that could find a place in the most serious of his works (for example at 'Is this all you can bring?'). The threnody plumbs a grief wholly at variance with a situation known to be absurd: a compositional tour de force in its climactic superimposition of many individual laments, it is also the opera's emotional peak. The finest examples (Mozart's above all) offer support for such ambivalence, but do not help Britten to combat the anti-climactic effect of the mourned hero's return. Albert points a moral, but the development of character heard earlier in his cautious assimilation of Sid's vein of heady popular song seems to be forgotten here, and the victory over a censorious society appears provisional. Britten's chamber scoring is in striking contrast to that of *Lucretia*. A fine range of incisively ridiculous effects is overshadowed in the memory by the sonorous idealization of prosaic situations: the eerily attractive children's-games music, for example, and the nocturne in the darkened fruit shop. The same instrumental resources were used yet again in 1948 for Britten's version of *The Beggar's Opera*, to surround the original arias with a wealth of exuberant or pathetic detail; sometimes they are built into spans that transcend the nature of the musically unpretentious 'ballad opera'.

At the furthest remove from chamber opera, *Billy Budd* (1951) is Britten's biggest, most densely written opera. Its menace stems from much more than the large orchestra and chorus, though their weight is deployed overpoweringly at such moments as the muster before the execution scene. Whereas the sombre theme of *Peter Grimes* was softened by the trivia of Borough life, here the only escape from oppression and violence lies in the sweet, hopeless shanties and the promise of action against the enemy. The restriction to an entirely male vocal range and predominantly small melodic intervals

278

creates the obsessive tone, and elaborate motivic usages intensify this; they are often laconic – a single F minor chord can re-establish Claggart's brutal dominance, a single saxophone note recall the novice's despair. The harmonic range is unusually wide for Britten, but the symbolic role of the triad is elevated as never before in the orchestral interlude during which, offstage, Vere must make his peace with the boy he is to sacrifice. At the other extreme, semitonal major–minor conflicts within the harmony are worked out as semitonal key oppositions in some of Britten's most dramatic tonal structures. The three central characters are incisively drawn: Vere, the intellectual among men of action, is a subtly refined portrait, but the demoniac Claggart, with his anguished intimations of a beauty that he must crush, is no villainous stereotype; Billy, the victim armed only with the strength of innocence, is more difficult to present convincingly, though his ardent lyricism makes its effect unfailingly in the intra-musical drama.

Billy Budd was not recognized at first to be a peak in Britten's operatic career; only after it was re-cast from four into two acts, in 1960, did its granite quality secure the admiration that now keeps it firmly in British repertories. The next opera, *Gloriana*, fared still worse, being comprehensively misunderstood by an audience assembled to celebrate (a coronation) rather than to experience. Yet, despite the searching character study of Elizabeth which is central to this work, it remains Britten's most 'public' opera, startlingly so after the hermetic world of *Budd*. The extreme integration of that opera is exchanged for set pieces so divisible from their contexts as to be numbered and titled; the connecting material is sometimes rather perfunctory. But the blocks of pieces that form great tableaux (the choral dances at Norwich and the instrumental dances at court), even if they reduce the action's urgency, contribute vitally to the portrait of Elizabeth with her subjects. The character of Essex, though well developed, serves ultimately to create dramatic situations that further reveal his queen. Musically, *Gloriana* has a wide range of archaic reference, none of it fastidiously precise, but congruity stems from the modality that permeates this score. An audience sustained by some knowledge of the historical background will savour the opera's musical richness, but it has made little progress on foreign stages.

Britten returned to chamber opera in 1954 with *The Turn of the Screw*. Though Myfanwy Piper's adaptation of Henry James necessarily required the invention of words for ghosts who in the original are silent, the opera captures, and in some respects intensifies, the fevered atmosphere of the story. Its ambiguities, of innocence touched with worldly wisdom, terror mounting in a serene environment, led Britten here towards a music that hints at profound emotional substrata. The plot unfolds through many short scenes, but across their diversity a single musical argument is conducted in orchestral interludes that are variations on, progressive turns of, a 'screw' theme which is Britten's first 12-note proposition. In fact, tonal centres had never been more important to him: setting out from an initial A, associated with the Governess's moral resolution, the theme's statements are based on 'tonics' which steadily rise throughout Act 1 to the A♭ consistently associated with the ghosts' evil allurement: by an inverted series of moves the 'tonics' of the Act 2 variations descend from that pitch until, within the final scene, a tonal conflict between A and A♭ appears as the logical (and powerful) representation of the battle waged between the Governess and Quint for the soul of young Miles. The ramifications of this scheme are complex, but its dramatic force is direct. Other themes, like the sinuous 'corruption of innocence' symbol, have more immediate prominence within the story, but all remain audibly referable to the 'screw' theme's basic shape (ascending 4th, falling minor 3rd); highly distinctive instrumental colourings, as in the ghosts' music, augment the dramatic force of this restricted intervallic source material. The children's music is subject to Britten's distortion techniques; of a less grotesque order than those of *Herring*, they suggest frightening vistas of self-knowledge. But, as in James, it is through the Governess's emotional development that one is drawn most tensely into this psychological drama.

The next opera followed, after the longest gap in the succession, in 1960. Meanwhile, a full-length ballet, *The Prince of the Pagodas* (1956), offered a formidable challenge, denying the composer the precise verbal stimuli and the complex dramatic situations of opera. It makes use of recurrent material, varied or developed, but to programmatic as much as structural ends; neither the closeness of motivic weave nor the dramatically forceful tonal relations of Britten's operas are esssayed. A colourful scenario has been used as a pretext for some brightly coloured orchestral invention. Direct echoes of Tchaikovsky and Stravinsky (*Apollo*) pay apt tribute, but there is also a strong debt to the pentatonicism of Balinese gamelan music, its delicately percussive sonorities being reconstructed from Western resources. The final pas de six is playable as a concert piece, and conductors have assembled various suites to give wider currency to a neglected score.

For *A Midsummer Night's Dream* (1960) Britten employed a larger chamber orchestra than his original group, facilitating blends of wood, brass and strings; a range of bright percussion, two harps and harpsichord, contribute to one of Britten's most individual scores. Shakespeare's text was virtually halved, by Britten and Pears, and all the action takes place in the wood until the middle of the final (third) act; so the arrival at Theseus's court signifies a major shift, to mundane existence after the dreamlike happenings that, contrived by the fairies, have befallen both lovers and mechanicals. These three orders of being remain on musically independent planes: the fairies' music, glittering or eerily enchanting (ostinato and inversion both serve magical ends; countertenor and coloratura soprano dominate), is frequently shaped into set pieces; the four lovers, whose fates are so confusingly linked up, share in the fretful development of a single leading theme; and the mechanicals employ an earthy parlando against cryptic orchestral commentary. This diversity is set into frames – in Act 1 a slow-breathed ritornello, symbolizing the wood, and in Act 2 a prelude, interlude and postlude, symbolizing sleep. Both these unifying ideas have a 12-note basis, as do the hunting-call interlude (which contrives the major transition in Act 3) and many other contexts, all fundamentally tonal. The most memorable, the sleep music, constructs four simple chords from a set, wonderfully contrasted in timbre, and makes variations upon the succession, finally as background to the fairies' benediction. The fairies' later blessing, on the household, marks a highpoint of their luminous music, and restores an enchantment lost during the parody of 19th-century Italian opera that the mechanicals consider appropriate to their play.

No Britten opera is less preoccupied by a moral or more generous in its musical variety than *A Midsummer Night's Dream*. In the light of his later work it seems like the celebration of riches he was shortly to renounce. Of operas in the traditional sense he wrote none for a decade, and the 'parables for church performance' appeared ascetic in much more than their restriction to the small circular ramped stage on which Colin Graham's productions were mounted. *Curlew River* (1964), directly based on the noh play that had caught Britten's imagination in 1956, established a ritual conducted in stylized gestures by masked male singers, accompanied by a small group of instruments (treated discretely rather than orchestrally), that was followed in two later works. Specific Japanese reference was abandoned in William Plomer's librettos and the parables were as if enacted by monks in a setting of medieval Christendom: each work is framed by a plainsong hymn, and an instrumental fantasy on this leads into and out of the inner action. In the heterophony of these fantasies Britten discarded the harmonic movement of his earlier style, and the elevation of melodic properties throughout the three works makes harmony no more than an aggregate, often of a complete 'mode'; within this, exact alignment of the voices is no longer essential, and the musical discourse floats free of metrical constraints. Without blurring the definition of characters, the close network of melodic relationships and the clear pattern of recurrences makes of each work a unified span of

26. *Autograph sketch ('On the river bank') from Britten's church parable 'Curlew River', composed 1964*

highly individual experience – above all, *Curlew River*. Its obsessive quest mounts to a despair from which a consoling vision brings release: the use of a great Christian hymn, *Custodes hominum*, at this access of divine grace is reproduced in the shaping of the other two parables. *The Burning Fiery Furnace* (1966) notably extends the range of the new manner in representing the vanities of Nebuchadnezzar's court: the barbarous processional music in praise of the heathen god is brilliant in its multi-tonal superimpositions, and the whole work reinstates the semitonally opposed fields (D/Eb) of earlier Britten. In *The Prodigal Son* (1968) the contrast is rather between the chromatic wiles of the Tempter and the diatonic Bb world of the Father's home.

The three parables offer morals at differing levels – personal, political and domestic – but are facets of a single stage of the composer's development. Their textural and temporal innovations were assimilated into Britten's technical armoury and on his return to opera, in *Owen Wingrave* (1970), were applied to contexts otherwise more reminiscent of his earlier dramatic works. The most remarkable of several freely related textural (rather than merely linear) superimpositions is the interview at which Sir Philip disinherits Owen, and the rest of the company, overhearing, add their reactions. In an earlier fantasy scene the whole family hurl their accusations in a freely aligned fugato. Its nightmarish eruptions depend for their full effect on the techniques of television, for which the opera was written, but transfer to the stage represents a compensating gain in musical depth. The fugato creates 12-note fields of a consistency Britten had rarely used before, and material throughout the opera derives audibly from the 12-note succession of three chords which, like the clangour of battles long ago, opens the work; the diminished triad stamps the Wingraves' warlike fixations (and the family portrait themes) whereas Owen's apostrophe to peace, the opera's overt climax, touches on all 12 perfect (usually major) triads. Despite the obvious similarity in the dénouements (a simple ballad creating, like 'Malo' in *The Turn of the Screw*, a pathetic irony), *Wingrave* operates at a less shadowy level than the earlier James adaptation; the expectations of a television audience may have prompted Britten to develop even the lesser characters into quite lavish portraits.

Death in Venice (1973) thrusts a formidable weight on to the central character, Aschenbach, whose thoughts, visions and dreams are the essence of Mann's narrative, skilfully converted into a libretto by Myfanwy Piper. Much of this huge role is soliloquy, for the great writer makes little contact with those around him. Tadzio, the beautiful Polish boy he idealizes, is silent (he acts in balletic terms, as do his mother and their friends) and all other characters are glimpsed through their effect on Aschenbach: by using a single baritone for many of them, Britten follows Mann's hint that these messengers of fate have no separate identity. But the workings of fate are still more pervasive: a single motivic cell (at the outset D–C–E–E♭) breeds throughout the music of the opera, symbolizing on the physical level the hidden growth of the plague and on the emotional level the corruption of Aschenbach's proud idealism into abject passion. Venice, represented by a variant form of this motif, harbours the canker, yet its capacity to allure is wonderfully realized in the gondola

27. *Benjamin Britten in 1976*

music that articulates much of the action. The only independent material is Tadzio's – exotic in the Locrian bias of its A major and its bright percussive sounds, but inert in relation to the restless motivic developments of Aschenbach's pursuit. The two acts offer pointed correspondences: the sunlit scene of beach games (choral music and ballet), of which Aschenbach makes an Apollonian vision, and the dark dream of Dionysiac orgies; his aspiring hymn to Apollo and a harrowingly clear-eyed view of the Dionysiac abyss, foreshadowing his end. Though this opera is Britten's most sustained study of obsession, monotony of tone never threatens. Even his distortion techniques are relevantly used for the piazza café orchestra and the sinister strolling player's music. But rounded arias are few, and Aschenbach's prized detachment is conveyed in piano-accompanied recitative. Though the melodic conflations of the parables are not habitual, the opera is characterized by textures thin enough for the motivic concentration and interaction to impinge forcefully. Britten's several sketches for the orchestral postlude confirm the significance he attached to this profoundly moving operatic swan-song; as it washes away the corruption that has festered throughout the second act, the specific erotic nuances of the opera appear far less fundamental than the ideal of beauty it reaffirms against the threats of intellectual desiccation and lacerating frenzy.

WORKS

Numbers in right-hand margins denote references in the text.

STAGE

op.		
17	Paul Bunyan (opera, prol. 2, Auden), 1941: New York, Brander Matthews Hall, 5 May 1941; withdrawn; revived, BBC, 1 Feb 1976, Snape Maltings, 4 June 1976	241, 247, 273
33	Peter Grimes (opera, prol. 3, M. Slater, after Crabbe), 1944–5; cond. Goodall, London, Sadler's Wells, 7 June 1945	115, 241, 244, 249, 250, 265, 273, 274, 275–6, 277, 278
37	The Rape of Lucretia (chamber opera, 2, R. Duncan, after A. Obey), 1946, rev. 1947; cond. Ansermet, Glyndebourne, 2 July 1946	243, 261, 268, 276–7, 278
39	Albert Herring (comic chamber opera, 3, E. Crozier, after Maupassant), 1947; cond. Britten, Glyndebourne, 20 June 1947	243, 277–8, 281
43	The Beggar's Opera [after John Gay] (ballad opera), 1948; cond. Britten, Cambridge, Arts, 24 May 1948	278
45	The Little Sweep [originally part of Let's Make an Opera] (chamber opera, 1, Crozier), 1949; cond. Del Mar, Aldeburgh, Jubilee Hall, 14 June 1949	44, 269–70
50	Billy Budd (opera, 4, Forster, Crozier, after Melville), 1951; cond. Britten, London, Covent Garden, 1 Dec 1951; rev. in 2 acts, 1960; cond. Britten, BBC, 13 Nov 1960	244, 257, 262, 276, 278–9
53	Gloriana (opera, 3, W. Plomer), 1953; cond. Pritchard, Covent Garden, 8 June 1953	244, 279–80
54	The Turn of the Screw (chamber opera, prol. 2, M. Piper, after H. James), 1954; cond. Britten, Venice, Fenice, 14 Sept 1954	244, 262, 280–81, 286
57	The Prince of the Pagodas (ballet, 3, Cranko), 1956; cond. Britten, Covent Garden, 1 Jan 1957	244, 281–2
59	Noye's Fludde (children's opera, 1, Chester miracle play), 1957; cond. Mackerras, Orford Church, 18 June 1958	243, 262, 270, 271
64	A Midsummer Night's Dream (opera, 3, Britten, Pears, after Shakespeare), 1960; cond. Britten, Aldeburgh, Jubilee Hall, 11 June 1960	244, 281, 282–3
71	Curlew River (church parable, 1, Plomer), 1964; directed Britten, Orford Church, 12 June 1964	36, 243, 244, 257, 283, 284, 285
77	The Burning Fiery Furnace (church parable, 1, Plomer), 1966; directed Britten, Orford Church, 9 June 1966	36, 243, 257, 283, 285
81	The Prodigal Son (church parable, 1, Plomer), 1968; directed Britten, Orford Church, 10 June 1968	36, 243, 257, 283, 285
85	Owen Wingrave (opera, 2, Piper, after H. James), 1970; cond. Britten, BBC television, broadcast 16 May 1971; stage première cond. S. Bedford, Covent Garden, 10 May 1973	245, 276, 285–6
88	Death in Venice (opera, 2, Piper, after Mann), 1973; cond. Bedford, Snape Maltings, 16 June 1973	245, 252, 276, 286, 288

ORCHESTRAL

op.		
1	Sinfonietta, chamber orch, 1932: London, 31 Jan 1933	247
4	Simple Symphony, str, 1933–4; cond. Britten, Norwich, 6 March 1934	240, 247–8, 251
9	Soirées musicales [after Rossini], 1936	
10	Variations on a Theme of Frank Bridge, str, 1937; Boyd Neel Orch, Salzburg, 27 Aug 1937	248
12	Mont Juic [after Catalan dances], 1936–7, collab. Berkeley	
13	Piano Concerto, 1938, Britten, BBC SO, cond. Wood, London, Queen's Hall, 18 Aug 1938	190–91, 241, 248–9
15	Violin Concerto, 1939, rev. 1958; Brosa, New York PO, cond. Barbirolli, 28 March 1940	241, 249, 250
16	Young Apollo, pf, str, 1939, Toronto, Aug 1939	
19	Canadian Carnival (Kermesse canadienne), 1939; cond. Raybould, BBC, 6 June 1940	
20	Sinfonia da requiem, 1940; New York PO, cond. Barbirolli, 30 March 1941	241, 249
21	Diversions, pf left hand, orch, 1940, rev. 1954; Wittgenstein, Philadelphia Orch, cond. Ormandy, 16 Jan 1942	
24	Matinées musicales [after Rossini], 1941	

CHORAL.

No.	Work	Pages
26	Scottish Ballad, 2 pf, orch, 1941; E. Bartlett, R. Robertson, Cincinnati SO, cond. Goossens, 28 Nov 1941	
—	An American Overture, 1942	
29	Prelude and Fugue, 18 str, 1943; Boyd Neel Orch, London, 23 June 1943	
33a	Four Sea Interludes, from Peter Grimes	
33b	Passacaglia, from Peter Grimes	
34	The Young Person's Guide to the Orchestra (Variations and Fugue on a Theme of Purcell), speaker (text by Crozier) ad lib, orch, 1946; Liverpool PO, cond. Sargent, Liverpool, 15 Oct 1946	243, 250
38	Occasional Overture, C, 1946; BBC, 29 Sept 1946	
—	Men of Goodwill, variations on a carol, 1947	
48a	Lachrimae, va, str [arr. of op.48], 1976	
53a	Symphonic Suite 'Gloriana', T/ob, orch; Pears, City of Birmingham SO, cond. R. Schwarz, Birmingham, 23 Sept 1954	
57a	Pas de six from The Prince of the Pagodas; City of Birmingham SO, cond. Schwarz, Birmingham, 26 Sept 1957	
68	Cello Symphony, vc, orch, 1963; Rostropovich, Moscow PO, cond. Britten, Moscow, 12 March 1964	244, 251
79	The Building of the House (Ps cxxvii), ov. SATB/org/brass, orch, 1967; East Anglian choirs, English Chamber Orch, cond. Britten, Snape Maltings, 2 June 1967	
90	Suite on English Folk Tunes 'A Time There Was', chamber orch, 1966–75; English Chamber Orch, cond. Bedford, Snape Maltings, 13 June 1975 [incl. Hankin Booby, 1966, written for opening of Queen Elizabeth Hall, 1 March 1967]	245

CHORAL.

No.	Work	Pages
—	A Hymn to the Virgin (c1300), unacc., 1930, rev. 1934; Lowestoft, St John, 5 Jan 1931	
—	Three Two-part Songs (de la Mare), boys'/female vv, 1932: The Ride-by-nights, The Rainbow, The Ship of Rio; London, 12 Dec 1932	
3	A Boy was Born (15th- and 16th-century carols), choral variations, boys' vv, male vv, female vv, 1932–3, rev. with org ad lib, 1955, BBC, 23 Feb 1934: Corpus Christi Carol from variation 5 arr. Tr solo/unison, org, 1961	264
—	Two Two-part Songs, SATB, pf, 1933: I Lov'd a Lass (G. Wither), Lift Boy (Graves); London, 11 Dec 1933	
7	Friday Afternoons, 12 songs, children's vv, pf, 1933–5	269
—	May, unison vv, pf, 1934	
—	Te Deum, C, Tr, SATB, org/(str, harp/pf), 1934; London, 27 Jan 1936	267
—	Two Ballads, 2vv, pf, 1937: Mother Comfort (Slater), Underneath the Abject Willow (Auden)	
—	Advance Democracy, (R. Swingler), SSAATTBB, 1938	
14	Ballad of Heroes (Swingler, Auden), T/S, chorus, orch, 1939; cond. Lambert, Queen's Hall, 5 April 1939	240, 264
17	Hopkins settings, withdrawn [17 reassigned to Paul Bunyan]	
27	Hymn to St Cecilia (Auden), SSATB, 1942; BBC Singers, cond. L. Woodgate, London, 22 Nov 1942	264
28	A Ceremony of Carols, Tr vv, harp, 1942; Fleet Street Choir, G. Mason, cond. T. B. Lawrence, Norwich Castle, 5 Dec 1942	241, 264–5
30	Rejoice in the Lamb (Smart), Tr, A, T, B, SATB, org, 1943; Northampton, St Matthew, 21 Sept 1943	241, 265
—	The Ballad of Little Musgrave and Lady Barnard, male vv, pf, 1943; Eichstätt, Feb 1944	269
32	A Shepherd's Carol (Auden), SATB, 1944; BBC, 1944	
—	Festival Te Deum, SATB, org, 1944; Swindon, St Mark, 24 April 1945	267
—	Old Joe has Gone Fishing, from Peter Grimes, SATB, pf	
—	Song of the Fishermen, from Peter Grimes, SATB, pf	
42	St Nicolas (Crozier), T, SA, 4 Tr, SATB, str, pf 4 hands, perc, org, 1948; Pears, Aldeburgh Festival Chorus, cond. Woodgate, Aldeburgh, 5 June 1948	243, 269
44	Spring Symphony (various poets), S, A, T, boys' vv, mixed vv, orch, 1949; Vincent, Ferrier, Pears, Dutch Radio Chorus, Concertgebouw, cond. Van Beinum, Amsterdam, 9 July 1949	243, 265, 272
46	A Wedding Anthem (Amo ergo sum) (Duncan), S, T, SATB, org, 1949	267–8
47	Five Flower Songs, SATB, 1950	
—	Choral Dances from Gloriana, unacc.	
56a	Hymn to St Peter, Tr, SATB, org, 1955	
56b	Antiphon (Herbert), SATB, org, 1956	

62	Cantata academica, carmen basiliense (compiled B. Wyss), S, A, T, B, chorus, orch, 1959; Giebel, Cavelti, Pears, Rehfuss, Basle Chamber Orch, cond. Sacher, Basle University, 1 July 1960	244, 265-6
63	Missa brevis, D, boys' vv, org, 1959; Westminster Cathedral, 22 July 1959	268
—	Jubilate Deo, SATB, org, 1961; Leeds Parish Church, 8 Oct 1961	267
—	Fancie (Shakespeare), unison vv, pf, 1961	
66	War Requiem (Requiem, Owen), S, T, Bar, boys' vv, mixed vv, orch, chamber orch, 1961; Harper, Pears, Fischer-Dieskau, Coventry Festival Chorus, City of Birmingham SO, Melos Ensemble, cond. M Davies, Britten, Coventry Cathedral, 30 May 1962	244, 266-7
67	Psalm cl, children's chorus 2vv, insts, 1962; Northgate School children, cond. Britten, Aldeburgh, Jubilee Hall, 24 June 1963	270
—	A Hymn of St Columba – Regis regum rectissimi, SATB, org, 1962	
69	Cantata misericordium (P. Wilkinson), T, Bar, small chorus, str qt, str orch, pf, harp, timp, 1963; Pears, Fischer-Dieskau, Motet de Genève, Suisse Romande Orchestra, cond. Ansermet, Geneva, 1 Sept 1963	267
75	Voices for Today (Virgil), boys' vv, mixed vv, org ad lib, 1965; simultaneous premières in London, New York and Paris, 24 Oct 1965	245, 267
—	Sweet was the Song the Virgin Sung (W. Ballet), SSAA, 1931, recomposed 1966	
78	The Golden Vanity (C. Graham), boys' vv, pf, 1966; Vienna Boys' Choir, Snape Maltings, 3 June 1967	272
—	The Oxen (Christmas Eve, and Twelve of the Clock) (Hardy), female chorus 2vv, pf, 1967	
—	The Sycamore Tree (trad.), SATB, 1930, recomposed 1967	
—	A Wealden Trio: the Song of the Women (F. M. Ford), SSA, 1929, recomposed 1967	
82	Children's Crusade (Kinderkreuzzug) (Brecht, trans. H. Keller), children's vv, perc, 2 pf, org, 1968; Wandsworth School Choir and Orchestra, cond. R. Burgess, London, St Paul's Cathedral, 19 May 1969	272
91	Sacred and Profane (8 medieval lyrics), 5vv, 1974-5; Wilbye Consort, Snape Maltings, 14 Sept 1975	245, 267
95	Welcome Ode (T. Dekker, J. Ford, H. Fielding, anon.), young peoples' vv, orch, 1976; Ipswich, 11 July 1977	245, 272

CHAMBER AND INSTRUMENTAL

—	Quartettino, str qt, 1930	240, 247
—	String Quartet, D, 1931; Gabrieli Qt, Snape Maltings, 7 June 1975	251
—	Phantasy, f, str qnt, 1932	248
2	Phantasy, ob qt, 1932	240, 248
—	Alla Marcia, str qt, 1933	
5	Holiday Diary, suite, pf, 1934	248
6	Suite, vn, pf, 1934-5; Brosa, Britten, Barcelona, 21 April 1936	248
—	Two Insect Pieces, ob, pf, 1935	
—	Temporal Variations, ob, pf, 1936	
—	Three Divertimenti, str qt, 1936	
—	Reveille, vn, pf, 1937	
23/1	Introduction and Rondo alla burlesca, 2 pf, 1940	
23/2	Mazurka elegiaca, 2 pf, 1941; E. Bartlett, R. Robertson, New York, Town Hall, 1941	241, 249-50
25	String Quartet no.1, D, 1941; Coolidge Qt, Los Angeles, Sept 1941	
36	String Quartet no.2, C, 1945; Zorian Qt, London, 21 Nov 1945	243, 250
—	Prelude and Fugue on a Theme of Vittoria, org, 1946	
48	Lachrymae, reflections on a song of Dowland, va, pf, 1950; Primrose, Britten, Aldeburgh, 20 June 1950: arr. va, str orch, 1976	250, 251
49	Six Metamorphoses after Ovid, ob, 1951; J. Boughton, Thorpeness, The Meare, 14 June 1951	250
—	Morris Dance, from Gloriana, 2 descant rec	
—	Alpine Suite, rec trio, 1955	
—	Scherzo, rec qt, 1955	
65	Fanfare for St Edmundsbury, 3 tpt, 1959	
—	Sonata, C, vc, pf, 1961; Rostropovich, Britten, Aldeburgh, Jubilee Hall, 7 July 1961	244, 250-51
—	Night Piece (Notturno), pf, 1963	
70	Nocturnal after John Dowland, gui, 1963; Bream, Aldeburgh, 12 June 1964	251
—	Russian Funeral, 3 tpt, 4 hn, 3 trbn, tuba, perc, 1963	

72	Suite no.1, vc, 1964; Rostropovich, Aldeburgh, 27 June 1965	244, 251
73	Gemini Variations, fl, vn, pf [4 players in all], 1965; Z. and G. Jeney, Aldeburgh, 19 June 1965	272
80	Suite no.2, vc, 1967; Rostropovich, Snape Maltings, 17 June 1968	244, 251
83	Suite, harp, 1969; Ellis, Aldeburgh, Jubilee Hall, 24 June 1969	251
87	Five Waltzes (Waltzes), pf, 1923-5, recomposed 1969	244, 251
94	Suite no.3, vc, 1972	246, 252
	String Quartet no.3, 1975; Amadeus Qt. Snape Maltings, 19 Dec 1976	253-63

SOLO VOCAL

—	Three Early Songs (various poets), male v, pf, 1922-6	
—	Quatre chansons françaises (Hugo, Verlaine), S, orch, 1928	
—	The Birds (Belloc), Mez/Bar, pf, 1929, rev. 1934	
—	The Ship of Rio (de la Mare), 1932, arr. 1v, pf, 1963	
8	Our Hunting Fathers (Auden), sym. cycle, S/T, orch, 1936; S. Wyss, LPO, cond. Britten, Norwich, 25 Sept 1936	240, 249, 254
11	On this Island (Auden), cycle, S/T, pf, 1937; Wyss, Britten, London, Broadcasting House Concert Hall, 19 Nov 1937	254, 273
	Fish in the Unruffled Lakes (Auden), S/T, pf, 1937	254
18	Les illuminations (Rimbaud), cycle, S/T, str, 1939; Wyss, Boyd Neel Orch, cond. Neel, London, 30 Jan 1940	241, 254-5, 256
22	Seven Sonnets of Michelangelo, cycle, T, pf, 1940; Pears, Britten, London, Wigmore Hall, 23 Sept 1942	240, 255
31	Serenade (various poets), T, hn, str orch, 1943; Pears, Brain, cond. Goehr, London, Wigmore Hall, 15 Oct 1943	241, 255-6, 259
—	Three Arias, from Peter Grimes: Peter's Dreams, T, pf/orch; Embroidery Aria, S, pf/orch; Church Scene, S, pf/orch	
35	The Holy Sonnets of John Donne, cycle, S/T, pf, 1945; Pears, Britten, London, Wigmore Hall, 22 Nov 1945	243, 256
—	Three Arias, from The Rape of Lucretia: Flower Song, A, pf/orch; The Ride, T, pf/orch; Slumber Song, Mez, pf/orch	
40	Canticle I 'My beloved is mine' (Quarles), S/T, pf, 1947; Pears, Britten, 1 Nov 1947	261
41	A Charm of Lullabies, cycle, Mez, pf, 1947; N. Evans, F. de Nobel, The Hague, 3 Jan 1948	256
51	Canticle II 'Abraham and Isaac' (Chester miracle play), A, T, pf, 1952; Ferrier, Pears, Britten, Nottingham, 21 Jan 1952	261-2

52	Winter Words (Hardy), cycle, S/T, pf, 1953; Pears, Britten, Harewood House, 8 Oct 1953	256-7
55	Canticle III 'Still Falls the Rain – the Raids, 1940, Night and Dawn' (E. Sitwell), T, hn, pf, 1954; Pears, Brain, Britten, London, Wigmore Hall, 28 Jan 1955	262
58	Songs from the Chinese (trans. Waley), cycle, S/T, gui, 1957; Pears, Bream, Aldeburgh, Great Glemham House, 17 June 1958	257
60	Nocturne (various poets), T, 7 obbl insts, str orch, 1958; Pears, BBC SO, cond. Schwarz, Leeds, Town Hall, 16 Oct 1958	259
61	Sechs Hölderlin-Fragmente, cycle, 1v, pf, 1958; Pears, Britten, Schloss Wolfsgarten. 20 Nov 1958	257, 259
—	Bottom's Dream, from A Midsummer Night's Dream, B-Bar, pf/orch	
74	Songs and Proverbs of William Blake, cycle, Bar, pf, 1965; Fischer-Dieskau, Britten, Aldeburgh, 24 June 1965	259-60
76	The Poet's Echo (Pushkin), cycle, S/T, pf, 1965; Vishnevskaya, Rostropovich, Moscow Conservatory, 2 Dec 1965	245-260
—	Tit for Tat (de la Mare), cycle, 1v, pf, 1928-31, recomposed 1968; Shirley-Quirk, Britten, Aldeburgh, 23 June 1969	
84	Who are these Children? (Soutar), cycle, T, pf, 1969; Pears, Britten, Edinburgh, National Gallery of Scotland, 4 May 1971	260
86	Canticle IV 'The Journey of the Magi' (Eliot), Ct, T, Bar, pf, 1971; Bowman, Pears, Shirley-Quirk, Britten, Aldeburgh, 26 June 1971	262-3
89	Canticle V 'The Death of St Narcissus' (Eliot), T, harp, 1974; Pears, Ellis, Schloss Elmau, 15 Jan 1975	245, 263
92	A Birthday Hansel (Burns), high v, harp, 1975; Pears, Ellis, New Hall, Cardiff, 19 March 1976	245, 261
93	Phaedra (Racine, trans. R. Lowell), Mez, str, perc, vc, hpd, 1975; Baker, English Chamber Orch, Bedford, Snape Maltings, 16 June 1976	246, 261

INCIDENTAL MUSIC

Easter 1916 (Slater), London, Phoenix, 1935; lost
Timon of Athens (Shakespeare), London, Westminster Theatre, 1935
Agamemnon (trans. MacNeice), London, Westminster Theatre, 1936
Stay down Miner (Slater), London, Westminster Theatre, 1936
The Ascent of F.6 (Auden, Isherwood), London, Mercury, 1937

Out of the Picture (MacNeice), London, Westminster Theatre, 1937

Pageant of Empire (Slater), ?1937

Old Spain (Slater), London, Mercury, 1938; lost

On the Frontier (Auden, Isherwood), Cambridge, Arts, 1938

The Seven Ages of Man (Slater), London, Mercury, 1938; lost

Johnson over Jordan (Priestley), London, New, 1939

The Rescue (MacNeice), BBC radio, 1943

This Way to the Tomb (Duncan), London, Mercury, 1945

The Dark Tower (MacNeice), BBC radio, 1946

The Duchess of Malfi (Webster), New York, 1946; lost

The Eagle has Two Heads (Cocteau, trans. Duncan), Hammersmith, Lyric, 1946

Stratton (Duncan), Brighton, Theatre Royal, 1949; lost

Am Stram Gram (A. Roussin), London, Toynbee Hall, 1954, song pubd in *Tempo*, no.107 (1973), 9

The Punch Revue, London, Duke of York's, 1955

For details of numerous film and other radio scores see Mitchell and Keller (1952)

ARRANGEMENTS ETC

(folksong arrangements)

5 vols. for 1v, pf: British Isles; France; British Isles; Moore's Irish Melodies; British Isles

1 vol. for S/T: gui: England

For 1v, orch: La belle est au jardin d'amour; The Bonny Earl o' Moray; O can ye sew cushions?; Come you not from Newcastle?; Eho! Eho!, Fileuse; Little Sir William; La noël passée; Oliver Cromwell; The Ploughboy; Quand j'étais chez mon père; Le roi s'en va-t en chasse; The Salley Gardens; O Waly, Waly

For chorus: The Holly and the Ivy, SATB; King Herod and the Cock; Oliver Cromwell, The Salley Gardens, unison vv, pf

For 1v, harp: 8 Folksongs, 1976

(Purcell realizations)

with I. Holst: Dido and Aeneas; cond. Britten, Hammersmith, Lyric, 1 May 1951

with I. Holst, P. Ledger and P. Pears: The Fairy Queen [concert version]; cond. Britten, Aldeburgh, 25 June 1967

with P. Pears: *Orpheus britannicus*: Five Songs, 1v, pf; Six Songs, 1v, pf; Seven Songs, 1v, pf; Six Duets, 2vv, pf; Suite of Songs, S/T, orch; Three Songs, S/T, orch

——: *Harmonia sacra*: The Blessed Virgin's Expostulation, S/T, pf; Job's Curse, S/T, pf; Saul and the Witch at Endor, S, T, B, pf; Three Divine Hymns, 1v, pf; Two Divine Hymns and Alleluia, S/T, pf

——: *Odes and Elegies: The Queen's Epicedium*, S/T, pf

Other works: When night her purple veil had softly spread, Bar, 2 vn, bc; Chacony, g, str ql/str orch; The Golden Sonata, 2 vn, vc, pf

(other arrangements)

The National Anthem, SATB, orch; Leeds Festival Chorus, Royal Liverpool PO, cond. Pritchard, Leeds, Town Hall, 7 Oct 1961

J. S. Bach: Five Spiritual Songs (trans. Pears), S/T, pf; Pears, Britten, Blythburgh, 18 June 1969

God Save the Queen, orch; Snape Maltings, 13 June 1971

G. Mahler: What the Wild Flowers Tell me [Sym. no.3: 2nd movt], reduced orch, 1941

(concerto cadenzas)

J. Haydn: Cello Concerto in C, 1964; Rostropovich, Blythburgh Church, 18 June 1964

W. A. Mozart: Piano Concerto in E♭ K482, 1966; Richter, July 1966

Principal publishers: Boosey & Hawkes (opp.1–69), Faber (opp.70–95)

For further details see *Benjamin Britten: a Complete Catalogue of his Published Works* (London, 1973) and Boosey & Hawkes catalogue (London, 1963)

WRITINGS

'An English Composer sees America', *Tempo*, i (New York, 1940)

'On Behalf of Gustav Mahler', *Tempo*, ii (New York, 1942)

with I. Holst: *The Story of Music* (London, 1958/R1968 as *The Wonderful World of Music*)

'On Realizing the Continuo in Purcell's Songs', *Henry Purcell: 1659–1695*, ed. I. Holst (London, 1959)

On Receiving the First Aspen Award (London, 1964/R1978)

'Frank Bridge (1879–1941)', *Faber Music News* (1966), aut. 17

BIBLIOGRAPHY
MONOGRAPHS AND COLLECTIONS OF ARTICLES

E. W. White: *Benjamin Britten: a Sketch of his Life and Works* (London, 1948, rev. 2/1954; Ger. trans., 1948)

Music Survey, ii (1950), 217–82 [Britten issue]

D. Mitchell and H. Keller, eds.: *Benjamin Britten: a Commentary on his Works from a Group of Specialists* (London, 1952)

A. Gishford, ed.: *Tribute to Benjamin Britten on his Fiftieth Birthday* (London, 1963)

Tempo, nos.66–7 (1963) [Britten issue]

I. Holst: *Britten* (London, 1966, rev. 2/1970)

M. Hurd: *Benjamin Britten* (London, 1966)

P. M. Young: *Benjamin Britten* (London, 1966)

E. W. White: *Benjamin Britten: his Life and Operas* (London, 1970; rev. 2/1983)

D. Mitchell and J. Evans, eds.: *Benjamin Britten, 1913–1976: Pictures from a Life* (London, 1978)

P. Evans: *The Music of Benjamin Britten* (London, 1979)

M. Kennedy: *Britten* (London, 1981)

D. Mitchell: *Britten and Auden in the 'Thirties: the Year 1936* (London, 1981)

R. Duncan: *Working with Britten* (London, 1982)

A. Whittall: *The Music of Britten and Tippett: Studies in Themes and Techniques* (Cambridge, 1982)

C. Palmer, ed: *The Britten Companion* (London, 1984)

GENERAL ARTICLES

H. Boys: 'The Younger English Composers, v: Benjamin Britten', *MMR*, lxviii (1938), 234

J. A. Westrup: 'The Virtuosity of Benjamin Britten', *The Listener*, xxviii (1942), 93

C. Mason: 'Britten: Another View', *MMR*, lxxiii (1943), 153

H. Keller: 'Britten and Mozart: a Challenge in the Form of Variations on an Unfamiliar Theme', *ML*, xxix (1948), 17

C. Mason: 'Benjamin Britten', *MT*, lxxxix (1948), 73, 107, 139

P. Hamburger: 'Mainly about Britten', *Music Survey*, iii (1950–51), 98

E. Stein: 'Britten seen against his English Background', *Orpheus in New Guises* (London, 1953)

P. Tranchell: 'Britten and Brittenites', *ML*, xxxiv (1953), 124

D. Brown: 'Stimulus and Form in Britten's Works', *ML*, xxxix (1958), 218

A. Whittall: 'Benjamin Britten', *MR*, xxiii (1962), 314

P. Evans: 'Sonata Structures in Early Britten', *Tempo*, no.82 (1967), 2

Bibliography

F. Routh: 'Benjamin Britten', *Contemporary British Music* (London, 1972)

P. Evans: 'Britten's Fourth Creative Decade', *Tempo*, no.106 (1973), 8

A. Hutchings: 'Music in Britain: 1916–1960', *NOHM*, x (1974), 543

I. Holst: 'Working for Benjamin Britten', *MT*, cxviii (1977), 202

A. Whittall: 'The Study of Britten: Triadic Harmony and Tonal Structure', *PRMA*, cvi (1979–80), 27

W. Flynn: 'Britten the Progressive', *MR*, xliv (1983), 44

C. Mark: 'Simplicity in early Britten', *Tempo*, no.147 (1983), 8

M. Trend: *The Music Makers: Heirs and Rebels of the English Musical Renaissance, Edward Elgar to Benjamin Britten* (London, 1985)

LITERATURE ON OPERAS

E. Crozier, ed.: *Peter Grimes* (London, 1945)

E. Stein: 'Opera and "Peter Grimes" ', *Tempo*, 1st ser., no.12 (1945), 2

H. Keller: *The Rape of Lucretia; Albert Herring* (London, 1947)

E. Stein: 'Form in Opera: "Albert Herring" Examined', *Tempo*, new ser., no.5 (1947), 4

C. Stuart: *Peter Grimes* (London, 1947)

E. Crozier, ed.: *The Rape of Lucretia: a Symposium* (London, 1948)

F. Abbiati: *Peter Grimes* (Milan, 1949)

D. Mitchell: 'Britten's "Let's Make an Opera" op.45', *Music Survey*, ii (1959–50), 86

E. Stein: 'Benjamin Britten's Operas', *Opera*, i (1950), 16

Opera, ii/6 (1951) [Britten issue: chamber operas]

D. Mitchell: 'More off than on "Billy Budd" ', *Music Survey*, iv (1951–2), 386

A. Porter: 'Britten's "Billy Budd" ', *ML*, xxxiii (1952), 111

E. Stein: 'The Music of "Billy Budd" ', *Opera*, iii (1952), 206

Tempo, no.21 (1952) [Britten issue on *Billy Budd*]

J. Klein: 'Reflections on "Gloriana" ', *Tempo*, no.29 (1953), 16

A. Porter: 'Britten's "Gloriana" ', *ML*, xxxiv (1953), 277

E. Stein: ' "The Turn of the Screw" and its Musical Idiom', *Tempo*, no.34 (1954–5), 6

H. Lindler: *Benjamin Britten: das Opernwerk* (?Bonn, 1955)

E. Roseberry: 'The Music of "Noye's Fludde" ', *Tempo*, no.49 (1958), 2

E. Stein: 'Britten's New Opera for Children: "Noye's Fludde" ', *Tempo*, no.48 (1958), 7

P. Evans: 'Britten's "A Midsummer Night's Dream" ', *Tempo*, nos. 53–4 (1960), 34

P. Howard: *The Operas of Benjamin Britten* (London, 1969)

P. Evans: 'Britten's Television Opera', *MT*, cxii (1971), 425

——: 'Britten's "Death in Venice" ', *Opera*, xxiv (1973), 490

P. Brett: 'Britten and Grimes', *MT*, cxviii (1977), 995

D. Herbert, ed.: *The Operas of Benjamin Britten: the Complete Librettos Illustrated with Designs of the First Productions* (London and New York, 1979)

P. Brett, ed.: *Benjamin Britten: Peter Grimes* (Cambridge, 1983)

P. Howard, ed.: *Benjamin Britten: Turn of the Screw* (Cambridge, 1985)

LITERATURE ON OTHER WORKS

H. Keller: 'Benjamin Britten's Second Quartet', *Tempo*, new ser., no.3 (1947), 6

I. Holst: 'Britten's "Saint Nicolas" ', *Tempo*, no.10 (1948–9), 23

L. Berkeley: 'Britten's "Spring Symphony" ', *ML*, xxxi (1950), 216

E. Stein: 'Britten's "Spring Symphony" ', *Tempo*, no.15 (1950), 19

I. Holst: 'Britten's Nocturne', *Tempo*, no.50 (1958), 14

J. Noble: 'Britten's "Songs from the Chinese" ', *Tempo*, no.52 (1959), 25

S. Bradshaw: 'Britten's "Cantata academica" ', *Tempo*, nos.53–4 (1960), 22

D. Brown: 'Britten's Three Canticles', *MR*, xxi (1960), 55

E. Roseberry: 'Britten's "Missa brevis" ', *Tempo*, nos.53–4 (1960), 11

P. Evans: 'Britten's Cello Sonata', *Tempo*, no.58 (1961), 8

——: 'Britten's "War Requiem" ', *Tempo*, nos.61–2 (1962), 20

A. Robertson: 'Britten's "War Requiem" ', *MT*, ciii (1962), 308

A. Whittall: 'Tonal Instability in Britten's "War Requiem" ', *MR*, xxiv (1963), 201

J. Warrack: 'Britten's Cello Symphony', *MT*, cv (1964), 418

M. Boyd: 'Britten, Verdi and the Requiem', *Tempo*, no.86 (1968), 2

E. W. White: 'Britten in the Theatre', *Tempo*, no.107 (1973), 2

C. Matthews: 'Britten's Indian Summer', *Soundings*, vi (1977), 42

C. Mark: 'Britten's "Quatre Chansons Françaises" ', *Soundings*, x (1983), 23

Index

Acts of St John, 159
Adelaide, Dowager Queen, 1
Adler, Larry, 128
Aldeburgh, 246
——, Festival, 243, 244, 245
——, Moot Hall, *242*
Algeria, 157
America, 184; *see also* United States of America
American Academy and Institute of Arts and Letters, 177
Aristophanes: *The Wasps*, 113
Armenia, 245
Arnold, Matthew: *The Scholar Gipsy*, 128
Arts Council of Great Britain, 104
Arundell, Dennis, 127
Atkins, E. Wulstan: *The Elgar–Atkins Friendship*, 21
Atkins, Ivor, 21
Auden, W. H., 240, 241, 254, 264, 265
Augustine, St: *Confessions*, 226
Australia, 177

Bach, Johann Sebastian, 100, 184
——, Cantatas, 147
——, Fantasy and Fugue in C BWV537, 47
——, Passions, 100, 216
——, *St Matthew Passion*, 100
Baker, Janet, 187, 246, 261
Baker, W. Meath [squire], 9
Buku, 148
Bantock, Granville, 8, 15, 84
Barnes, William, 109
Bartók, Béla, 99, 118, 178, 239
Basle, University of, 244, 266
Bath Festival, 205

Bavaria, 14
Bax, Arnold, 73, 115
Bax, Clifford, 159, 162
Bayreuth, 27, 33
BBC, 22, 161, 164, 181, 184, 205
——, Television, 123, 245
——, Third Programme, 105
Beecham, Thomas, 72, 76, 78, 83
Beethoven, Ludwig van, 211, 212, 226, 228
——, Choral Fantasia op.80, 128
——, Overture, *Coriolan*, op.62, 47
——, String Quartet in A minor op.132, 210
——, Symphony no.5, 182
——, Symphony no.9, 228
Bell, George K. A., Bishop of Chichester, 153
Benjamin, Arthur, 239
Benson, A. C., 13
Berg, Alban, 178, 240, 254
——, Violin Concerto, 41
——, *Wozzeck*. 240, 276
Berlin, 98
——, Komische Oper, 76
Berlioz, Hector: *Grand traité d'instrumentation et d'orchestration modernes*, 145
——, Overture, *Benvenute Cellini*, 25
Berners, Lord (Tyrwhitt-Wilson, Gerald Hugh), 176
Birmingham, 3, 13, 14, 15, 18, 33
——, Triennial Festival, 10
——, University, 14
Bishop Auckland, 17
Bizet, Georges, 39
Blackpool, 147
Blackwood, Algernen: *A Prisoner in Fairyland*, 44

Blake, William, 105, 259–60
——, *Elegy*, 256
——, *Illustrations to the Book of Job*, 121
——, *Marriage of Heaven and Hell*, 207
Boosey & Hawkes, 12
Boughton, Rutland, 102
Boult, Adrian, 101, 159, 202
Bradford, 69, 73, 76
——, Grammar School, 69
Brahms, Johannes, 25, 40
——, Symphony no.3, 15, 25
Brecht, Bertolt, 272
Brema, Marie, 11
Bridge, Frank, 239, 248
——, *Oration*, 248
Bridges, Robert, 160
Brighton, 147
British Expeditionary Force, First Army, 101
Britten, (Edward) Benjamin, 162, 165, 187, 239–96
Britten (née Hockey), Edith Rhoda [mother], 239
Broadheath: *see* Lower Broadheath
Broadwood, Lucy, 156
Bruch, Max, 98
Bruckner, Anton, 40
Bunyan, John, 117
——, *The Pilgrim's Progress*, 105
Burley, Rosa, 17
Burne-Jones, Philip, 22
Burns, Robert, 245, 261
Bushes and Briars [folksong], 100
Busoni, Ferruccio, 13
Buths, Julius, 12, 72
Butt, Clara, 10
Butterworth, George, 114
Byrd, William, 117

Cable, George Washington: *The Grandissimes*, 75
Calne, Wiltshire, 202
Cambridge, 98, 99, 127
——, Trinity College, 98
——, University of, 12
Cannes, 201
Canterbury Cathedral, 161
Capell, Richard, 127
Carey, Thomas, *214*
Cassirer, Fritz, 72, 75, 76
Chabrier, Emmanuel, 30
Chaucer, Geoffrey, 186
Chekhov, Anton Pavlovich, 187
Chelsea, 176
Cheltenham, 145, 146, 151
——, Festival, 105
——, Grammar School, 145
——, Holst Festival, 151
Chicago, 13
——, Symphony Orchestra, 50th anniversary, 184
Chichester Cathedral, 153
——, 900th anniversary, 191
Child's Introduction to Thorough Bass, The, 97
Chopin, Fryderyk: Piano Sonata in B flat minor, 47
——, Waltz in E minor op. posth., 69
Claines, nr. Worcester, 2
Clark, Edward, 181
Cleveland Orchestra, 40th anniversary, 188
Coates, Albert, 81
Cobbett, W. W., 248
Colonne, Edouard, 13
Columbus, Christopher, 184
Colvin, Sir Sidney, 17
Composer's Guild of Great Britain, 176
Conder, Charles, 44
Constantinople (now Istanbul), 148
Cooke, Deryck: 'Symphony no.6 in E minor, by Vaughan Williams', 127
Cooper, Joseph, 118
Cork International Choral and Folk Dance Festival, 192
Cornell University, 105
Corsham, Wiltshire: Parkside, 202

Index

Cossart, Ernest: *see* Holst, Emil von

Cotswold Hills, 115

Council for the Encouragement of Music and the Arts: *see* Arts Council of Great Britain

Courtauld, Mrs Samuel, 176

Coventry Cathedral, 244

——, Friends of, 191

Cowen, Frederick Hymen, 8

Crabbe, George, 241

Craggs, Stewart R.: *William Walton: a Thematic Catalogue*, 192

Cross, John, 241, *274*

Crozier, Eric, *242*

Custodes hominum [hymn], 285

Czinner, Paul, 176

Daily Telegraph, 127

Dan [Sinclair's bulldog], 36

Danville, Virginia, 71

Darmstadt, 82

Darwin, Charles, 97

Davies, Walford, 8

Dean, Basil, 82

Debussy, Claude, 115

——, *La mer*, 115

——, *Prélude à l'après-midi d'un faune*, 84

Delhi Durbar, 44

Delibes, Léo, 30

Delius (née Krönig), Elise Pauline [mother], 69

Delius, Frederick [Fritz] (Theodore Albert), 22, 49, 69–94

Delius (née Rosen), Jelka [wife], 71, 72, *79*, 82, *85*

Delius, Julius Friedrich Wilhelm [father], 69, 71

Dieren, Bernard van, 176, 185

Dives and Lazarus [folksong], 111

Dobson, Frank, *180*

Dolin, Anton, *120*

Done, William, 3

Donne, John: Sonnets, 256

'Dorabella': *see* Powell, D. M.

Dorfman, Dr Ralph, 191

Dorking, 97, 105

Dorset, 109

Douglas, Roy, 106

——, *Working with R. V. W.*, 105,

Dover, 1

Dowland, John, 205, 251

Down Ampney, Gloucestershire, 97

Dulwich, James Allen's Girls' School, 147, 160

Duncan, Ronald, 268

Durham, University of, 177

Düsseldorf, 12

——, Lower Rhine Festival, 12–13

Dvořák, Antonín, 3, 35, 114, 155

Dyagilev, Sergey, 121, 179

Edinburgh: Fettes College, 201

Edward VII, King of Great Britain, 13, 14, 15

Elberfeld, 75

——, Stadttheater, 75

Elgar (née Roberts), (Caroline) Alice [wife], *4*, 5, 6, 7, 8, 9, 10, 12, 14, 18, 20, 23

Elgar (née Greening), Ann [mother], 1–2, 5, 20

Elgar, Carice [daughter], 6, 20, 23

Elgar, Edward (William), 1–65, 73, 104, 106, 110, 183

——, relations at Worcester, 21

Elgar, William Henry [father], 1, 2, 5, 7

——, children of, 2

Eliot, T. S.: *The Death of St Narcissus*, 263

——, *The Journey of the Magi*, 261, 262, 263

Elizabeth I, Queen of England, 244, 279

Elizabeth II, Queen of Great Britain, 244

Ellis, Osian, 245

England, 72, 73, 76, 80, 145, 147, 149, 150, 158, 240, 241, 245, 247, 254; *see also* United Kingdom of Great Britain

English Bach Festival, 191
English Folk Dance Society (later English Folk Dance and Song Society), 101, 102, 122, 161
English Hymnal, The, 100, 113, 156
English Music Theatre Company, 246
English Opera Group, 243, 246
Essen, 77
Essex, 100, 148
Europe, 77, 106

Far East, 244
Fauré, Gabriel, 254
Fenby, Eric, 72, 76, 82
——, *Delius*, 83
——, *Delius as I Knew him*, 72, 87
Fischer-Dieskau, Dietrich, 259
Fisher, Adeline: *see* Vaughan Williams, Adeline
Flecker, James Elroy: *Hassan*, 82
Florence: ISCM Festival, 240
Florida, 69, 71, 75, 80
Fontainebleau, 72
Forster, E. M., 241
Foss, Hubert, 126, 176, 182
Foster, Arnold, 204
Foster, Muriel, 13
France, 101, 116, 151
Franck, César, 32
Frankfurt, 80, 81

Gaisberg, Fred, 21
Gardiner, H. Balfour, 73, 159
Garnett, Richard, 121
Gauguin, Paul, 71, *85*
Gay, John: *The Beggar's Opera*, 203, 278
Geneva, 102
Germany, 8, 72
Gil, Susana: *see* Walton, Susana
Gilbert, W. S., 155
Gloucester, Cathedral, *38*
——, Three Choirs Festival, 3, *38*, 160
Gloucestershire, 151

Godalming: Charterhouse School, 97, 99
Gomez, Jill, *214*
Goossens, Leon, 124
Gordon, Charles George, General, 10, 12
Gounod, Charles, 8, 25, 28
Graham, Colin, 283
Grainger, Percy, 73
Gramophone Company, 21
Greek Anthology, 43
Greene, Henry Plunket, 11
Greening, Ann: *see* Elgar, Ann
Grez-sur-Loing, 22, 71, 72, 73
Grieg, Edvard, *70*, 71, 74, 155
Griffith, Troyte [architect], 9
Groveham, Edith [friend of Helen Weaver], 5
Groves, Charles, 81
Grynsban, Herschel, 213, 215

Halversen, Johan, *70*
Hamburg, University of: Shakespeare Prize, 104
Hammersmith, 164; *see also* London
Handel, George Frideric: *Messiah*, 216
——, Overture from Chandos Anthem no.2, 47
Hanley, 8, 13
Hardy, Thomas, 163, 256
——, *The Return of the Native*, 163
Harrison, Beatrice, 20
Harrison, Isobel: *see* Holst, Isobel
Harty, Hamilton, 182
Harvard University, 153
Hassall, Christopher, 186
Haydn, Joseph, 24
Haym, Hans, 72, 75, 76
Hedley, Percival, 22
Heifetz, Jascha, 183
Hemsley, Thomas, *214*
Herbert, George, 112
——, *Antiphon*, 191
Hereford, 13, 18
——, Cathedral, 9

Index

——, Plâs Gwyn [Elgar's home], 14, 15
——, Three Choirs Festival, 3
Herincx, Raimund, *214*
Heseltine, Philip: *see* Warlock, Peter
Hindemith, Paul, 181, 182, 190, 211
——, Cello Concerto, 190
——, *Mathis der Maler*, 190
Hockman, Vera, 21
Hölderlin, Johann Christian, 253, 257
Holst, Adolph von [Holst's father], 145, 146
——, second wife of, 145
Holst (née Lediard), Clara von [Holst's mother], 145
Holst, Emil von (Cossart, Ernest) [Holst's brother], 145
Holst, Gustav [Holst, Gustavus Theodore von], 49, 98–9, *103*, 121, 123, 145–71
Holst, Gustavus Valentine von [Holst's grandfather], 145
——, wife of, 145
Holst, Imogen [Holst's daughter], 162
Holst (née Harrison), Isobel [Holst's wife], 146, 147, 149
Holst, Matthias von [Holst's great-grandfather], 145
——, wife of, 145
Holst, Theodor von [Holst's great-uncle], 145
Homer, 222
Honegger, Arthur, 179
Hope and Glory [film], 22
Housman, A. E., 114
Howes, Frank: *The Music of William Walton*, 192
Huddersfield Choral Society, 125th anniversary, 191
Humperdinck, Engelbert: *Hänsel und Gretel*, 44
Hungary, 99

India, 5

Intermusical Society for Contemporary Music, 102, 178, 240
——, Festival (1934), 240
Ireland, John, 239
Ischia, 177
Isleworth, Middlesex, 69
——, International College, 69
Istanbul: *see* Constantinople
Italy, 14, 177

Jackson, Sir Barry, 22
Jacksonville, Florida, 69, 71
Jacob, Gordon, 102
Jacobsen, J. P. 78
——, *Niels Lyhne*, 78
Jadassohn, Alexander, 71
Jaeger, A. J., 9, 10, 11, 12, 20, *34*
James, Henry, 286
——, *The Turn of the Screw*, 280, 281
Jeans, Sir James: *The Mysterious Universe*, 151
Johnson, C.: *The Village Opera*, 202–3
Jonson, Ben: *The Devil is an Ass*, 22
——, *Hymn to Diana*, 256
Jung, Carl, 221

Keary, Charles, 75
Keats, John, 25, 160, 256
——, *Ode on a Grecian Urn*, 160
Keller, Gottfried: *Die Leute von Seldwyla*, 75
——, *Romeo und Julia auf dem Dorfe*, 75
Kemp, Isabel Clementine Binny: *see* Tippett, Isabel Clementine Binny
Kennedy, Michael: *Portrait of Elgar*, 43
——, *The Works of Ralph Vaughan Williams*, 106, 117, 126
Kent, Christopher, 48
——, *Edward Elgar, a Composer at Work*, 48
Kentner, Louis, 186
Keynes, Geoffrey, 121

Khartoum, 10
Kilburn, Nicholas, 15
Kipling, Rudyard: *Recessional*, 13
Kitson, C. H., 202
Kodály, Zoltán, 99, 272
Kreisler, Fritz, 17
Krönig, Elise Pauline: *see* Delius, Elise Pauline

Latvia, 145
Lambert, Constant, 115, 176, 179
——, 'Some Recent Works by William Walton', 179, 183
Leicestershire Schools Symphony Orchestra, 205
Lediard, Clara: *see* Holst, Clara von
Leeds, 18
——, Festival, 8, 160, 181
Leipzig, 5, 15, *70*
——, Conservatory, 2, 71
Leith Hill, Surrey, 97
——, Music Festival, 100, 101
Leith Hill Place, 97
Leningrad: *see* St Petersburg
Le Sage, Alain René: *Gils Blas*, 17
Limpsfield, Surrey, 73
Lincolnshire, 201
Liszt, Franz, 32
——, *Les préludes*, 25
Little Malvern: St Wulstan's Church, 23
Liverpool, 15, 81
——, Royal Liverpool Philharmonic Society, 188
Lloyd, Edward, 11
London, 1, 2, 5, 6, 7, 8, 10, 11, 13, 17, 18, 19, 20, 23, 25, 43, 69, 78, 81, 97, 102, 105, 106, 115, 120, 146, 147, 150, 151, 153, 201, 203, 204, 205, 245, *274*
——, Aeolian Hall, *180*
——, Athenaeum Club, 14
——, Avonmore Road, West Kensington, Elgar's home at, 6
——, Bach Choir, 101
——, British Library, 160, 164, 178

——, Brompton Oratory, 5
——, Camargo Society, 121
——, Carl Rosa Opera Company, 147
——, Crystal Palace, 3, 6, 25
——, Delius Festival (1929), 72, 82
——, (1946), 83
——, Elgar Festival, 14, 19
——, Grand Opera Syndicate, 19
——, Hammersmith Municipal Opera, 80
——, Hammersmith Socialist Choir, 146
——, Handel Society, 101
——, His Majesty's Theatre, 82
——, London Symphony Orchestra, 17, 22
——, Macnaghten–Lemare Concert, 240
——, Morley College, 147–8, 161, 203, 204, 205
——, Morley College Professional Orchestra, 203
——, National Brass Band Contest (1930), 48
——, National Gallery Concerts, 104
——, National Portrait Gallery, 22, 153
——, New Queen's Hall Orchestra, 159
——, Norwood, Elgar's home at, 6
——, Queen's Hall, 20
——, Royal Arsenal Co-operative Society, 203
——, Royal Ballet, 121
——, Royal College of Music, 98, 101, 146, 147, 150, 151, 202, 203, 239
——, Royal Festival Hall, 105, 205
——, Royal Opera House, Covent Garden, 14, 19, 25, 69, 105, 146, 186, 187, *214*, 244, 245
——, Royal Philharmonic Society, 73, 104, 151, 177, 190
——, Royal Society of Arts, 104

302

Index

——, Sadler's Wells Opera Company, 241

——, Sadler's Wells Theatre, 76, 241, *274*

——, St James's Hall, 10, 25

——, St Paul's Cathedral, 272

——, St Paul's Girls' School, Hammersmith, 147, 148, 150, 160

——, St Sepulchre, Holborn, 192

——, Savoy Orpheus Band, 179

——, Severn House, Hampstead, 18, 20

——, South London Orchestra, 203–4

——, University College, 146–7

——, Wandsworth School Boys' Choir, 272

——, Westminster Abbey, 23, 107

——, Westminster Cathedral, 13, 117, 268

——, Wigmore Hall, 20

——, White Viennese Band, 147

——, Wormwood Scrubs, 205

Longfellow, Henry Wadsworth, 26

——, *The Black Knight*, 26

——, *The Saga of King Olaf*, 26

Lower Broadheath, nr Worcester, 1, 2, 23

Lowestoft, 239

Lyke-wake Dirge (anon.), 256

Mackenzie, Alexander, 8

MacNeice, Louis, 184

Maconchy, Elizabeth, 102

Mahābharata, 147, 157

Mahler, Gustav, 37, 40, 41, 249, 254

——, Symphony no.10, 48

——, *Um Mitternacht*, 30

Maine, Basil: *Basil Maine on Music*, 48

Malvern, 5, 17

——, Festival, 22

——, Forli [Elgar's home], 6

Malvern Hills, 2

——, Birchwood Lodge [Elgar's home], 12, 20

Malvern Wells: Craeg Lea [Elgar's home], 12

Manchester, 13, 15

Mann, Thomas, 286

Manns, August, 3, 6

Marriner, Neville, 185

Masefield, John: *The Coming of Christ*, 161

——, *Where does the uttered music go?*, 192

Mason, Colin: 'William Walton', 182, 188

Massenet, Jules, 25, 36

Mellers, Wilfrid, 104

Mendelssohn, Felix, 24, 25, 155

——, *Elijah*, 27

——, *Hebrides* Overture, 25

Menuhin, Yehudi, 22, 186

Meredith, George, 160

Messiaen, Olivier, 32, 209

Meyerbeer, Giacomo, 25, 37

Michelangelo Buonarotti, 253, 255

Michigan, University of, 150

Middle East, 148

Middlesex, 201

Milan: La Scala, 186

Millais, John Everett, 18

Monteverdi, Claudio, 205

Moore, Jerrold Northrop, 48

——, *Elgar on Record: the Composer and the Gramophone*, 22

——, *Elgar: a Life in Photographs*, 22

Morley, Thomas: Madrigals, 146

Morris, R. O., 203

Morris, William, 146, 155

Morrison, Angus, 176, 179

Mozart, Wolfgang Amadeus, 278

Munch, Edvard, 71

Munich, 27

Musical Times, The [report, vol. xlii, p.388], 13

Musorgsky, Modest, 228

Newman, Ernest, 15

Newman, John Henry: *The Dream of*

Gerontius, 10, 32
New York, 13, 15, 81, 245, 273
——, Philharmonic Orchestra, 125th
    season, 190
New Zealand, 177
Nichols, Robert, 76
Nietzsche, Friedrich: *Also sprach
    Zarathustra*, 77, 78
Norfolk, 100
North America, 240; *see* also United
    States of America
North Staffordshire Festival, 8
Norway, 69, 72
Norwich Festival, 10, 239
Novello [publishers], 7, 9, 12, 27

O'Brien, Timothy, 214
Oldham, 175, 176
Olivier, Laurence, 184
Orford Church, 243
O'Shaughnessy, A., 43
Ottaway, Hugh: 'Scott and After: the
    Final Phase', 106
——, 'Walton Adapted', 186
Owen, Wilfrid, 266
Oxford, 102, 146, 176
——, Christ Church Cathedral, 175
——, Christ Church College Library,
    178
——, University of, 177
Oxford University Press, 176
Oxted, 202
——, Hazelwood School, 202
——, Oxted and Limpsfield Players,
    202
——, Police Court, 204

Paris, 22, 69, 71, 72, 98, 213, 245
Parry, Hubert, 8, 43, 98, 102, 106,
    110
——, Symphonic Variations, 28
——, Symphony no.4, 25
Pears, Peter, 240, 241, 244, 245, 253,
    258, 259, *274*, 282
Pennsylvania: Bryn Mawr College,
    102

Performing Right Society, 176
Peyton, Richard, 14
Piers Plowman, 11
Piper, Myfanwy, 280, 286
Plato, 118
Plomer, William, 283
Pollitzer, Adolf, 2, 3
Powell, D. M. ('Dorabella'), 17
——, 'The Words of "The Apostles"
    and "The Kingdom" ', 35
Powell, R.: *see* Powell, D. M.
Powick: Country Lunatic Asylum, 3,
    24
Prague, 102
Previn, André, 182
Prokofiev, Sergey, 181
——, Violin Concerto no.1, 181
Puccini, Giacomo, 42
Purcell, Henry, 107, 205, 210, 241,
    250, 256
——, *Dido and Aeneas*, 115
——, *The Fairy Queen*, 148
——, Partsongs, 146
——, Welcome Songs, 100
Pushkin, Alexander, 245, 253, 260
Pyatigorsky, Greger, 188

Quarles, Francis, 261

Rabelais, François, 19
Raikes, Julie; *see* Roberts, Julie
Rakhmaninov, Sergey, 42
Ramayana, 147
Ravel, Maurice, 98, 112, 178
Raverat, Gwen [Vaughan Williams's
    cousin], 98, 121
Raymar, Aubin, 202
Reading, 150
——, University College, 150
Red Cross, 267
Redmarley d'Abitot, 5
Reed, W. H., 17, 28
——, *Elgar as I Knew him*, 48
Reinecke, Carl, 71
Revelation of St John the Divine, 118
Richter, Hans, 10, 11, 15, 25

Index

Riga, 145
Rig Veda, 147
Rimband, (Jean) Arthur, 241, 253, 255
Roberts, Caroline Alice: *see* Elgar, (Caroline) Alice
Roberts, Major-General Sir Henry Gee [father of Alice Elgar], 5
Roberts (née Raikes), Julie [Elgar's mother-in-law], 5
Rochester, NY: St Paul's Church, 150th anniversay, 191
Rodewald, Alfred, 15
Rosen, Jelka: *see* Delius, Jelka
Rossetti, Dante Gabriel, 109
Rostropovich, Mstislav, 244, 245, 250, 251
Rottingdean, 97
Royal Army Medical Corps, 101, 116
Rubbra, Edmund, 165

St John's River, 69
St Petersburg (now Leningrad), 15
Saint-Saëns, Camille, 30
Salmond, Felix, 20
Salonica [Thessalonika], 101, 148
Salzburg, 102, 178
Samuel, Harold, 239
Sanford, Samuel Simon, 15
San Francisco Symphony Orchestra, 191
Sargent, Malcolm, 82, 182, 191, 201, 202
Scandinavia, 80
Schoenberg, Arnold, 37, 178, 239
——, First Chamber Symphony, 247
——, *Pierrot lunaire*, 178
Schubert, Franz, 24
Schumann, Robert, 25, 28
——, Symphonies, 48
Schuster, Frank, 17
Scott, Robert Falcon, 126
Scottish Orchestra, 147
Searching for Lambs [folksong], 111
Second Viennese School, 106

Shakespeare, William, 186, 259
——, *Hamlet*, 184
——, *Henry IV*, 42, 162
——, *Henry V*, 49, 183, 184
——, *The Merry Wives of Windsor*, 119
——, *The Merchant of Venice*, 123
——, *A Midsummer Night's Dream*, 282
——, *Richard III*, 183
Sharp, Cecil, 156
Shaw, George Bernard, 17, 22, *46*, 47
Shaw, Norman, 18
Sheffield, 13, 18
Shelley, Percy Bysshe, 41
Sibelius, Jean, 106, 182, 206, 212
Sicily, 151
Simon, Heinrich, 81
Sinclair, G. R., 9, 36
Sinding, Christian, *70*
Sitt, Hans, 71
Sitwell, Edith, 178, 192, 261, 262
Sitwell, Osbert, 176, 177, 185
——, *Laughter in the Next Room*, 178
Sitwell, Sacheverell, 176, 177, 178, 185
Six, Les, 181
Skelton, John, 122
Smart, Christopher, 265
Smetana, Bedřich: *The Bartered Bride*, 115
Snape Maltings, 245
Solana Grove, nr Jacksonville, 69, 71, 87
Song of Songs [*Song of Solomon*], 118
Sonzogno [music publishers]: International Competition, 76
Soutar, William, 260, 261
Spenser, Edmund: *Epithalamion*, 123
Spetchley Park, school at, 2
Speyer, Edgar, 17
Stainer, John: *A Theory of Harmony*, 97

Stamford, 201
——, Grammar School, 201
Stanford, Charles Villiers, 8, 98, 107, 110, 112, 146
——, *The Travelling Companion*, 203
Steinbeck, Fritz, 13
Stevenson, Robert Louis, 109
Stockley, W. C., 3
Stratford on Avon, 20
Strauss, Richard, 18, 36, 42
Stravinsky, Igor, 179, 208, 209, 211, 249, 254
——, *Apollo*, 281
Strindberg, August, 71
Strong, Thomas, Dean of Christ Church Cathedral, Oxford, 175
Stuart-Wortley, Alice, 17, 18
Stuart-Wortley, Charles, 18
Suffolk, 201, 241, 243
Sullivan, Arthur, 8, 155
Sumidagawa [noh play], 244, 283
Surrey, 73, 97, 202
Sussex, 97, 100, 202
——, Brinkwells [Elgar's home], 19
Synge, John Millington: *Riders to the Sea*, 119
Szell, Georg, 182

Tallis, Thomas, 113
Tasso, Torquato, 10
Tchaikovsky, Pyotr Il'yich, 32, 39, 281
Tear, Robert, 214
Teme, River, 23, 24
Terry, Sanford, 48
Tertis, Lionel, 119, 181
Thaxted, Essex, 148, 150, 161
Thessalonika: *see* Salonica
Three Choirs Festival, 47, 105, 181; *see also* Gloucester, Hereford, Worcester
Times, The, 149
Tinkler, Frances, 201
Tippett, Henry William [father], 201
Tippett (née Kemp), Isabel Clementine Binny [mother], 201

Tippett, Michael Kemp, 165, 201–36
——, governess of, 201
Tippett, Peter Kemp (Kemp, Peter) [brother], 201
Townshend, Richard Baxter [author], 9
Turner, Louisa: *see* Walton, Louisa
Tyrrwhit-Wilson, Gerald Hugh: *see* Berners, Lord

United Kingdom of Great Britain, 177, 183, 205; *see also* England
——, Festival of Britain, 243
——, General Post Office, 240
——, Home Office Committee for the Release of Interned Alien Musicians, 104
——, Labour Party, 203
——, Peace Pledge Union, 204
United Nations, 245
——, Save the Children Fund, 272
United States of America, 102, 105, 183, 205, 240; *see also* America
Union of Soviet Socialist Republics, 177, 244, 245
——, Composers' House, Armenia, 245

Valois, Ninette de, *120*
Vaughan, Henry: *Dialogue between the Body and the Soul*, 160
Vaughan Williams (née Fisher), Adeline [Vaughan Williams's first wife], 105
Vaughan Williams, Rev. Arthur [father], 97
Vaughan Williams, Sir Edward [grandfather], 97
Vaughan Williams, Ralph, 49, 97–142, 146, 150, 155, 156
——, brother and sister of, 97
Vaughan Williams (née Wood), Ursula [Vaughan Williams's second wife], 99, 105, 123, 130
Venice, 102, 252
——, Biennale, 244

Index

Verdi, Giuseppe, 35, 37, 221
Victoria, Queen of Great Britain, 8
——, Diamond Jubilee of, 7, 8
Vienna, 15, 240, 248
Vienna Boys' Choir, 272
Virgil, 267
Vishnevskaya, Galina, 245, 260

Waddell, Helen, 162
Wadhurst, Sussex, 202
——, Tidebrook Manor, 202
Wagner, Richard, 8, 28, 33, 74, 146, 155, 221, 228
——, *Der fliegende Holländer*, 25
——, *Die Meistersinger*, 25, 27, 33
——, *Lohengrin*, 33, 69
——, *Parsifal*, 27, 32, 33, 35
——, *Rienzi*, 25
——, *Ring* cycle, 27, 33
——, *Die Walküre*, 25
——, *Siegfried Idyll*, 84
——, *Tristan und Isolde*, 27
Waley, Arthur, 257
Walton, Charles [father], 175
Walton (née Turner), Louisa [mother], 175
Walton (née Gil), Susanna [wife], 177
Walton, William Turner, 175–97
Ward, Thomas, 69, 71
Warlock, Peter (Heseltine, Philip), 176
Weaver, Helen, 5, 7
——, family of, 5
Weber, Carl Maria von, 8
——, Overtures, 25
Wedgwood III, Josiah [Vaughan Williams's grandfather], 97
Wedgwood, Sophie [Vaughan Williams's aunt], 97
Weingartner, Felix, 13
Wembley: British Empire Exhibition, 48
Werneth: St John's Church, 175
Wetherden, Suffolk, 201

Whitman, Walt, 76, 77, 82, 105, 110, 111, 122, 160
——, *Dirge for two Veterans*, 122
Whittaker, William Gilles, 149
Wiltshire, 202
Wimborne, Lady, 176
Wolfe, Humbert, 157
Wood, Charles, 202
Wood, Henry, 98, 123, 192
Wood, Ursula: *see* Vaughan Williams, Ursula
Woodforde, Millicent, *152*, 153
Worcester, 1, 2, 3, 20, 21, 30
——, Amateur Instrumental Society, 2, 3
——, Cathedral, 23
——, Festival Choral Society, 8
——, Glee Club, 3
——, Guildhall, 22
——, High Street, the Elgars' home and shop in, 2
——, Littleton House School, 2
——, Marl Bank [Elgar's home], 20, 23
——, Philharmonic orchestra, 3
——, Public Hall, 6
——, St George's Roman Catholic Church, 1, 2
——, Three Choirs Festival, 3, 6, 8, 12, 13
Worcestershire Philharmonic Society, 8, 13, 21
World War I, 19, 43, 72, 101, 122, 148, 159
World War II, 104, 122, 184, 204–5, 213, 241
Worthington, Julia, 17
Wyss, Sophie, 259

Yale University, 15, 151
Yeats, W. B., 37
YMCA, 148
Yorkshire, 69, 203
——, East Cleveland, 203
Young, Percy: *Elgar O. M.: a Study of a Musician*, 36

307